BPM
Everywhere

BPM and Workflow Handbook Series

Published in association with the
Workflow Management Coalition

Workflow Management Coalition

W f M
f C

21 Years of Thought-Process Leadership

Edited by
Layna Fischer

Future Strategies Inc., Book Division

Lighthouse Point, Florida

BPM Everywhere: Internet of Things, Process of Everything

ISBN-13: 978-0986321412

Published by Future Strategies Inc., Book Division

3640 North Federal Highway B3
Lighthouse Point FL 33064 USA
954.782.3376 fax 954.719.3746
www.FutStrat.com; books@FutStrat.com

Publisher's Cataloging-in-Publication Data

ISBN: 978-0986321412

Library of Congress Control Number: 2015939201

BPM Everywhere: Internet of Things, Process of Everything

/Layna Fischer (editor)

p. cm.

Includes bibliographical references, appendices and index.

1. Business Process Management. 2. Intelligent Systems. 3. Big Data. 4. Business Intelligence. 5. Business Process Technology. 6. Adaptive Case Management. 7. Internet of Things. 8. Predictive Analytics 9. Process of Everything. 10. Electronic Commerce. 11. Process Mining

Palmer, Nathaniel; Swenson, Keith; Fingar, Peter; Reddy, Surendra; *et al* (authors)
Fischer, Layna (editor)

Table of Contents

Section 2: Appendices

Introduction
BPM Everywhere

Layna Fischer, Future Strategies Inc. USA

We are entering an entirely new phase of BPM – the era of *"BPM Everywhere"* or *BPME.*

BPME represents the strategy for leveraging, not simply surviving but fully exploiting the wave of disruption facing every business over the next 5 years and beyond. Without question, one of the single most disruptive events in the last decade was the introduction of the smartphone. Consider for a moment how great of an impact this has had on the relationship between businesses and their customers. Not even the emergence of the Web and Internet-based "digital native" business models can compare with the level of intimacy now available with your customers.

In the era of the Internet of Things where smart homes, appliances, cars, phones, virtually imaginable devices are all connected, BPM must, and will, be everywhere. As Peter Whibley discusses in *"The Internet of Things Will Be Invisible,"* by 2025 there are expected to be more than 26 billion or more connected devices.

In the chapter *"Digital Prescriptive Maintenance: Disrupting Manufacturing through IoT, Big Data, and Dynamic Case Management,"* Dr. Setrag Khoshafian introduces the "4 Vs" of "thing" data, specifically "Volume, Velocity, Variety and Value." From monitors and remote sensors, to appliances and vehicles, to tens of billions of other "things," connected devices are generating meaningful and informative data that would easily overwhelm any human being, but collectively they present critical context about processes and the state of operations.

"Big Data" has never been so large, nor presented such an acute role within enterprises and the processes that drive them. BPME as well as traditional BPM methods can already be found at the center of this. Its role will grow exponentially. Emergent factors such as process mining (see chapter *"Mining the Swarm"* by Keith Swenson, et al.) will be critical for uncovering engagement patterns and the need for process management platforms to coordinate interaction and control of smart devices. It is intelligent BPM that is expanding the window of what can be automated, by enabling adaptable automation.

The mobile strategies in far too many organizations seem to be the building of apps that presume that customers will use their smartphones like mini laptops. This avoids the fact that we now have a level of intimacy with our customer we've never had before. As discussed in the chapter *"BPM to Go – Supporting Business Processes in a Mobile and Sensing World,"* our customers are carrying around a device that offers a range of capabilities unlike any laptop. A smartphone produces volumes of meaningful data about our customers (think about the "4Vs") and is able to interact with that customer in ways that a laptop never can.

The growing ubiquity of connectivity always within reach combined with new services and capabilities such as mobile banking is a key part of driving constantly-changing expectations. Yet digital disruption is not limited to mobile devices, and is in fact disrupting everywhere BPM is otherwise found, and why *BPM everywhere* is becoming the new normal.

If you have ever used Siri and asked any particularly complex question, you immediately get a sense of the disadvantages. Rather than providing answers that understand multiple volumes of related information, it will deliver a set of query results with no understanding of how they relate. This is likely the level of what will be seen with another intelligent mediator. In contrast, as Peter Fingar explains in his chapter on *"Cognitive BPM,"* Watson will provide an intelligent answer that is a synthesis of multiple sources; Watson learns, gets smarter and provides the answer. Watson can also understand the context of the task or process step.

This is a *critical* difference for BPME, a difference which risks being lost in its subtlety.

Robots, sensors and other data-generating "things" require vertical integration to create managed, measured, and actionable feedback loops. Your refrigerator will probably not be directly connected to a BPM process anytime soon, but will inevitably participate in any number of processes ranging from maintenance to energy conservation.

BPM, and specifically **BPME**, is necessary to bring these innovations into mainstream business operations. New applications are being built to leverage this, yet traditional approaches to application development remain typically far more procedural and programmer-centric. A BPM-based application platform presents a declarative, model-driven development approach that favors configuration over coding. This type of "low code," model-driven approach is how the complex, data-driven systems of the "Internet of Everything" and IoT will continue to emerge.

Resolving the challenge of connecting the growing spectrum of intelligent things is what will drive the BPM investments and digital transformation initiatives of the next decade.

Overview of Chapters

IS YOUR BUSINESS READY FOR BPM EVERYWHERE?
Nathaniel Palmer, BPM.com and WfMC

The greatest impact on business process over the last five years has not come specifically from technology; or at least not technology alone. Instead, the one fundamental change that holds the greatest potential for business disruption, and similarly offers the greatest opportunity for innovation, is the dramatic shift in customer expectations. As we will discuss later in this chapter, the in-ability to adapt systems fast enough to keep pace with evolving customer ex-pectations is the single greatest challenge reported by companies we sur-veyed.

Resolving this challenge is what drives most IT investments and digital transformation initiatives today. Yet it is far from a stopgap measure. What we are seeing now is still the beginning of an inflexion point in the trajectory of change. This is the arrival of digital disruption, which recognizes no finite boundaries on what it will change. Everything today that we see, touch, buy, consume and require to live will all be affected in one capacity or another.

I, FOR ONE, WELCOME OUR NEW ROBOT OVERLORDS
Scott Francis and Lance Gibbs, BP3 Global, USA, David Brakoniecki, BP3 Global, UK

While pursuing the nirvana of BPM Everywhere in the future of the Internet of Things, let's not forget the basics. Business is about people. Customer experiences are differentiating. Customers experience your product and your company through your business processes. Waste should be minimized, efficiency maximized, and goals aligned. How do we apply the concepts of Lean, Six Sigma, and BPM to a world full of a surplus of events, data, and agents? How do we separate signal from noise and produce fantastic process outcomes?

THE INTERNET OF THINGS WILL BE INVISIBLE

Peter Whibley, KANA, United Kingdom

"The most profound technologies are those that disappear. They weave themselves into the fabric of everyday life until they are indistinguishable from it." Mark Weiser

The IoT will act as an airbag for our lives, ready to step in when you need it, not constantly competing for your attention. By freeing us from the mundane activities that today we would have to do manually on the web we are being freed from the internet itself. IoT solutions will make us less dependent on our current web interfaces. We will use the screen and keyboard interface to the web less and less as voice and gesture become more a more appropriate method of interacting with IoT devices. BPM and workflow technologies will orchestrate automatic processes triggered by smart devices, freeing users from mundane processes, interrupting our daily lives only when a decision is required.

WOOTS: SMART THINGS THAT CAN THINK, ACT, LEARN AND TALK.

Surendra Reddy, CEO, Quantiply, USA

We introduce a new concept called Web Of Open Things (Woots) that are everyday "Smart Things" with a specific identity, address and presence on the Internet and capabilities to self-organize and communicate with other things with or without human intervention. To make sense of the flow of information, activities, and rich interaction experience, Woots also embed a "tiny brain" to provide context awareness, autonomy, business process intelligence and reactivity. A semantic memory embedded into Woots stores a digital diary of an individual physical object in a persistent way and makes this information available to other devices, applications, and its environment. Woots would enable the creation of personalized software humanoids that will cater for our needs in private life, including shopping, smart home and public environments.

This paper discusses on the adoption of smart analytics and business process intelligence into Smart Things to realize the Web of Open Things (Woots), how to improve interoperability, reduce the overall architectural complexity, and facilitate the integration of processes, people, and things.

COGNITIVE BPM

Peter Fingar, USA

The era of cognitive systems is dawning and building on today's computer program-ming era. All machines, for now, require programming, and by definition program-ming does not allow for alternate scenarios that have not been programmed. To allow alternating outcomes would require going up a level, creating a *self-learning* Artificial Intelligence (AI). Via *biomimicry and neuroscience,* Cognitive Computing does this, taking computing concepts to a whole new level. Once-futuristic capabil-ities are becoming mainstream.

Organizations have a lot to learn about the impact of cognitive computing, so we we'll open with an Albert Einstein quote, "Once you stop learning, you start dying."

DIGITAL PRESCRIPTIVE MAINTENANCE: DISRUPTING MANUFACTURING VALUE STREAMS THROUGH INTERNET OF THINGS, BIG DATA, AND DYNAMIC CASE MANAGEMENT

Dr. Setrag Khoshafian and Carolyn Rostetter, Pegasystems Inc., USA

The holistic approach to maintenance is now augmented with Things that are increasingly intelligent and responsive. Connected devices and IoT are changing the dynamics of conventional TPM. Devices are now incorporating intelligent software that is becoming a key enabler for diagnostics and maintenance. Prescriptive maintenance goes beyond the realm of descriptive and predictive. With prescriptive maintenance the devices are pro-active participants in their own maintenance.

The paper highlights a number of use cases from key industries that are leveraging IoT (aka "Industrial Internet"). These include automotive OEMs, home appliances, healthcare devices and utility devices. The disruptive digitization approach to maintenance from descriptive, to predictive, to prescriptive with digitized decisions, cases, and IoT applies to any industry.

WHEN HARRY MET R2D2: CONNECTING HUMANS AND MACHINES IN THE FLOW OF WORK

Larry Hawes, Dow Brook Advisory Services, USA

Nearly every day in the technology press we are reminded that sensors, robots and software are taking jobs from low-skilled workers. However, the reality is that not all work can be automated and that machines will augment humans' capabilities as the Internet of Everything grows. As a result, how humans and machines will collaborate to get work done becomes a critical issue.

BPM and, especially, Case Management solutions are already beginning to connect humans and machines in the flow of work. Many current enterprise social technologies integrate event-related data generated by sensors and software systems, posting it as notifications in activity streams seen by relevant individuals. Increasingly, people can share that data, communicate and collaborate to gather additional information needed to make decisions and craft responses, and take action – all from within the activity stream.

This chapter provides current examples of humans and machines working together, and imagines some additional ways that the two might collaborate using social-enabled BPM and Case Management principles and technologies. The requirement for social interoperability standards is also discussed.

WEARABLE WORKFLOW, THE INTERNET OF THINGS, AND THE MAKER MOVEMENT

Charles Webster, MD, MSIE, MSIS

Wearable technology and the Internet of Things have incredible potential for improving healthcare workflow. From the original calculator watch to today's smart glasses and smart clothing accessories, wearable technology seeks to weave (sometimes literally!) information and communication technology into everyday life and work, making it pervasive, intimate, and, metaphorically, friction free. Especially promising are applications in healthcare. These, for example, include patient monitors for the well and unwell and wearable user interfaces to health information systems. However, wearable tech will not succeed unless we get the workflow right. Getting the workflow right means understanding the relationship of wearable tech to the Internet of Things, driving workflow at the point-of-care, and analyzing and optimizing this workflow. Inexpensive Maker-style prototyping of 3D-printed wearable and Internet of Things gadgetry is a great way to explore Wearable Workflow. This presentation is based on the Dr. Webster's recent 2015 keynote at the Society for Health Systems, Institute of Industrial Engineering Healthcare Systems Process Improvement Conference.

PROCESS ORIENTED ARCHITECTURE FOR DIGITAL TRANSFORMATION

Vinay Mummigatti

Estimates from Cisco, Intel, GE and McKinsey consulting predict that more than 25-50 Billion (predictions vary by each) connected devices will exist by 2020 and the value creation through IOE can vary between $5-15trillion in the next decade.

The disruptions caused by this trend will impact the business processes and models offered by every large firm. Adding to this trend the demands of a connected customer makes it even more challenging as we need to provision goods and services in real time. It is a struggle for many firms to deal with the boundaries of Digital transformation that will decide their sheer existence in the next 3-5years. The social media user base has already crossed 1Billion and this is the market that is mainly consisting of Generation X – the digitally savvy, always connected, real time action oriented and driven by a sense of community.

As we navigate the digital paradigm and establish a seamless connection between social media, IOE and channels, we will come across major challenges as well as opportunities to grow and expand the business. The sheer size of the value that will be created through these disruptive trends can give birth to many new firms which will thrive on the emerging connected world.

MANAGING BPM TOWARD THE SINGULARITY

Roy Altman, Memorial Sloan Kettering Cancer Center, USA

The Singularity describes when ordinary computers exceed the capacity of the human brain. Moores Law, which states that computing power increases at an exponential rate, has held constant since the dawn of the computer age. If one extrapolates forward, experts agree that the Singularity will be reached within 15-30 years. We are entering the age leading up to the Age of Intelligent Machines. Big Data Analytics and Artificial Intelligence are already having a profound impact on business and society. As the lines blur between our work and private time, and our physical and digital lives, BPM will become pervasive by providing a framework for managing interactions including both predetermined and uncertain processes. Once The Singularity is reached and exceeded, there will be profound impacts on society. We need to plan for the implications of the redefined role of humans, and management of a robotic workforce. We currently manage to the technology we have today or in the near future. We need to manage BPM along the technology curve toward The Singularity, with an eye toward the powerful technologies that are just around the corner

STANDARDS AND TECHNIQUES FOR DATA-DRIVEN, DECISION-CENTRIC PROCESS INNOVATION

James Taylor, Decision Management Solutions, USA

In an era of Big Data, organizations are applying analytics so they can become data-driven. Cookie cutter treatment of customers is being replaced with personalized, targeted communication and offers. Pay and chase fraud recovery is giving way to the prevention of fraud before it gets into the system. And post-transaction risk monitoring is being replaced with dynamic, transaction by transaction risk-based pricing and management. New data sources, better management of corporate data and the growing power of analytics are combining to create a new generation of data-centric decision-making.

Process-centric organizations need to adopt new standards and techniques so they can use data-driven decision-making to radically innovate their business processes. Proven techniques allow organizations to discover the decisions in their processes. Adopting the new Decision Model and Notation standard lets them clearly model this decision making, simplifying their process models and identifying clear and compelling analytic opportunities. Focusing on decisions and processes as peers creates innovative decision-centric processes with higher rates of straight through processing, more customer-centricity and improved operational effectiveness.

This paper introduces operational decisions, discusses how to find them in a business process and shows how they can be modeled effectively in the new Decision Model and Notation (DMN) standard. How to use these models to frame analytic requirements is covered as is the opportunity for process innovation created by changing the role of decisions in business processes.

VALUE STREAMS DRIVING THE BUSINESS INTERNET OF THINGS

Joseph B. Lail and Gregory T. Taylor, Raytheon USA

The direction towards global markets and operations places stress on many business processes that originated in the days of primarily domestic business and occasional international operations. The potential of a broader set of customers across more regions carries a set of complications where in-country policies, acquisition rules, leadership expectations and differing infrastructure challenge carrying a domestic business model into the global scene. The Raytheon Company is stepping back to look at new value streams, or models across marketing, engineering, suppliers, manufacturing and information systems, which lead to improved business outcomes and improved affordability in the more complex global market. We will demonstrate how the key shifts in business capabilities tied to this value stream will enable new business processes, then how that use case drives new technology and more efficient business operations. This specific case leads to the Internet of Things (IoT), but in a context relevant to our defense business with specific policies and mission needs that we have labeled the "Business IoT". The Business IoT combined with advanced analytics brings powerful new agility and business efficiency driven throughout by rigorous application to the new business process and direct relation to the future value stream.

MINING THE SWARM

Keith D. Swenson, Sumeet Batra, Yasumasa Oshiro, Fujitsu America

Data mining and process mining are both tools used by the BPM professional in order find out how an organization is currently operating and to get an objective measure of how efficiently the organizaiton is operating. Big data is a style of data analysis that reflects a return to large, centralized data repositories. Processing power and memory is getting cheaper, while the bandwidth between all the smart devices remains a barrier to getting all the data together in one place for analysis. If we look at common technological trends, we might predict that more and more processing power will remain at the device level. In a way similar to how Google distributed web search queries across a grid of computers, it is reasonable to see analytics functions distributed to the devices that form the Internet of things. Swarms of devices will be mined in order to retrieve intelligence about what those devices have been involved in. There are potentially very disturbing aspects of this: who owns this data when it is distributed over millions of devices? How can one protect privacy? Whether centralized or distributed, how can one assure the quality of the data? On the flip side, devices that mine information from other devices might be able to provide better service, and a better quality life than without. Like all technology advancements we should not let fear rule our actions, yet we should move forward with our eyes open.

BPM TO GO: SUPPORTING BUSINESS PROCESSES IN A MOBILE AND SENSING WORLD

Rüdiger Pryss, Manfred Reichert, Alexander Bachmeier, Johann Albach, Ulm University, Germany

The growing maturity of smart mobile devices has fostered their prevalence in various business areas. As a consequence, BPM technologies need to be enhanced with sophisticated and configurable mobile task support. Along characteristic use cases from different application domains (e.g., healthcare, logistics), this chapter will give insights into the challenges, concepts and technologies relevant for integrating mobile task support with business processes. Amongst others we will show how mobile task support can be enhanced with location-based data, sensor integration, and task configuration support. The latter is based on a 3 D model for configuring mobile tasks on smart mobile devices.

UNLOCKING THE POWER OF THE INTERNET OF THINGS THROUGH BPM

Stuart Chandler, Virtusa, USA

Business Process Management (BPM) enables businesses to harness the power and speed of the Internet of Things (IoT). Capitalizing on data enriches customer relationships by converting data into information so the organization can interact intelligently. The data explosion sets up businesses for understanding behavior and needs. However, only with the right platform, can real-time data be effectively used for intelligent decision making. BPM makes this possible by enabling orchestration, and improving process efficiencies which would lead to higher revenues and increased margins. While many businesses are already employing BPM, true success requires not only a foundational BPM platform but also orchestrating various processes across the customer value chain, integrating with other key application/data platforms, and making processes transportable across platforms. It's also critical to develop industry standards for exchanging BPM processes and procedures to allow value chain partners to interact closely—where the value chain disappears as customers experience seamless relationships across many providers. This article also presents legal sector and travel industry case studies highlighting how two businesses went through a paradigm culture shift. BPM helped them raise the way they service customers and interact with partners to a whole new level.

CREATING THE INFORMATION FOUNDATION FOR iBPM

David RR Webber, Horizon Industries, USA

When creating predictable information assets solution architects face a bewildering array of competing approaches and theoretical philosophies. What choices make the most sense in the context of iBPM, and what are their pros and cons? How can we handle multilingual needs in a pluralistic distributed workforce? Big strides are being made in the ability to semantically package knowledge and information that can be processed logically and predictably. Tools that integrate into BPM solutions can provide a smooth and rapidly deployable information infrastructure. Existing open source and open standard software assets are considered along with complementary industry products. Use cases and examples are examined with respect to a selection of major industry challenges and needs including healthcare and multinational government collaboration. Particularly in regard to mobile device deployment and enabling collaborative team environments both domestically and internationally.

ADVANCED COMPLEX ADAPTIVE ORGANIZATIONAL SYSTEMS BPM/WORKFLOW DESIGN

Mark Casey, Miyian.com, USA

A new theoretical model and software design based on recent CAOS (complex adaptive organization systems) science research has been developed, integrating business management, workflow optimization, and operational and scientific systems. With federated big data and supercomputer support, self-organizing dynamic software dynamically rebuilds and optimizes itself in real and near real time to integrate and optimize the hundreds of current simultaneous BPM, Workflow, Learning, and engineering/technology CAS systems that make up an organizational system. The new model and software design integrates existing software, informational, and process frameworks to encompass all the changing states within an organization. Longitudinal, temporal, and hierarchical process and workflow layers are auto-dynamically defined and modeled to produce optimal outcome and states using coordinated goal seeking strategies. Embedded 2D and 3D virtual reality interfaces based on natural human audio, video, and data interface patterns are ubiquitous throughout the design. Healthcare is one of the first target industries.

VIEWING THE INTERNET OF EVENTS THROUGH A PROCESS LENS

Wil van der Aalst, Eindhoven University of Technology, The Netherlands

The spectacular growth of event data is rapidly changing the Business Process Management (BPM) discipline. It makes no sense to focus on process modeling (including model-based analysis and model-based process automation) without considering the torrents of factual data in and between today's organizations. Hence, there is a need to connect BPM technology to the "internet of events" and make it more evidence-based BPM. However, the volume (size of data), velocity (speed of change), variety (multiple heterogeneous data sources), and veracity (uncertainty) of event data complicate matters.

Mainstream analytics approaches are unable to turn data into insights, once things get more involved. Therefore, they tend to focus on isolated decision problems rather than providing a more holistic view on the behavior of actors within and outside the organization. Fortunately, recent developments in process mining make it possible to use process models as the "lens" to look at (low) level event data. Viewing the internet of events through a "process lens" helps to understand and solve compliance and performance related problems. In fact, we envision a new profession—the process scientist—connecting traditional model-driven BPM with data-centric approaches (data mining, statistics, and business intelligence). Process mining provides the process scientist with a powerful set of tools and prepares BPM for a highly-connected world where processes are surrounded by devices emitting events.

Section 1

Is Your Business Ready for BPM Everywhere?

Nathaniel Palmer, BPM.com and WfMC

1. ABSTRACT

The greatest impact on business process over the last five years has not come specifically from technology; or at least not technology *alone*. Instead, the one fundamental change that holds the greatest potential for business disruption, and similarly offers the greatest opportunity for innovation, is the dramatic shift in *customer expectations*. As we will discuss later in this chapter, the inability to adapt systems fast enough to keep pace with evolving customer expectations is the single greatest challenge reported by companies we surveyed.

Resolving this challenge is what drives most IT investments and digital transformation initiatives today. Yet it is far from a stopgap measure. What we are seeing now is still the beginning of an inflexion point in the trajectory of change. This is the arrival of digital disruption, which recognizes no finite boundaries on what it will change. Everything today that we see, touch, buy, consume and require to live—will all be affected in one capacity or another.

We are entering an entirely new phase of BPM – the era of "*BPM Everywhere*" or *BPME*.

BPME represents the strategy for leveraging, not simply surviving but fully exploiting the wave of disruption facing every business over the next 5 years and beyond. Without question, one of the single most disruptive events in the last decade was the introduction of the smartphone. Consider for a moment how great of an impact this has had on the relationship between businesses and their customers. Not even the emergence of the Web and Internet-based "digital native" business models can compare with the level of intimacy now available with your customers.

Tell me, where is your phone right now? Whatever time or day of the week it is, chances are it is there by your side. With it are threads back to the businesses that have leveraged the mobile platform to establish an unprecedented level of customer intimacy.

Yet, as disruptive as smartphones and the mobile platform have been, the impact of the Internet of Things (IoT) and the opportunity for BPME will happen far faster, and on a scale of many orders of magnitude larger than that of mobility alone. Rather than to have one new digital interface, IoT and BPME represent many new levels of interaction, from smart devices to intelligent agents, from connected cars to social robots. To devices that have no category today, but are about to become ubiquitous in our homes and businesses. All of the new channels are competing for your customers, as well as for you, to reach them.

Is *your* business ready for **BPM Everywhere**? Ready or not, here it comes!

2. THE FIRST PHASE OF BPME AND THE EMERGENCE OF INTELLIGENT AUTOMATION

In the era of the Internet of Things and Process of Everything, where smart homes, appliances, cars, phones, virtually imaginable devices are all connected, BPM must, and will, be everywhere. As Peter Whibley discusses later in "*The Internet of Things Will Be Invisible*," by 2025 there are expected to be more than 26 billion or more connected devices. If history is any guide, this number is likely far too low. Yet whatever the number of connected devices will be in a decade, or in just the next five years, what we do know today is that there will be far too many, and far too complex interactions, to keep pace with traditional software techniques. Once a dirty word in BPM circles, "automation" has begun to return to the forefront, with adaptive and data-driven processes automated by intelligent and distributed software agents managed through an "intelligent hub" of BPM.

The data-driven transformation, now well underway, parallels a volume of data generated that is already nearly incomprehensible, yet merely a fraction of what it will soon become. Consider all data produced from the beginning of history to the year 2002 – that entire volume is now produced every 10 minutes. This is largely due to the data generated by connected, physical devices.

Yet within five years, the same volume will take less than a second.

In the chapter "*Digital Prescriptive Maintenance: Disrupting Manufacturing through IoT, Big Data, and Dynamic Case Management,*" Dr. Setrag Khoshafian introduces the "4 Vs" of "thing" data, specifically "Volume, Velocity, Variety and Value." From monitors and remote sensors, to appliances and vehicles, to tens of billions of other "things," connected devices are generating meaningful and informative data that would easily overwhelm any human being, but collectively they present critical context about processes and the state of operations.

"Big Data" has never been so large, nor presented such an acute role within enterprises and the processes that drive them. BPME as well as traditional BPM methods can already be found at the center of this. Its role will grow exponentially. Emergent factors such as process mining (see chapter "*Mining the Swarm*" by Keith Swenson, et al.) will be critical for uncovering engagement patterns and the need for process management platforms to coordinate interaction and control of smart devices. It is intelligent BPM [1] that is expanding the window of what can be automated, by enabling adaptable automation.

The *Bank of Tokyo-Mitsubishi UFJ*, the largest bank in Japan, recently debuted robots in its front office operations, greeting customers.

Figure 1. Nao ("now") is an Autonomous Robot from Aldebaran Robotics, used to greet customers (and film them) at the largest bank in Japan

---

[1] See iBPMS: Intelligent BPM Systems (Future Strategies Inc).
http://futstrat.com/books/iBPMS_Handbook.php

These robots (the *Nao* shown above) may be cute with their cherubic expressions, but inside of that button-like mouth is a high definition camera – used by the bank to record every customer's reaction via the combination of facial recognition and sentiment analysis; something a human teller would find difficult to do once, nonetheless consistently every time with every customer. These little robots are beating human co-workers when it comes to capturing meaningful customer data (and lots of it).

Today, robot greeters for most organizations are likely more of a novelty than a strategic tool. Yet in the not-too-distant future, the majority of customer-facing interaction will happen via some form of robot, whether physical or virtual as an intelligent software agent, and increasingly among the agents themselves. My prediction is that it will take less than five years before the majority of customer interactions via intelligent agents will exceed those with human beings. Yet this will also be nearly impossible to measure with the rapidly-blurring lines between human and machine interaction.

Looked at through the lens of what is in place in most organizations already, this all may sound like science fiction, or least exaggeration; robots in the workforce, materials delivered by drones, self-optimizing intelligence processes, collaborating via wearable devices and in your car (through your car). But it's not science fiction; it is business reality, delivered today, in part, by the mind-blowing array of innovations showcased in the last few months alone.

Cool devices and smart machines by themselves do not equate to digital transformation any more than smartphones alone changed how we work. It is BPM that is the real leverage point. We need to measure and evaluate BPM not by what it looks like, but how it is enabling digital transformation. Ready or not, we face a new generation of customers, whose expectations are changing faster than can be responded to using traditional IT development tools and practices.

3. MEET YOUR CUSTOMERS FOR THE NEXT 20 YEARS

Who are your customers for the *next* 20 years? Here's the hyper-connected digital family from 20 years ago; Dad with his *Motorola DynaTAC 8000X*, Junior's got two phones going on, everybody's got a device. Well, obviously this picture is included partly in jest, but the point it drives home is that this family from the 1990s represents the first generation now taking hyper-connectivity for granted.

They're the Millennial Generation or perhaps *Generation Z* (the individuals born after Millennials) who have grown up knowing that connectivity is always within reach. This generation hates computers, but they love phones (even if they rarely use them for verbal communication). To them, computers are for work, their personal life, their commercial relationships; these are all through their phones. They would no sooner use a laptop for matters such as online banking than they would use dial-up for Instant Messaging.

This shift toward the expectation of being constantly connected, always within reach, is perhaps one of the best examples of what has been

driving the notion of "digital disruption." But the reality is that digital disruption isn't just about having expectations change. This is not a "once and done" proposition, but the reality of digital disruption involves constantly-changing expectations.

A Tale of Two Popes and Digital Disruption

In the two pictures below, both show the crowd assembled in Saint Peter's Square outside of the Vatican, awaiting the announcement of the Pope. In 2005 it was Pope Benedict XVI, and eight years later in 2013, it was Pope Francis. Having two new Popes in such a short period of time is, of course, unusual, but what is most remarkable is the difference in the crowd. In 2005, no doubt everyone had phones in their pockets and cameras in their hands but the two devices had little in common and no awareness of the other. By 2013, the devices were one and connected; thousands of amateur photojournalists streamed and shared their experiences for the rest of the world to see. Today we live our lives through our devices. This is how expectations are changing.

Figure 2. Within eight years of the iPhone's introduction the lens through which we view the world was changed forever (Source: Morguefile.com)

Just how profound is this shift already? Consider a study done in 2014 by Alix Partners that examined customers who switched banks. What they found was that among those smartphone customers who switched, electing to go through the personal upheaval of changing their banking, 60% switched specifically because of mobile banking capabilities. What is perhaps even more remarkable, however, prior to this study and just six months earlier, less than half had switched. That's about a 30% change in just six months. Just imagine what was like 12 months later.

The good news is you have to worry only about customers that happen to have a phone or a tablet, or that might in the future. The bad news is that's all of your customers. There is a war for your customers happening right now on their phones.

But what does *your* strategy look like?

The mobile strategies in far too many organizations seem to be the building of apps on the presumption that customers use their smartphones like mini laptops. This avoids the fact that we now have a level of intimacy with our customer we've never had before. As discussed in the chapter "*BPM to Go – Supporting Business Processes in a Mobile and Sensing World*," our customers carry around a device that offers a range of capabilities unlike any laptop. A smartphone produces volumes of meaningful data about our customers (think about the "4Vs") and is able to interact with that customer in ways that a laptop never can.

Smartphones are not mini-laptops and ultimately it's not about the app, it's about the *process*.

Beyond Mobility to Process Dematerialization

The growing ubiquity of connectivity always within reach combined with new services and capabilities such as mobile banking is a key part of driving constantly-changing expectations. Yet digital disruption is not limited to mobile devices, and is in fact disrupting everywhere BPM is otherwise found, and why *BPM everywhere* is becoming the new normal.

An example of this happening right now is the move toward a fully-automated bank branch where everything you could do in a regular staffed branch, you can now do in a fully digital capacity. In the picture below on the screen is clearly a teller, an actual live human being, yet their location could be anywhere, inevitably in many cases an entirely different continent.

Figure 3. The automated branch is changing face-to-face banking from a "banker's hours only" to a 24/7 experience (Source: Bank of America)

Nearly all the interaction customers would otherwise expect access to any branch that is available there in an automated branch 24/7. The picture shows a full document scanner, on the left there is a large screen that's a page-size monitor, all the capabilities you would need normally if you're interacting face-to-face with a teller or somebody else in the bank.

This is **process dematerialization**, another key dimension to **BPME**. What enables this level of branch automation is not simply the technology visible in the picture. Rather, it is the fact that underneath there is a managed process; in one form or another that is BPME. You could go to the next automated branch and do exactly the same thing, or more importantly, continue the same process (e.g., the process you're participating in as a customer is not linked to any fixed location).

This, more than any development in the last 20 years, holds the potential to disrupt the consumer banking industry, which previously now has competed on, as well as been regulated, in terms of geography and real estate.

For example, while you're making a deposit with an automated teller, the human teller pops up and suggests that in light of the balance on the credit card you just paid, you would likely be better served by a Home Equity Line of Credit (HELOC) which has an introductory Annual Percentage Rate (APR) of just 2.9%. Or perhaps the bank is running a special on new credit cards and you can transfer that balance over for a year at zero interest What is the cost to that bank of soliciting customers cold-called by phone or mail? What is the conversion rate of those methods? There is no question that the transaction costs and conversion rates are far better when this is executed in real-time during another banking transaction.

Yet while the automated branch is great for customers who prefer going to the bank but find their biggest hurdle banker's hours, the automated bank is still a bank. It is just the first tier of process dematerialization, and arguably already a tad anti-quated because you nonetheless must travel to a physical site. So what is the next tier? If you've used a *Kindle Fire HDX* you probably have an idea.

If you have hit the "Mayday Button" then you've experienced the next tier of process dematerialization, where a service representative greets you in real-time. They can't see you but you can see them, you're having a live conversation and most notably they now can do anything to or with your device that you request; they can config-ure it, help you with any sort of transaction. Amazon reports that 75% of customer contacts for Fire HDX now come via Mayday.

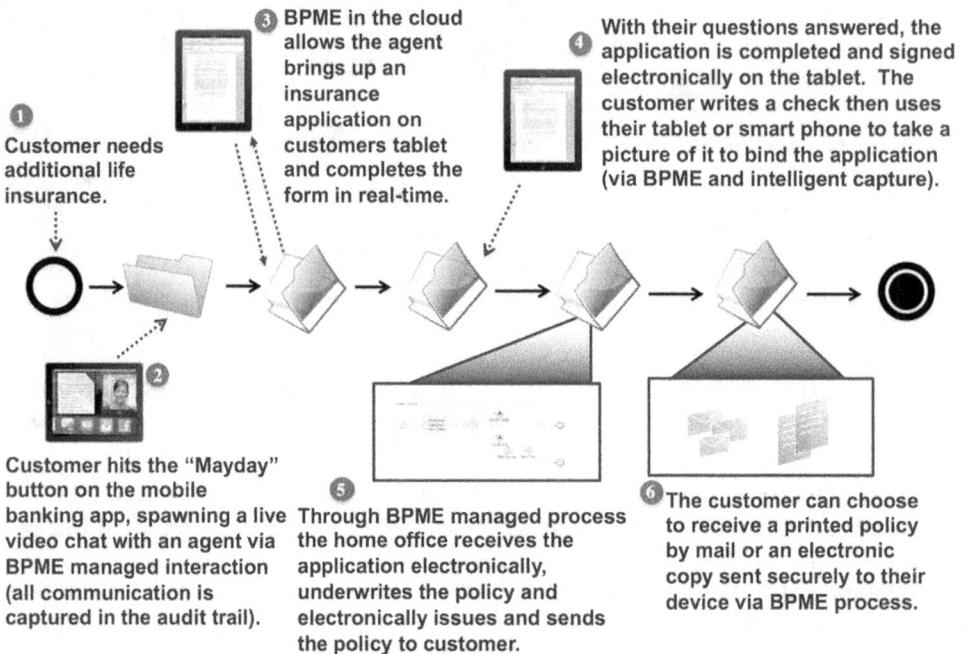

Figure 4. With the "Mayday scenario" customers have access to the same capabilities of the automated branch at home or anywhere else

What's not on any device that's otherwise at the automated bank? There's no ability to deliver physical money, but you have a scanner (e.g., camera) and access to a printer, and the ability to connect with teller who can see your account. Virtually everything that can be done at the automated branch can be done on the Fire HDX (or any another thus-enabled device; this just happens to be pioneered by Amazon). Rather than simply offering tech support, how difficult would it be to extend this to selling high-value products such as life insurance? Not at all.

When you combine commodity and widely available mobile capabilities with BPME you have the ability to do nearly everything on that device you otherwise can do at traditional bank branch or automated branch. Again, access to physical money is one of the few limitations, yet money transfers and check deposits are already commonplace. While there are not likely be cash dispensers on iPod or iPhones any time soon, cash itself is becoming dematerialized[2] just rapidly as financial processes are. One of the most promising advances that offers the greatest potential to disrupt financial services, is how BPME leverages mobility to deliver high-value and highly complex products and services.

As of this writing, this full capability is not yet offered in a true on-demand, self-service capacity as shown in *Figure 4*. Yet there is no technical or regulatory hurdle preventing it. It is not only inevitable; it will likely be in place by the time you read this book. The automated branch, which has been in the making for decades, can be leapfrogged virtually overnight by BPME, because all the pieces are there and regulatory-sensitive pieces of the equation are still managed securely in the same way. The main technical challenge, one that is fundamental yet relatively straightforward, is whether the BPM capabilities are abstracted so as to enable this level of interaction (see *The Architecture of BPME* later in this chapter).

After the second tier of process dematerialization, what comes next? What is the next source or target of digital disruption? Have you seen the *Amazon Echo*? It's basically "*Siri in a box*" (or a tube more accurately). Today it has about the same level of functionality as Siri, however, while few would really credit either tool as the

type of intelligent agents Peter Fingar describes in "*Cognitive BPM*"... that is not where Amazon is going with *Echo*. Its mission is far more commercially driven.

What Echo provides is the ability for you to have that same kind of interaction, removing the requirement for human contact, having a 24/7 real-time connection. It goes by the name of "Alexa" (which works well if no one else in your household has the same name) and is always connected, ready to go. Echo is listening, waiting for your instructions, right there in your home, offering real-time contact, just like you would find with the Mayday button on your Fire HDX – and similarly connected to Amazon.com and your Amazon account. Like Siri, Echo will accept basic voice commands, provide access to various Amazon services, but most of all it will automate purchases. Echo is there to facilitate buying stuff; ultimately just about anything.

Figure 5. Echo accepts basic voice commands, provides access to various amazon services, as well as automates purchases via amazon.com

---

[2] Apple Pay is a mobile payment and digital wallet services from Apple Inc., allowing users to make secure payments via their iPhone just as they use cash in a local transaction.

Think for a moment, about what business Amazon is in. Is it selling books?

No. It's in the business of *customer experience*. Amazon exists, and the Echo exists, to make it easier to buy stuff. And not just books. Increasingly anything —and with Echo you simply say it out loud and it arrives, *via drone* (eventually).

What does Echo mean for you and your business? If you're selling products of any kind, it will likely mean a lot (soon if not today). Presently it has not evolved to the point where it can do complex transactions (of any level complexity, although this will certainly change). But in its current form, it already holds the potential to drive another order of magnitude change in expectations – for both your **customers** and **users**. For customers, achieving the level of intimacy where Echo is in their homes and part of their conversations, they are able to have that contact 24/7. That is certainly a hard act to compete with, and once that level of instant gratification is firmly in place, there's no going back. The level of intimacy, the expectation for access, the expectation for expediency; that's never going to change.

From a user experience (UX) perspective, it also offers a compelling push in the direction of interaction via natural language, voice-based commands. In fact, these commands are logged on whatever device (smartphone, *et al.*) your Echo is linked to. Unlike Siri, Echo uses this log of historic questions and commands to learn, and become smarter (theoretically). This is life imitating science fiction, interaction with IT resources by simply speaking out loud, rather than into a specific microphone or device (swap "Alexa…" with "Computer…" and the scene is straight out of the original *Star Trek*, and countless scenarios since). Yet as novel or kitschy as it may sound, it is easy to underestimate the extent by which this type of interaction will radically alter expectations for interaction. Yet even Echo is parochial compared to what comes next. Get ready for *JIBO!*

Figure 6. Dr. Cynthia Breazeal with JIBO, the world's first social robot for the home (source: JIBO, Inc.)

The person on the left is Cynthia Breazeal, a professor and founder of the *Personal Robots Group* at MIT, as well as the founder and Chief Scientist of Jibo, Inc. What's on the right is JIBO, one of the most fascinating, and some may argue also, one of the creepiest devices you'll ever meet. Indeed, you really need to see its debut video[3] to truly appreciate it, but JIBO is the first mainstream *social robot* for the home. It's not a robot butler; rather it's an interface just like Echo. Although a better comparison may in fact be a smartphone, because it's increasingly what's going to stand between you and customers, even your employees. Just as it would have seemed unlikely only decade ago that mobile phones would be a critical interface between employees and customers, the idea of social robots as market and process disruptors today may seem far-fetched. To be clear, JIBO alone is not an example of BPME, however, JIBO, Echo, as well as other new forms of intelligent interfaces not yet released, and certainly many not yet even conceived are all key drivers for both digital disruption and the need for BPME. We have already seen robotics introduced into the workforce in areas otherwise assumed out of reach to automation. These roles (those held by robots) need to be factored into process designs. That notion is probably not too hard to accept, but what does this mean for JIBO?

JIBO is not going to manage your processes; that's science fiction, at least for the moment. What this will do (and not simply JIBO but the rapidly-evolving space of intelligent assistants), is drive a new form of mediated interaction. The types of use cases where BPME will be applied increasingly will drop the work list metaphor in favors tasks that JIBO and its robotic/AI brethren – *Cortana, Cubic, Echo, Google Now, Pepper, Siri*, et al. – all of these are mediators. They will increasingly stand between your processes and your customers, partners, and employees.

You will ask *"JIBO, can I take a later flight today?"* To act on this, it will need access to not just your personal details, travel systems, other service-based interfaces, but likely a host of third-party intermediary services (Expedia 2.0) that are designed to interface with these new intelligent entities. Many organizations face this now with mobile; how often have you heard employees (or customers) complain that it is easier to book a flight or perform some other service with a mobile than to request approval to do so using the internal company workflow system? As JIBO-like actors take on more responsibility, it is naïve to assume your internal processes will remain immune to this kind of pressure.

The cynics among us may still claim this is irrelevant to BPM. Yet we have seen this play out many times before. It may begin in retail, but will quickly disrupt other customer interaction points. Customers are not going to go to a web page or call a contact center if JIBO can do it. So customers are going to be ready for JIBO faster than we know it. The question is: *are your processes ready?* Because if they're not, your customers are going to go somewhere where they are.

4. BPME AND PROCESS MATURITY

Where are you today with your ability to responding to changing expectations among customers and employees? Probably not unlike most companies are with their processes, as identified through a recent survey we completed of about 1,000 mid-sized organizations. The focus of this survey was what problems are these organizations trying to solve and what specific challenges are they dealing with today. The top three results were:
- ✓ *"Older IT systems cannot be changed or adapted as fast as we would like"*
- ✓ *"Growing maintenance burden on existing legacy applications consumes precious resources and budget better spent elsewhere"*

---

[3] Visit http://www.jibo.com/ to see an introductory video about JIBO

✓ *"Customers expect easier ways to interact with us and our systems (such as via web and mobile apps)"*

As the survey results show, the third most critical challenge organizations face is dealing with the fact that while they recognize customer expectations are changing, their ability to keep pace with those changes lags behind. Second, and in most organizations, is the challenge of simply dealing with the maintenance burden, all the resources that go into keeping legacy systems running. Just keeping the lights on is consuming more resources, more money, that they would otherwise be putting into creating innovation. Overwhelmingly, however, the number one issue reflected in both of those, are that existing systems simply aren't agile enough. They just cannot adapt them fast enough to be able to keep up with the requirement for change. For this reason, either the ability to adapt existing infrastructure, even simply the lack infrastructure itself (i.e., the absence of legacy burden) has become the key dividing line in competitive advantage, in particular between large firms and emerging digital natives.

20th Century	21st Century
Infrastructure Ownership	*Infrastructure Access*
Economies of Scale	*Network Effect*
Supply Chain Control	*Technology Innovation*
Customer Lock-in	*Happy Customers*
Wage Arbitrage	*Billions of Customers*

Figure 7. Drivers of competitive advantage shifting between centuries with digital transformation

The large brands built in the last century, the traditional *Fortune 500®* firms, owe their success in no small part to building proprietary infrastructure, where the firms with best fleets, factories, supply chains or channels dominated. Economies of scale were realized through the ability to leverage infrastructure across vertical-integrated organizations, using it to apply control over the supply chain, to establish lock-in of customers and, ultimately seeking to maximize economies of efficiency. That's largely defined by IT investments and competitive advantage for 20th century organizations.

For 21st century organizations and digital natives, like *Uber* or *WhatsApp*, whose valuations just a few years after they were created already exceeds that of their most established competitors is based in no small part on the **lack** of infrastructure.

Why did Facebook buy WhatsApp for $22 billion despite its lack of any meaningful revenue? Because its value as a communication platform with virtually no infrastructure but millions of customers, means the cost to service the customers is not dependent on costly infrastructure as is otherwise the case with a 20th century telecomm provider offering essentially the same service.

Digital natives are competing on an entirely different set of economics. Access to infrastructure is a commodity. The reality is that these digital natives have access to the same capabilities as any Fortune 500 firm. But *more importantly, so do you and so do your competitors.* How are you leveraging that?

Are you going to be disrupted or are you going to be the disruptor? as we saw in that survey, it comes down to how we are we able to keep pace with legacy and move beyond that. What needs to occur to all new innovation into the organizations, to be able to leverage new channels and interfaces such as JIBO and Echo, and ultimately to keep pace with rapidly-changing expectations.

The answers to these questions get to the heart of the very architecture of BPME.

5. THE ARCHITECTURE OF BPME

The *architecture of BPME* is the focus of the rest of this chapter; the same focus of a lot of what we've been seeing in our recent research, the notion of a BPM platform as a way to not only more quickly and more cost-effectively adapt processes, but also to build and deliver better applications. This involves a fundamental shift in the way applications are currently built, as well as shift to understanding BPME as a next-generation application development platform.

Despite many advances (as well as growing market fixation) with Integrated Development Environments or IDEs, we still see mostly siloed applications where the processes, the workflow, even if not the data repositories but the data model, is all wrapped up into the application. IDEs were effective at allowing developers to build small applications quickly, but not allowing these applications to scale horizontally or connect to our processes. With a BPM platform you have the advantage of having a shared process, being able to have a process go across multiple applications, having shared rules, shared resources in terms of data, integration points and other aspects of infrastructure, while also having a common interface.

To be clear, however, the word "interface" is used to mean much more than skin around existing or legacy applications; which in truth describes most BPM-based application development over the last few years. Rather the context intended here is building an interface to information and capabilities used by the organization. Simply put, the terms "interface" and "application" are essentially interchangeable in this context, but not because the interface is wedded to the application, but because both are dynamically driven by the *process*, *rules* and *data* involved, delivering an optimal and consistent user experience.

Delivering a Consistent User Experience

The User or Customer Experience (UX/CX) must be unified and consistent, both requiring common interfaces as well as continuity of underlying processes, rules and data. One of the strategies we can pattern and adapt from the success of Digital Natives is the shift from the way applications are built. This is largely represented by the shift from "Web architecture" to "Cloud architecture" with application development and delivery. BPME is not necessarily "cloud-based" in terms of procurement and delivery, but in the core underlying architecture and design.

Over the last 10 years with the introduction of the three-tier architecture—unlike the previous generation where you had the presentation tier connected to the application—three-tier architecture moved toward the ability to separate the interface from the application itself. Every BPM system that's been built in the last 10 years, probably the last 15 years, follows this sort of three-tier model where you're able to have a completely separate interface from the application logic which is where the rules and the processes reside. But this doesn't allow you to deal with the change in expectations for how customers are interacting with applications.

Applications designed to follow a cloud-based architecture, e.g., those with an actual user interface, not just programmatic interface true model-driven development approach, which at the interface level extends the traditional "MVC" (*Model–View–Controller*) architectural pattern. This is accomplished in part by abstracting how data is managed from how it is viewed. But in modern, BPM-based application platforms, the traditional MVC pattern is extended through a common interface layer, which is controlled by the process state (e.g., the context of what is happening in the process at any given time).

This approach, which is closer to the more advanced *Model-View-View-Model* or "MVVM" pattern, offers the ability to define how an interface looks in any instance with each new application, and ensures each view is appropriate to the context of the specific moment. Thus it is not a single, static view-imposed on each application, but a data-driven and context-driven view, where the user has a consistent experience across multiple apps, as well as a personalized experience based on the device they are using or the task they are performing.

BPME as development platform provides a framework for app construction to define how content and data are presented, according to the design objectives for the app, regardless of where it is accessed. Then, utilizing a "write-once, deploy-any-where" model, the app can be deployed to and accessed from any desktop, web or mobile platform. This requires declarative UI, for both the acceleration of app development, as well as a richer user experience by dynamically generating the apps native to each target platform. Thus apps can offer a *consistent look and feel*, while also leveraging the native platform capabilities. For example, the same app can have a consistent interface whether it is deployed to iOS for Apple devices or otherwise for Android; by deploying natively (not in mobile browser) it is able to leverage local (device resident) data and capabilities.

The Emergence of the Four-Tier Architecture

The formalization of the cloud-based or cloud-oriented architecture pattern that extends the traditional three-tier architecture of App Server platforms is increasingly referred to as "4-Tier Architecture." It abstracts not only the Presentation, Application, and Data tiers (the traditional 3-tier model, nominally illustrated below) but introduces a fourth tier by separating "Presentation" into "Client" and "Delivery." This results in four new tiers: *Client, Delivery, Aggregation,* and *Services.*

3-TIER ARCHITECTURE   4-TIER ARCHITECTURE

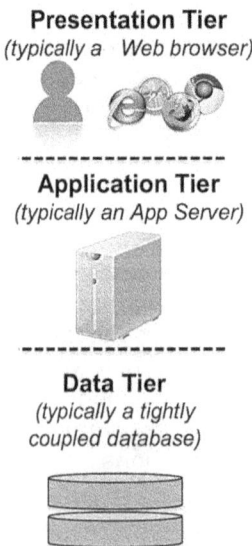

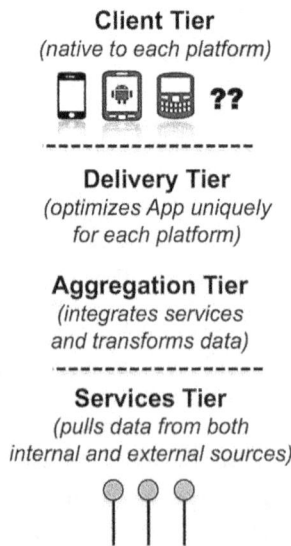

Presentation Tier
(typically a Web browser)

Client Tier
(native to each platform)

Client Tier and Delivery Tier are Separate to Allow Data and Application Capabilities to be Delivered Specific the Client-side Environment

Application Tier
(typically an App Server)

Delivery Tier
(optimizes App uniquely for each platform)

Aggregation Tier
(integrates services and transforms data)

The Data Tier and Aggregation Tier Replace More Tightly-coupled Data and Application Containers With Microservices

Data Tier
(typically a tightly coupled database)

Services Tier
(pulls data from both internal and external sources)

Figure 8 – BPME and the New "Four-Tier Architecture"

Looking at the model above, imagine an application that can be accessed via an iPhone, an iPad, a PC Web browser, a Blackberry (seriously, it could happen), or otherwise autonomous robots and intelligent mediators. Each of these need to access applications, not simply data but applications. Yet the presentation of the application itself needs to be tuned to user (e.g., the consumer of the application service, whether it's presented with an actual UI or a programmatic interface). It would be impossible (or at best very ill-advised) to design this into the presentation tier within a traditional Web MVC framework. This would be fine for the user of a PC-based Web browser, but likely have horrible UX with any mobile device, and would certainly fail with the JIBO-type mediators.

This is how applications must be built to be ready for JIBO, to be ready for other intelligent interfaces, where in that fourth tier you have a separation between the delivery of the application and how it's being accessed. And this is critical for, not just the modernization of existing application, but having applications *be ready to be*, to use a term that frankly has been probably misapplied. We were talking about future-proofing applications when we were talking about the three-tier architecture, but they weren't future-proofed. They're completely antiquated by today's standard. To truly future-proof our applications we need to follow this four-tier architecture, building better applications faster and in a more agile way.

In light of this, the 3-Tier architecture is inevitably on its way out, and consistent with the reasons described above, most interpretations of the 4-tier architecture model are relatively data-centric. In basic terms this means emphasizing the need to have data presented in the way that makes the most sense for the platform on which it is accessed, as well as the premise that data can come from any source. It also means that data must be transformed and aggregated into a single composite in *Aggregation Tier*, abstracted and separate from the *Delivery Tier*.

One approach might be to assume whatever intelligence is applied to the data should also be the source of integration. Yet this has limits and disadvantages.

If you have ever used Siri and asked any particularly complex question, you immediately get a sense of the disadvantages. Rather than providing answers that understand multiple volumes of related information, it will deliver a set of query results with no understanding of how they relate. This is likely the level of what will be seen with another intelligent mediator. In contrast, as Peter Fingar explains in his chapter on "*Cognitive BPM,*" Watson will provide an intelligent answer that is a synthesis of multiple sources; Watson learns, gets smarter and provides the answer. Watson can also understand the context of the task or process step.

This is a *critical* difference for BPME, a difference which risks being lost in its subtlety. Consider, however, the various patterns discussed throughout this book, and this chapter specifically. Use cases such as *Digital Prescriptive Maintenance* described by Dr. Khoshafian involve enormous amount of "thing data" to be combined with more structured data (such as maintenance cycles) as well as unstructured information, such as maintenance logs and pictures or video used to assess condition of assets.

Certainly the best case is for this content to be combined in the *Aggregation Tier* so that the aggregated data can be applied to rules and policies within the application, and the combination of that (process, rules, data) is what is made available to be acted on by a human being or an intelligent mediator. Just as it is hugely inefficient for a human being to do extraction and integration of data manually, then also manually apply this to business rules, so too it is enormously inefficient to push this burden onto an autonomous robot or intelligent agent.

What *is* effective, however, is to have a multi-agent system, to have some agent dedicated extraction and transformation of data, another to analysis, and others to act in the context of a BPM-driven process (see Fingar chapter for more on this).

BPME in the "Age Of The Customer"

Earlier this year Forrester Research released a report entitled *"Predictions 2015: The Age Of The Customer Is Set To Disrupt The BPM Market,"* authored by lead analysts Clay Richardson and Craig Le Clair (among a few others). This report presents a change in traditional BPM market segmentation. Specifically, it argues for a shift away from characterizing BPM in terms of how it is designed (in Forrester's terms "Human-centric" vs "Integration-centric" vs "Document-centric") to instead splitting it according to whether the intended use is "Operations-centric" or "Customer-centric."

This segmentation doesn't imply that customers are not part of business operations. Rather, it suggests that BPM as a middleware platform, whether focused on content management or data integration or process automation, traditionally supported the operations side of business, and focused foremost on driving costs out of production and operations (read "process efficiency"). In most cases these processes and applications were rarely touched directly by customers outside of the firewall.

In contrast, Forrester argues that in 2015 and beyond, BPM will be used increasingly for front-office versus back-office benefits, and will indeed be touched directly by the customer, and that customer experience teams and "design thinking" will displace the traditional "efficiency expert" orientation of process improvement teams and IT-centric roles traditionally driving BPM initiatives.

This shift represents not so much a change in direction, but more the expansion of BPM's mission and potential benefits. Today the most innovative, successful, and certainly the largest firms in the world run their businesses on BPM; specifically leveraging BPM as the fundamental application platform responsible 24/7/365 for generating revenue, managing the customer the experience, and enabling innovation.

Thus, if we view "Operations" and "Customer-facing" as the two distinct hemispheres of business activity—internal and external functions, together forming the whole—BPM is today addressing the entire organization. As Forrester points out, this does require further evolution of BPM offerings. Notably, as roles involved in BPM shift from IT to business, the manner by which applications are built on BPM must also evolve. In particular, this points to the emergence of "low-code" platforms that favor configuration over coding; with users building applications via drag-and-drop rather than sitting in front of a complier.

Although some have touted a "codeless" orientation, this is a bit of a *non sequitur* for building actual, mission-critical applications. New capabilities can be introduced onto a BPM platform without requiring code, but the end-to-end delivery is going to require at least a modicum of coding at some point. Yet what modern application platforms enable is a clean separation of concern, where most work is done through drag-and-drop configuration, and actual coding is kept to a minimum.

BPME and Agile Development Patterns

One of the most important measures for modern application development is the ability to develop and release applications in individual modules. This is the foundation of all Agile software development, from Extreme Programming (XP) to Scrum, with each focused on improving software quality and application design by closely aligning and validating the requirements of the customer (whether internal or external) through iterative releases of often 30 days or less.

Analysts such as Gartner heavily emphasize support for *Iterative and Incremental Development* or "IID" as a metric for evaluating application platforms and frameworks for application development. Yet what is perhaps the most critical measure, and one too often overlooked in analyst round-ups, is how the parts come together to form the whole. Specifically, how are individual releases combined and made to work together?

Part of this is the actual build and release process. An advantage that BPM platforms offer of traditional IDE is support for a "one-click" build process once the app has been designed and configured. Yet as development orientation shifts from monolithic applications to a more agile "app store" model, maintaining alignment and consistency between each app are essential. It is not a matter of simply performing regression testing or confirming they are compatible.

Data-Driven vs Data-Centric

With traditional application development, most often you will find the orientation is framed around an e-form linked to a data table, where the data model is largely defined by the fields in the form. The application is designed from the perspective that user interaction is simply data entry. For example, an Order Entry application may likely be focused on completing an order, and where there is workflow within the app, it is based on what predefined fields are required to be completed. This is a data-centric approach, rather than data-driven or event-driven.

This type of data-centric scenario is what the first generation of BPM emerged to address. For example, the Order Entry task is just one step (or at most a handful of steps) in a broader process involving the customer, from sales to on-boarding to fulfillment of the order. So BPM initially offered (and in many cases still does) a process-centric approach to complete the various tasks involved in an end-to-end process, such as order-to-cash or procure-to-pay.

The process is not defined simply by the steps needed to complete the form, but is aware of how the data in the form is used to perform the process. These types of processes are deterministic, where all possible paths are pre-determined or known in advance, no matter how complex the pathways may be. The direction of the process is determined by the pre-defined path and current state, where state is determined by the preceding activity (e.g., where the process is relative to its completion).

Yet while process-centric apps offer advancement over data-centric apps, modern BPM, and what we expect from a modern BPM-based application platform is the ability to support data-driven and event-driven apps. Case Management apps, for example, are both data-driven and event-driven. In contrast with process-centric apps, Case Management processes are specifically non-deterministic, where the objective is known when the case starts, but the specific pathway for reaching it, is determined by what happens at each stage – and in particular what data is captured and added to the case. Unlike the traditional BPM process where state is defined by a predetermined sequence of steps, the state of the case is determined by the content of the case and rules and policies applicable to it.

> BPME is, *by definition, an* event-driven and data-driven BPM platform, and must be able to support the types of dynamic processes involved with case management. Cases evolve over time in the direction of achieving a goal, often in unpredictable directions, requiring

the ability to jump forward, jump back, re-do or otherwise perform work in a sequence that can't be determined in advance.

Adaptive Case Management and BPME

A case is different than a standard process; not just in regard to the qualities described earlier, but in terms of its overall lifecycle. It is typically longer-lived, as a case may be restarted at any time, or remain "living" in its current state for any duration until another event occurs.

Where an executed BPM process provides a transactional thread across various others systems (i.e., the order-to-cash example cited earlier), a case captures the context of "what happened" in a virtual case folder that serves as the long-lived system of record of the case. Knowledge captured during the performance of the case, because it is not simply following a predefined path, provides both a critical business record as well as a launch point for new tasks and sub-processes.

This is where case management meets BPME, but providing full engagement of information within a BPM-based app, facilitating consumers of data (e.g., agnostic to being used by an application, intelligent mediator, or human being) including data from both internal and external sources, within an intelligent container where meaning and context can be captured and made actionable.

6. Summary

2015 has already proven to be a breakout year for the sibling technologies of BPME; with the simultaneous arrival robotic assistants (both physical such as *JIBO* and *Pepper* plus many flavors of virtual assistants like *Cubic, EmoSPARK,* and others) the mainstreaming of IoT, wearables such as *Apple Watch,* and new milestones in cognitive computing platforms such as IBM *Watson* and Google *DeepMind.*

Collectively these represent very positive indicators for the next five years of BPM. Each year for the last decade BPM has advanced year over year, continuously transforming not only itself but the environments in which it is applied. In light of this, its "banner years" are hard to distinguish from any other, yet in no year has BPM failed to deliver. At this moment, as we look forward over what's left of 2015 and the next few years to come, there can be no doubt it will again prove to be a banner year for BPM. The proof-points, once elusive, are now easy to find and impossible to ignore. At the same time, however, it is also indisputably different. This will be better than what we have seen before.

Robots, sensors and other data-generating "things" require vertical integration to create managed, measured, and actionable feedback loops. Your refrigerator will probably not be directly connected to a BPM process anytime soon, but will inevitably participate in any number of processes ranging from maintenance to energy conservation.

BPM, and specifically **BPME**, is necessary to bring these innovations into mainstream business operations. New applications are being built to leverage this, yet traditional approaches to application development remain typically far more procedural and programmer-centric. A BPM-based application platform presents a declarative, model-driven development approach that favors configuration over coding. This type of "low code," model-driven approach is how the complex, data-driven systems of the "Internet of Everything" and IoT will continue to emerge.

Resolving the challenge of connecting the growing spectrum of intelligent things is what will drive the BPM investments and digital transformation initiatives of the next decade.

I, For One, Welcome Our New Robot Overlords

Scott Francis and Lance Gibbs, BP3 Global, USA
David Brakoniecki, BP3 Global, UK

ABSTRACT

While pursuing the nirvana of *BPM Everywhere* in the future of *Internet of Things,* let's not forget the basics. Business is about people. Customer experiences are differentiating. The fact is that customers experience our product and our company through our business processes. Waste should be minimized, efficiency maximized, and visibility dramatically increased.

How do we apply the concepts of Lean Flow, Six Sigma, Voice of Customer, and BPM to a world full of a surplus of events, data, and agents? How do we separate signal from noise and produce fantastic process outcomes?

IT'S A BRAVE NEW WORLD. THE BPM CHALLENGES ARE NEW, AND THE SAME.

The premise of this book is *BPM Everywhere*, in the age of the Internet of Things and BPM. The Internet of Things addresses two historic challenges to BPM and process improvement practitioners; being aware of *location* and presence of the participants in the process and being plugged into all the possible *measurements* that might inform the performance of the process.

In the first case, when our process participants were not on a factory floor it used to be hard to know where they would be and whether they could be "present" in the process. In the second case, a key risk in all processes has been measurement risk - detecting the problems in the first place. In many cases accurate measurements at the point of the problem weren't possible – but those cases are fewer and farther between with the advent of IoT. IoT disrupts both of these technical barriers to getting accurate information into BPM process applications. Now it is up to us to take advantage.

However, with all the attention on the bright shiny objects of IoT, we run the risk of losing focus on the thing that matters most: customer experience. We need to determine how, exactly, IoT will impact a customer experience and the intimacy a company has with its customers.

It is our contention that without a focus on people, customers, and process, adopters of IoT risk squandering a generational opportunity to create lasting value.

First, Technology

In this context, BPM practitioners have estimated Takt time[1] and other measures using various methods because direct measurement isn't always possible in a knowledge worker environment.

With the advent of widespread mobile devices running modern operating systems, problem solved. With the advent of IoT, BPM practitioners and systems now have access to all the measurements, events, and incidents they could

---

[1] http://en.wikipedia.org/wiki/Takt_time

possibly want. A single tweet in the Twitter stream could trigger a process or a change in the process execution.

And therein lies the problem. Our future promises an embarrassment of data riches: the flood of information in Twitter is only a small sample of the sheer volume of data that will become available via IoT. The challenge is no longer how to collect good data about our processes, our systems, and our world - the challenge of the future is to find the good data among the rivers of noisy data flowing by. That's a new problem for BPM advocates, but it won't feel like a new problem in 5 years.

But Business Is Human

At the same time, nothing has changed: Business is and will be a fundamentally human endeavor; with possible notable exceptions like trading algorithms, business likely won't be conducted by automated "bots" negotiating with each other on our behalf. The price of something is determined by the market of human desire and need, not by automation. What price do we put on art, on craftsmanship? What price do we put on trust? On shared responsibility? How does automation pick our artwork, our furniture, our clothes? More importantly, what is the **value** that automation is offering to its human masters in such situations? Our robot overlords will have to wait.

The conundrum is that, as technology capabilities continue to help expand the historical boundaries of social interactions between individuals and groups, it also increases the expectations of intimacy and immediacy; an unavoidable side effect, humans by nature are social creatures. Today more than ever, customers expect fast and effective interactions on their terms and not on the terms of any given company. Customers want a meaningful dialogue. This puts enormous pressure on businesses to evolve because the fact is that customers experience our products and our companies as the sum of our business processes. As the barriers continue to fall, the expectations will continue to rise.

The humanity of business will come under assault from the very people trying to improve it. We'll be inundated by rivers of data that are mostly noise rather than signal. We are increasingly depending upon automation to filter that noise to find the signal, and even to make decisions about how to respond, because our data intake is too large for humans to process. The option technologists hold in front of us is to increase our dependency on automation of "intelligent" behaviors.

It doesn't have to be this way. Business is still about people, and the proliferation of devices, events, and data doesn't change that. We don't have to accept the path laid out before us, we can lay out an alternate. Let's explore these themes in the context of IoT, and then bring it back to the people.

WHAT'S OLD IS NEW AGAIN

We have methodologies that have evolved over decades, like Lean-Six Sigma, to incorporate voice of customer into the business of doing business. Do we have to reboot how we do business in the context of the IoT? Are these methods now rendered moot by the data volumes inherent in IoT measurements? It turns out, rather than root out these pillars of BPM, we can turn the tables and apply BPM methods to the technical problems of measurement and analysis. When we look at the vast data collected from an IoT world, we see a few obvious applications of Lean theory.

Overproduction

First of all, the collection of all this data from our IoT devices, Twitter fire hoses, and other data sets violates one of the eight Lean wastes: overproduction. Overproduction is waste in a manufacturing context because it requires storage of inventory, and effectively parks the money that went into building that inventory. However, the analog to the digital world is absolutely there, for example in the context of IoT, all of the measurement data is stored, requiring vast processing power to filter and mine that data.

Lean Six Sigma: 8 Wastes

Defects	Overproduction	Waiting	Non-Utilized Talent
Efforts caused by rework, scrap, and incorrect information.	Production that is more than needed or before it is needed.	Wasted time waiting for the next step in a process.	Underutilizing people's talents, skills, & knowledge.

Transportation	Inventory	Motion	Extra-Processing
Unnecessary movements of products & materials.	Excess products and materials not being processed.	Unnecessary movements by people (e.g., walking).	More work or higher quality than is required by the customer.

goLEANSIXSIGMA   www.GoLeanSixSigma.com

Figure 1: the 8 wastes

Lots of brain power in the software industry goes into how to collect even more of this data from the edges. The rivers of data will become oceans[2]. Imagine the equivalent of a GoPro video feed on every device.

We can understand why so little thought goes into why we're collecting the data: storage is cheap, and no one calculates the cost of processing that data in the future. It is intellectually easier (and lazier) at design time to "collect everything" in case it is useful later, than it is to "collect the important things". But there are consequences to production with little planning...

---

[2] The rivers of data will become oceans: http://sloanreview.mit.edu/article/if-you-think-big-datas-challenges-are-tough-now/

Defects Due to Incorrect Information

Advocates of machine learning will tell us that these "unimportant" data items may turn out to be useful to machine learning and inferences. But real-world data sets are full of correlations that not only lack causation, but even lack a relationship. The quality of our filtering and mining can decline as a consequence of seeing correlations in irrelevant data - which can contribute to defects caused by misunderstanding the data (incorrect information, another of the 8 wastes). We see this tug of war all the time with spam filtering software, and with stock charts super-imposing a correlation in the movements of two unrelated securities – often with an implied prediction of future correlated behavior.

Lean principles would argue that we should spend, on balance, more time designing and thinking through which data (inputs) are useful to our business and business processes from the standpoint of the customer which is the epitome of Outside-In thinking - thus avoiding the waste of collecting data we don't need.

Extra Processing

BPM practitioners are no strangers to this sort of optimization. Often we're presented with mountains of data that the process "might need." We've witnessed whole projects aimed at gathering all the data into one repository - whether it is structured or unstructured data, needed or not. Often our tools will automatically track or log reams of data that we just don't need. And later, we'll have to sift through the sand for one speck of quality information. Combing through irrelevant data is a classic case of extra-processing.

Waiting

Often part of a BPM project revolves around eliminating wait times for a company's employees; reducing the amount of time someone is staring at the spinning dial, or web page refreshing, or a database query result waiting for a response. If analysis can't be done in near-real-time, if the data is delivered in batches, or if the dataset is so large that responses to queries take longer than they should, then we incur the additional waste of human waiting.

A human waiting for something to happen is one of the 8 wastes that Lean dictates we minimize. It disrupts their concentration and the flow of work, it maximizes opportunities for distractions, and it costs money.

Voice of Customer

One way to avoid the traps identified above is to keep the voice of customer top of mind. The more we understand the voice of the customer and their key drivers, the higher the confidence when it comes to meaningful measurement capture – and avoidance of wasted data capture. This data is to serve the business in making decisions in how best to serve the customer. The name of the game is to exceed the customer's expectations at the lowest possible cost.

Whatever the business processes may be or whatever the measurement system may be capable of there are two critical measurement-type notions to keep in mind. One, can I repeat the measurement when the conditions are the same and two, can I reproduce the measurement when the conditions are not the same. Said another way, if my customer interacts with me via one channel and I get insight into their needs, can I do this just as easily, read cheaply, if the channel or mechanism changes?

In the IoT + BPM world this is what is going to be really interesting to see evolve. A customer may fire off a tweet complaining about a service issue with their satellite radio and maybe the satellite company knows who that customer is, or maybe they don't. But the radio should know and if enabled could provide some diagnostic data back to the company. Even better, perhaps the radio sends information back indicating a problem and proactively the company engages the customer to verify their experience. Same macro measurement: "Service Good" - but different conditions.

It is this very notion of specific data, mapped to a key driver of Voice of Customer, and instrumented in the business processes to understand the event and more importantly, actually do something about it that makes things very interesting. The last thing we want is to be churning through thousands and thousands of variables, across huge amounts of data seeking insight. We are humans, customers, and businesses. We are social by nature; we want a dialogue, relevance, and intimacy. Businesses have a long way to go to be on the actionable end of things as it is today. Everyone running to catch up. And now, here is even more data to comprehend. Very interesting indeed!

DATA SCIENCE – IT'S ABOUT THE METHOD, NOT THE DATA

The trends are all there:

- The Internet of Things and social media creates more data than ever before
- Big Data technologies like Hadoop make that information more accessible
- Cloud computing is driving the cost of storage and processing huge data sets downward
- In this world, it is easy to get excited about how all of this information will change your business, how it's really going to change the world.

But, having data and understanding it are still two fundamentally different things. To understand data, to put it to use in context - this is a human endeavor. Even machine learning or cognitive computing technologies still need people to direct and define the problem sets and context.

While progress can be made by making data broadly available in your organization, these advances are limited. At scale, to find your answer in the data requires knowledge of mathematics and statistics as well as computer science. Further, it may require specific knowledge of the business domain. When you have millions of data points, it is a huge haystack. So, how do people find their needle?

The emerging field of data science is one key. Understanding which correlations are important and proving it requires a scientific approach to the data. **It's the science that is important, not the data.**

In scientific research, the Scientific Method[3] is used to systematically form hypotheses and design experiments to validate them. It is an iterative problem-solving methodology and the only way to find real understanding in massive data sets. Statistics can tell you if your experiment is valid, if it's proof. But it will not help to form a hypothesis in the first place.

---

[3] http://en.wikipedia.org/wiki/Scientific_method

So, where in the business world are people that have the right mindset to pick up this challenge? Are data scientists these people?

The research tells us that they are part - but not all - of the solution. While excellent programmers and statisticians who can find insight in numbers, data scientists also tend to be 'outside' the business context:

> A common complaint[4] is that data scientists are aloof and seem uninterested in the professional lives and business problems of less-technical coworkers; they don't see a need to explain or talk about the implications of their insights, which makes it difficult for them to partner effectively with professionals whose business expertise lies outside of the technical realm.

Interestingly, Lean techniques are already well suited to bridge the gap with the data scientists. They are focused on the business context and the value chain. They should be able to help frame the problem to be solved.

But, they also understand iterative problem-solving.

The Deming Cycle of Plan-Do-Check-Act (PDCA)[5] has been a cornerstone of lean thinking since Edward Deming developed it in Japan during the 1950s. PDCA is just the scientific method adapted to business operations.

Further, the mantra of continuous improvement that flows from the Deming Cycle has lead to more recent innovations like agile development which provides a fantastic method to realize the benefits of Big Data. After all, insight only becomes valuable in execution. Knowing something is not enough. You also need to change the business to respond, to adapt, to that knowledge.

Between Big Data and Lean principles – applied to the context of IoT - business should have a blueprint to dramatically improved customer experiences and to solve previously intractable problems. Doing so will require coordination across disciplines. Fortunately, aligning cross-functional teams around value streams is not a new idea. In fact, it might be the core observation of the Lean movement in manufacturing. We just need to bring it into the digital age.

IT'S THE CUSTOMER EXPERIENCE. PERIOD.

As we're looking to extract value from the Internet of Things, Lean methods, and Data Science, we can't lose sight of the ultimate goal: a great customer experience.

History has a way of repeating itself. Looking back to the nineties, when the World Wide Web rolled out in earnest, there was an immense focus on the disruptive nature of web-based technologies on traditional businesses. Largely these "born after the Internet" businesses failed - arguably because they were absorbed in the amazing new world of the internet, and lost sight of the primacy of customer experiences. The customer wasn't front and center, she was an afterthought.

The next wave of "born after the Internet" businesses have succeeded largely on the basis of providing a superior and differentiated customer experience - Uber, Instacart, Warby Parker, WP Engine, Lyft, Slack, Nest - while each had product innovations, and took advantage of technology tides, they didn't lose sight of the primacy of customer experience. The primary interactions with

---

[4] http://sloanreview.mit.edu/article/getting-value-from-your-data-scientists/

[5] http://en.wikipedia.org/wiki/PDCA

some of these companies is mobile, or online, and not physical premise. And yet, they each have a great reputation for customer service.

One could argue that ride-sharing businesses like Uber and Lyft are primitive early entrants in the IoT space -where each "thing" is a moving vehicle or a rider. And they manage the data flows so that you know when your car is picking you up, and the driver knows how to find you, from request to ride to payment at the end. But they aren't relying on how cool the technology is. They're tweaking business models to reach more customers, they're tweaking technology to improve the experience, and they're competing on the basis of superior customer engagement. The whole point of their business isn't the cool technical achievements – the point of their business is the customer experiences those technical achievements support and sustain.

Warby Parker and Zappos are examples of traditionally offline businesses (glasses and shoes) that work online *because of the great customer engagement and intimacy*. Their customer service overcomes time and distance and is partly enabled by technology and the vast logistics networks that are our shipping companies.

WP Engine and Nest pride themselves on offerings that are easy enough to use - but when you need help their product support teams are among the best we've ever worked with as customers.

Go Forth and Build Experiences

The opportunities exist, with IoT, to form new customer services experiences for maintenance - whether it is lawn care, pool maintenance, AC/Heat maintenance, or other electronics. It is just a matter of new and existing businesses putting the customer experience around the technology to make it interesting.

For businesses who can maintain core values around differentiated customer experience – IoT, BPM, and the technology wave - will only open up new opportunities for these businesses to augment their core value propositions and improve their customer intimacy. These customer experience focused enterprises will get increased leverage from Lean insights and practices. This is the opportunity in front of us: customer experiences that create lifetime customer relationships, enabled and augmented by an array of supporting technological innovations. It's an amazing opportunity we don't want to miss.

References

"If You Think Big Data's Challenges Are Tough *Now...*" Randy Bean, MIT Sloan Review: http://sloanreview.mit.edu/article/if-you-think-big-datas-challenges-are-tough-now/

"The Digital Universe of Opportunities: Rich Data and the Increasing Value of the Internet of Things"
http://www.emc.com/leadership/digital-universe/2014iview/index.htm

IDC, April 2014 -- http://www.emc.com/leadership/digital-universe/2014iview/internet-of-things.htm

Accenture Tech Vision 2015 – "Digital Business Era: Stretch Your Boundaries"
http://techtrends.accenture.com/us-en/business-technology-trends-report.html

[MIT Loan Management Review] (http://sloanreview.mit.edu/article/getting-value-from-your-data-scientists/)

The Internet of Things Will Be Invisible

Peter Whibley, KANA, United Kingdom

"The most profound technologies are those that disappear. They weave themselves into the fabric of everyday life until they are indistinguishable from it." Mark Weiser

INTRODUCTION

I already spend too much time on the Web, so what's it going to be like in 2025 when another 26 billion smart devices are connected to the Internet?

In 2014, research by Pew[1] looking at digital life in 2025, gave some pointers to what life might be like once all these smart devices come online. The Pew report reflects that this is a market in the very earliest stages of its evolution, with little overall consensus and concerns being expressed around the social (privacy, exclusion) as well as technical implications of Internet of Things (integration). One word, however, that pops up frequently in the Pew report is "invisible".

As humans, we've pretty much mastered our ability to generate data, and the emergence of the Internet of Things (IoT) takes our ability to create data to another dimension. What we haven't mastered, however, is our ability to increase time. Human attention is a limited, scarce resource. Do we really want to be alerted and prompted on a regular basis by multiple frivolous IoT devices all competing for our attention?

At the moment, discussion of the commercial IoT has focused on the devices or things themselves rather than the services that can be triggered by connecting sensors and devices to the Internet. Many of the commercial and smart home technologies we see today are really just gimmicks as already available sensor and Wi-Fi technology wait on other essential components of the IoT ecosystem to catch up. This chapter discusses two of these essential components of the future IoT ecosystem — business process management (BPM) and voice recognition.

The IoT will be notable for being invisible; BPM and voice recognition will help make this happen.

THE INTERNET...

The IoT market can be, very broadly, broken into two market segments — the industrial IoT and the commercial IoT. The industrial IoT has been alive and well for years, connecting critical machines and sensors as well as providing monitoring and control services in high-stakes industries, such as energy, healthcare and aerospace, where failures can result in emergency or life threatening situations. One of the key characteristics of the industrial IoT is that it provides these services with little or no human interaction. Often, the industrial IoT is providing services that must happen quickly, reliably and frequently without human involvement or in situations where human involvement would actually reduce service quality.

Discussion of the commercial IoT, however, has been heavily focused on the "things" rather than the "Internet," on the devices themselves and less so on the services that could be delivered through their connection to the Internet. Unlike their industrial cousins, the first generation of commercial IoT devices are, for the most part, providing frivolous and non-essential services where breakdowns or issues do not immediately create critical or emergency situations. They are mostly connected to the Internet for control, monitoring and software update purposes rather than for the provision of services.

When we start thinking of the commercial IoT not in terms of devices, but instead in terms of services that could be triggered through connection to the Internet, more compelling use cases start to emerge. Already some of the most successful commercial IoT solutions are providing services rather than simply devices to consumers. In-car telematics[2] is now widely used in the insurance industry today to monitor driver performance and to adjust insurance premiums accordingly. In medicine, heart implants[3] are being used that send data to physicians that can be analyzed to identify any slowing of heart rhythm or rapid heartbeats. Once installed, it requires no further action from the patient. Looking forward in the public realm, IoT will be used within Smart Cities to provide services to constituents that will, for example, reduce congestion, optimize energy use and support public safety. The common theme in all of these examples is that the IoT is being used to provide services with little or no input required by the individual. The IoT and the devices themselves are for the most part invisible.

...OF THINGS

To date, much of the discussion of commercial IoT has been dominated by the connection of everyday things to the Internet, for example, smart refrigerators, wearables, thermostats, automatic pet feeders, kettles, sprinklers and even smart toilets[4]. As with most nascent technologies, it appears we are learning on the job. The success of the smartphone was, in part, because it combined the functionality of multiple devices into a single handset. The music player, phone and personal organizer have all disappeared to be replaced by a single smart mobile device. Automobiles are incorporating technologies that were previously separate devices, such as satellite navigation, entertainment and telephony. Record players and DVD players have slowly disappeared from our homes to be replaced by a music and video on demand business model. It seems that the evolutionary endpoint of personal IT is that it ultimately disappears.

The consumer IoT market today, however, stands in direct contrast to this trend of eventual invisibility. In the smart home and consumer space, the sprawl of IoT devices already threatens to overwhelm us. The failure of Google Glass and the difficult birth of the smart watch reflect that both technologies have attempted to reverse the trend for miniaturization and invisibility by introducing rather than eliminating devices.

I already have a cupboard of old gadgets, a tech graveyard that includes old satellite receivers, food processors, old mobile phones and a spaghetti of chargers and power supplies. Gartner[5] estimates that the typical family home could have up to 500 smart devices by 2022. This device tsunami poses significant challenges from complexity to interoperability and ultimately cost. It threatens to widen the digital divide between those who have access to information and communication technology (ICT) and the skills to make use of ICT, and those who do not have the access or skills to use those same technologies.

... WILL BE INVISIBLE

I don't look forward to a future where I'm constantly interrupted with messages telling me that I've run out of milk, my toaster has a comms problem, I'm not brushing my teeth correctly, my grass needs to be watered or that I haven't exercised enough. Yet, rather than freeing us from the Internet, the current generation of commercial IoT devices is drawing us further and further into the Web for provisioning, integration, alerts, notifications and software update requests. Rather than simplifying our lives, the initial commercial IoT devices have arguably made our lives more complicated.

The sheer volume of potential IoT solutions is such that machine to machine (M2M) rather than machine to human (M2H) communications will dominate the IoT. Future commercial IoT services and solutions will, for the most part, be invisible, acting as an airbag for our lives, ready to step in when we need it, not constantly competing for our attention. Like their industrial counterparts, commercial IoT will provide either critical services, such as personal security and health monitoring, or help to eliminate repetitive or mundane processes, such as insurance renewals or car service scheduling.

The current focus on devices rather than services is inevitable, as sensor and Wi-Fi technology wait for other essential parts of the IoT ecosystem to catch up. Like the smartphone, the things themselves will slowly disappear or be consumed by other applications. The commercial IoT will evolve to an invisible services role in our lives.

IoT solutions will include a mix of technologies that include sensors, Wi-Fi networks, database management systems and data analytics applications. Two additional technologies will, however, be critical to delivering the next generation of commercial IoT services as well as the ultimate invisibility of the IoT — BPM and voice recognition.

BPM AND THE INTERNET OF THINGS

Process isn't just something businesses do. Only last weekend, I sold an old mobile phone on eBay. The process of putting it up for sale took maybe 15 minutes. I also visited a price comparison site to obtain a car insurance quote, a process which took a bit longer. My wife searched for and booked a flight. Car insurance and home insurance renewals loom on the horizon. In our individual lives, we are regularly performing mundane, sometimes important, often repetitive processes that many of us would gladly outsource to third-party applications.

Process will be absolutely fundamental to the future of the IoT. The IoT already has the potential to create vast floods of data with sensors and devices capturing data about themselves, their environment, their context or their user's behavior. To make sense out of this chaos, we require applications that can extract value from this data. The value of IoT data can only be fully realized if it is first analyzed and then used, if necessary, to trigger a follow-up action or process. In the heart implant example previously discussed, the detection of an irregular heart rhythm or rapid heartbeats could be used to alert the physician and automatically schedule a doctor's appointment. Already we see emerging IoT and process use cases, such as smart pill bottles[6] that remind the patient to take their pills and trigger follow-up actions, such as phone calls or text messages to the patient or their care giver if the medicine isn't taken.

Data has always been the blood in the veins of BPM solutions, used to trigger processes, recommend next-best actions and guide employees. Both in a personal and business IoT context, BPM applications are perfectly suited to orchestrate the flow of information and actions between the smart devices, the consumer and businesses.

The business process management suite (BPMS) was originally designed and deployed as a back-office application. In its original incarnation, the role of the BPMS was to automate and optimize mundane and repetitive processes, thus eliminating or freeing employees to focus where they could add more value. In recent years, as organizations have turned their attention toward how they acquire, serve and retain customers, the BPMS moved to the front of the house to be deployed alongside or embedded within CRM applications and used to optimize customer service processes. The eventual integration of processes within IoT solutions represents the next stage of the BPM journey that started in the back office. Process orchestration will be a crucial component in the delivery of IoT services.

While inevitable, the integration of process within IoT solutions still remains a few years away. The BPMS currently has an identity crisis. In common with other enterprise software applications, it has struggled to adapt to the social, mobile, analytics and cloud (SMAC) industry megatrends. It remains an extremely complex hybrid of multiple applications from process modelling, business rules, Web form design, business intelligence and, more recently, mobile apps and enterprise collaboration software. In recent years, the emergence of industry frameworks, accelerators and smart process applications[7] (SPAs) is a response by BPM vendors to address this complexity, to simplify process delivery and move the BPMS from a long-term strategic play to a short-term tactical play. Evolution of the BPMS or a mechanism by which high volume, pre-configured processes can be delivered rapidly to IoT devices and solutions is still required.

The most significant BPMS development in recent years, and the most important from an IoT perspective, has been the transition of the BPMS to the cloud. Today, many BPMS vendors offer multitenant versions of their on-premises BPMS. Multitenant cloud deployment opens the door for almost instant provisioning of BPM solutions or smaller process snippets that could be deployed with or embedded within IoT solutions.

Business process outsourcing (BPO) organizations have been delivering tailored and more standardized processes to clients for years. Business process services, such as human resources, payroll, policy administration and insurance claims, are provided by BPO organizations today. As the BPMS moves to the cloud, Business Process as a Service (BPaaS), or the delivery of multitenant BPO services, represents the evolution of this trend of process outsourcing. A multitenant BPMS has the capability to deliver high-volume, automatically scalable, highly standardized on-demand processes that will be necessary for the high-volume IoT services market.

The IoT is an opportunity for BPM to shed the layers of skin, to shed the mobile and social baggage it has built up over the years and get back to basics — the delivery and orchestration of high volume, repetitive processes. We are potentially looking at a process future very different from today's complex BPMS to a much leaner BPMS platform whose role is to mostly coordinate M2M communication, operating for the most part invisibly and only reaching out to humans when an authorization is required. It is the consumerization of BPM and the delivery of BPaaS, where embedded processes work with sensors and IoT devices in an attempt to eliminate mundane or repetitive processes or trigger critical services.

Examples of IoT services that could be supported by integrated or embedded processes include automatic car service scheduling, utility metering and payments, and ambient customer service where organizations detect product problems and deliver customer service directly to devices themselves without any human involvement. Going beyond devices, I would happily subscribe to a service from my financial service provider that would ensure my savings or loans were automatically on the best rate of interest or subscribe to a service that scanned the market for the best insurance deal and carried out the renewal automatically. These IoT services could be delivered using process applications, working invisibly in the background of our lives, only reaching out to us when a decision or an approval is required.

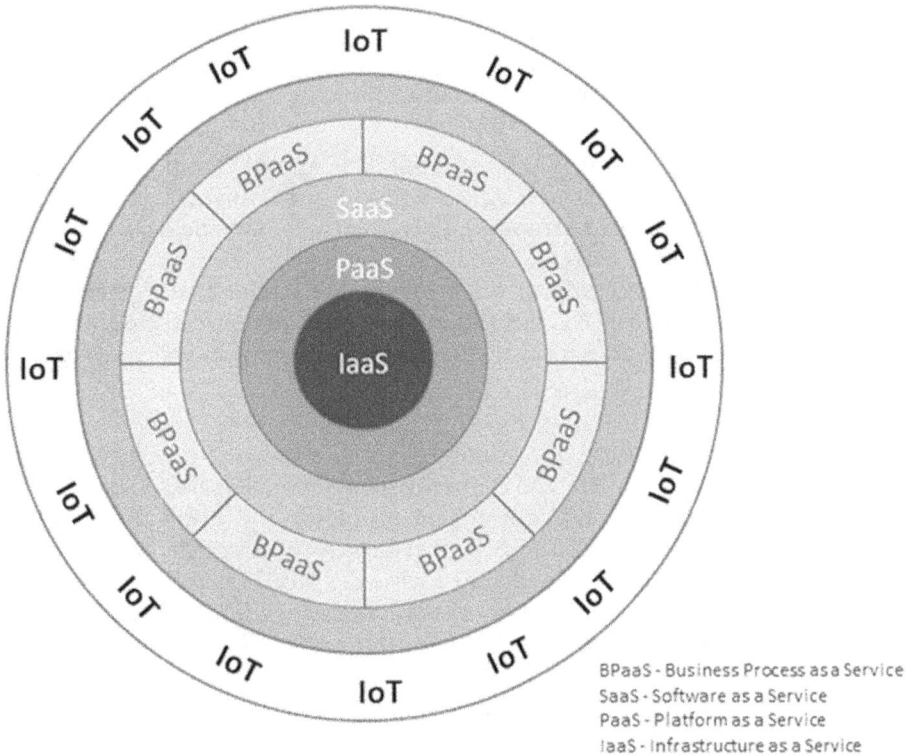

BPaaS - Business Process as a Service
SaaS - Software as a Service
PaaS - Platform as a Service
IaaS - Infrastructure as a Service

Figure 1: IoT Cloud Service Layers

VOICE RECOGNITION AND THE INTERNET OF THINGS

July 10, 2008 was a watershed date in personal computing. On this date, Apple launched the App Store, marking the first time that software applications could be purchased and installed onto a mobile device without having to sync with a PC or laptop. The App Store, launched with 552 applications, has now more than 1 million apps. The app store has had a profound impact on our perception of software and consumer technology. The ability to download a game or a lifestyle software application in seconds and use it intuitively without recourse to a user guide is now taken for granted in our personal lives. And our personal technology experience has changed our business IT expectations. Software should be simple, on demand, require no training and, in many cases, be free.

Yet already it appears that app fatigue is starting to set in. I currently have about 40 apps on my smartphone, yet I use only about 10 of them frequently. The vast majority of the 2 million apps on the Apple and Google app stores make no money. Today, many IoT devices are delivered with a mobile app for control. Apps have emerged for fridges, kettles, toothbrushes, thermostats and fitness devices, all sending alerts and all competing for our attention. This is the classic "basket of remotes" problem where instead of having a remote control for every new device within our homes, we now have a mobile app.

Apple HomeKit[8] and Samsung SmartThings[9] are attempts by leading IT organizations to address the emerging issue of multiple apps and disconnected IoT home devices. HomeKit attempts to unify all the different IoT devices into one system via an iPhone or iPad. Yet, this assumes that all IoT devices will consolidate within a single platform. It also narrowly views the IoT in terms of devices, to be controlled via a user interface, rather than as services. With an estimate that the typical family home could have up to 500 smart devices by 2022, we need to look beyond the app.

Today, three of largest global IT organizations — Apple, Google and Microsoft — offer voice recognition software. Apple was the first mover with Siri. Google followed with its own natural language user interface, Google Now, and finally Microsoft came to market with Cortana. Despite having an iPhone, apart from asking Siri a few stupid questions when I'm bored, I seldom use Siri. Yet here we have three of the largest IT companies on the planet investing heavily on speech recognition. Why do we have this sudden interest in voice recognition? The answer lies with the IoT.

With so many potential IoT devices, sensors and services, voice control provides a simpler, quicker and more convenient method of interaction rather than an app and a UI. With the iOS 8 operating system, Siri became completely hands free, with the "Hey Siri" command replacing initiation of Siri via the home button. In addition, from iOS 8, Siri began to integrate with the apple IoT HomeKit features. Apple stated that Siri users would soon be able to issue a single command "and have the lights turn on in specific rooms, the thermostat adjust the temperature and the garage door open."[10] Here we have Apple indicating that voice recognition will have a key role to play in the IoT.

"Hey Siri" follows on from the introduction of Google's "OK Google" search command on Google Now earlier this year. While both the "OK Google" and "Hey Siri" commands may seem trivial or frivolous features, due to app fatigue, voice initiation of our interactions with smart devices will be a critical component of personal IoT solutions. Having an app or having to access a UI for every smart device is unsustainable.

But why stop at the control of smart devices using voice command? As voice recognition improves, what is stopping many of our other interactions with the Internet from moving toward voice command rather than via a user interface (UI)? In the future, will we really need a UI to book a flight, transfer money, book a ticket or obtain an insurance quote? What if we could go "Hey Siri, can you put this coat up for sale on eBay?" or "Hey Siri, can you book me a flight to London on March 17?" What if we could say "OK Google, can you get me a home insurance quote?" or "OK Google, can you transfer my credit card balance to the lowest possible interest rate?" What if we could make these voice commands anywhere in our homes or while we are on the move? These are mundane, yet sometimes essential, activities and processes we'd all love to be able to outsource. These voice-activated processes will require a mix of voice recognition, smart devices and sensors, as well as process automation.

Figure 2: Voice Initiated IoT Services

CONCLUSION

To date, the most significant acquisition in the IoT space was Google's purchase of Nest in 2014. Following the acquisition by Google, Nest CEO Tony Fadell told WIRED[11] "Both companies believe in letting the technology do the hard work behind the scenes so that people can get on with their lives." The statement recognizes that IoT solutions will be mostly invisible and that process automation will be a crucial component.

We are at the very early stages in the development of the commercial IoT market, but ultimately it will follow its industrial counterpart and begin to provide services rather than devices. Successful IoT solutions will be those that remove complexity from our lives rather than add to it with yet another app or UI that demands our attention. Today's focus on devices and apps will change as voice recognition and process enable new services and alternative methods of interaction with the IoT. The speaker and mic could emerge as the most critical IoT devices in our daily lives. Voice rather than the UI may become the predominant way we engage with processes.

The IoT potentially won't have its Apple iPhone moment or a tipping point when demand soars. Instead, the IoT may silently and invisibly weave its way into our lives, providing an increasing portfolio of services that act as an airbag for our lives, ready to step in when problems occur. Just like the most profound technologies today, the IoT will disappear.

REFERENCES

1. The Internet of Things Will Thrive by 2025 http://www.pewinternet.org/2014/05/14/internet-of-things/
2. http://en.wikipedia.org/wiki/Telematics
3. http://www.bbc.co.uk/news/uk-northern-ireland-20991986
4. http://www.dailymail.co.uk/sciencetech/article-2384826/Satis-smart-toilets-Japan-hacked-hijacked-remotely.html
5. http://www.gartner.com/newsroom/id/2839717
6. http://www.theverge.com/2014/1/8/5289022/adheretech-smart-pill-bottle
7. https://www.forrester.com/Smart+Process+Applications+Fill+A+Big+Business+Gap/fulltext/-/E-RES77442
8. https://developer.apple.com/homekit/
9. http://www.smartthings.com/
10. https://www.apple.com/uk/pr/library/2014/09/09Apple-Announces-iOS-8-Available-September-17.html
11. http://www.wired.com/2014/01/googles-3-billion-nest-buy-finally-make-internet-things-real-us/

Woots: Smart Things that Can Think, Act, Learn and Talk

Surendra Reddy, CEO, Quantiply, USA

ABSTRACT

We introduce a new concept called *Web Of Open Things* (Woots) that are everyday "Smart Things" with a specific identity, intelligence, address and presence on the Internet and capabilities to self-organize and communicate with other things with or without human intervention. To make sense of the flow of information, activities, and rich interaction experience, Woots also embed a "tiny brain" to provide context awareness, autonomy, business process intelligence and reactivity.

A semantic memory embedded into Woots stores a digital diary of an individual physical object in a persistent way and makes this information available to other devices, applications, and its environment. Woots also integrates dial tone by which other Woots or applications can engage in social networking and co-operating machine learning process. This is called *flocking* and *mating* of Woots.

Another novel idea that is integral part of Woots architecture is the Enterprise Digital Genome (EDGE). The EDGE, using advanced machine learning techniques and process mining, characterizes the personalities of systems or system of systems in which Woots are embedded or integrated. There are number of scenarios where Woots could be revolutionary in enabling brilliant factories and smart cities. Woots would also enable the creation of personalized software humanoids, like Wootsup app described in this chapter, that will cater to our needs in private life, including shopping, smart home and public environments.

INTRODUCTION

Two billion people are connected to the Internet. Almost $8 trillion exchange hands each year through e-commerce. In some developed markets, about two-thirds of all businesses have a Web presence of some kind, and one-third of small and medium-sized businesses extensively use Web technologies. The Internet has transformed the way we live, the way we work, the way we socialize and meet, and the way our countries develop and grow [1]. The Internet has quickly become the de-facto global repository of knowledge and information as well as a continuing source of new opportunities as the primary global means of collaboration and co-creation.

And even with the Internet's tremendous impact to date, more and more people and things continue to be connected to the Internet every day. Additionally, the people, processes and things that connect via the Internet are leaving behind exponentially expanding digital footprints of their interactions, as well as, the organic daily rhythms of society itself.

As a result of the Internet's unprecedented success, growth and interconnectivity, it has become a vast repository of mostly unstructured and untapped digital traces of just about anything we can imagine. When these collective digital records of our behavior are fully leveraged they will help us to better understand consumption patterns, interactions with brands, people, and things, public opinion, and to form communities of interest to communicate and influence both social and market patterns for the benefit of individuals, organizations and societies more easily than ever before. Continuous measurement of these digital footprints will help us to better understand the invisible aspects of these smart objects and individual's interactions with these objects [15].

This never-before available volume, breadth, depth, and timeliness of data – digital traces – provide the opportunity to help detect new patterns, associations, and correlations in markets, public opinions, and even health and safety. Most exciting is that the rapid discovery and diffusion of these insights will be fast enough, even continuous and real-time, to be both actionable and of very high value.

The Internet itself, much like the revolution sparked by the printing press, has become a powerful tool to persuade, connect and engage humans and things alike, serving as the common fabric of interconnection [3,4] between anything and everything in our day-to-day lives and businesses. The Internet's potential as a powerful measurement tool to be fully leveraged by society, however, is yet to be realized. For decades, researchers, marketing departments and statisticians have all been using traditional surveys to measure and identify critical trends and strategies. Yet, these traditional methods are very expensive and take weeks or months to design, test and implement.

In the next wave of Internet evolution, happening now, the increasing volume, variety and velocity of data produced by the Internet of Things (IoT) – including connected cities, enterprises and factories – will continue to fuel the explosion of data and the high-value digital traces this data provides, for the foreseeable future. Enterprises are deploying smart labels, intelligent sensors, tags into everyday products to enable them to manage the life cycle and interactions with these smart things. Artificial intelligence added to these smart things enables them to think, act, and talk to other devices or humans.

Smartphones equipped with a plethora of sensors and significant processing power act as a data aggregator of network traffic from these sensors and serve as a gateway to platforms offering diversity of services. Smartphones play a crucial role in aggregating multiple sources and/or as computing platforms for artificial intelligence algorithms to learn from the data and intelligent sensing from the surrounding environment [11]. By enabling the social networking of these smart things, large numbers of people and/or machines can provide more accurate answers to complex problems than an individual or a machine can do [12].

People, Things and Processes that run in this connected world leave behind vast digital footprints of these processes, things, people, interactions, and daily rhythms of the society. As a result, the Internet is a powerful tool to persuade, connect and engage humans and things alike serving as the common fabric of interconnection among everything.

This chapter discusses the adoption of smart analytics and business process intelligence into Smart Things, called Woots, and the Enterprise Digital Genome (EDGE) service, a cloud-based smart things operating system to improve interoperability, reduce the overall architectural complexity, and facilitate the integration of processes, people, and things. The EDGE service described in this chapter is part of the experimental open innovation platform, Big Data Foundry, the author co-founded with PARC, Cisco, and Hitachi and will be part of the Global Real-time Analytics Centers of Excellence (Global RACE) being setup in USA, Singapore and Australia to promote open innovation for connected enterprises, smart cities, and smart environments.

BUSINESS DRIVERS AND CHALLENGES

Web and Internet technologies first helped connect people, society, enterprises, and various commerce infrastructures to radically simplify the distance between the reach and access. As people, things, and the world gets more interconnected, the vision of smart environments has moved into reality and the interlinking of these physical worlds allows for the creation of larger systems or System of Systems, which integrates systems into complex systems that offer better functionality and performance than simply the sum of the constituent systems [2]. This digital transformation not only changed the Customer's expectations but also accelerated the knowledge and information diffusion across and beyond the organizational boundaries. Information that was accessible only to a select set of people is now widely available. Consumerization and Globalization are turning enterprises upside down and demanding customer-focused business operating system.

Driven by these trends, companies have invested heavily in implementing ERP, CRM or other technology-enabled changes. Though these systems improved process efficiency and provided better financial data for strategic decisions, they became overly complex and have not yet fully engaged their stakeholders and ecosystem partners for real-time sensing and anticipatory decision support. These companies can derive much more value by integrating with smart environments, and driving digital transformation excellence to reap larger returns from their foundational investments. Retailers and other service firms gather detailed information on buyer behavior, but lack the analytics capabilities and real-time feedbacks into their business processes [6,7] to truly understand the power of the data.

Business processes are the critical link between strategy and execution [7]. In the past, businesses relied on market and customer segmentation to guide their sales and customer acquisition strategies. However, the digital transformation revolution shifted the power in favor of the customers in terms of what they buy, when they buy, through which channel and what price - disrupting the Product, Price, Place, and Promotion (4P) marketing models. The one-time transaction oriented model is almost dead; instead, customers need to be continuously engaged, educated, and entertained to drive engagement with the brands and the products. This continuous experience based engagement presented many opportunities to consumers to interact with a particular brand. Digital transformation and connectivity of the Internet also offered whole new set of opportunities to businesses to satisfy the ever-increasing demands of their customer base, strengthen the brand engagement and ultimately boost sales and engage profitable customers.

The connectivity of the Internet is changing the way products and services are made. Emergence of IoT is transforming factories from process-defined production facilities into agile digital manufacturing centers of excellence. Customers, designers, engineers, and even factories and machines can collaborate unlike never before to innovate, streamline, and maintain quality products, evolving service from a model of break-fix to self-aware machines and factories. This level of connectivity accorded by IoT increases reach, reliability, sustainability, and efficiency by improved access to information and active engagement of stakeholders.

IoT is one of the key technologies to enable the creation of cyber physical systems and realize the vision of connecting everything and turning everything smart. The IoT paradigm is therefore changing, and will continue to change, the lives of people worldwide, whether its effects are obvious to the user or not. IoT is rapidly expanding to different application domains due to ever-increasing number of connected mobile and wireless devices and their increasing capability not only to observe but also to actuate on the real world. Through the cooperative sensing, coordination and action, the IoT enables the development of collective intelligence applications.

The increasing volume, variety, and velocity of data produced by the IoT, including connected cities, enterprises and factories, will continue to fuel the explosion of data for the foreseeable future. The volume of the data will help detect new patterns, associations, and correlations in markets, public opinions, and even health and safety. To reap the full benefits, any successful solution to build context-aware data-intensive applications and services must be able to make this valuable or important information transparent and available at a much higher frequency, to substantially improve the decision making and prediction capabilities of the applications and services.

Smart Enterprise and Systems Thinking

Systems thinking [10] is purported as being highly germane for dealing with complex systems and problems. Systems thinking enables better understanding of the interconnections and the interactions of business processes, systems, people, things, the variables affecting processes, and the overall effects of the actions and decisions. Therefore, by thinking systematically, we challenged the current systems architecture and models by:

- actuating awareness of the current system,
- whenever possible reduce the computational complexity, thus leading to a simpler system which needs less time and often energy,
- understanding the interactions, structures and interconnections among various systems,
- challenging the current system boundaries to seamlessly integrating emerging trends in the technologies, and
- conceptualizing and defining the attributes of an improved and successful system state

Figure 1.1 shows the system of systems [9] view of a modern connected enterprise.

Smart Environment

Smart environments [5] are physical worlds that are interwoven with sensors, actuators, processes or applications, systems, displays and computational elements, embedded seamlessly into everyday objects and connected through a network enabling continuous sensing, discovery, and distribution of information.

System

A system is an organization of connected parts, where each part and the overall system exhibits some behavior [9]. A system is placed in an operating environment and may have a function or process and produce some outcome according to a system's objectives. The parts of a system are themselves systems. Enterprise Systems are organizational systems which may be observed on different levels, ranging from humans undertaking a collaborative enterprise, departments of a single organization to companies being part of supply networks [2]. These complex systems poses an interoperability barriers [19] that obstruct the collaboration of enterprise systems with respect to their conceptual, technological, as well as organizational disparities. In addition, the collaboration can take place at various different levels within an enterprise including data, service, and process interactions [7].

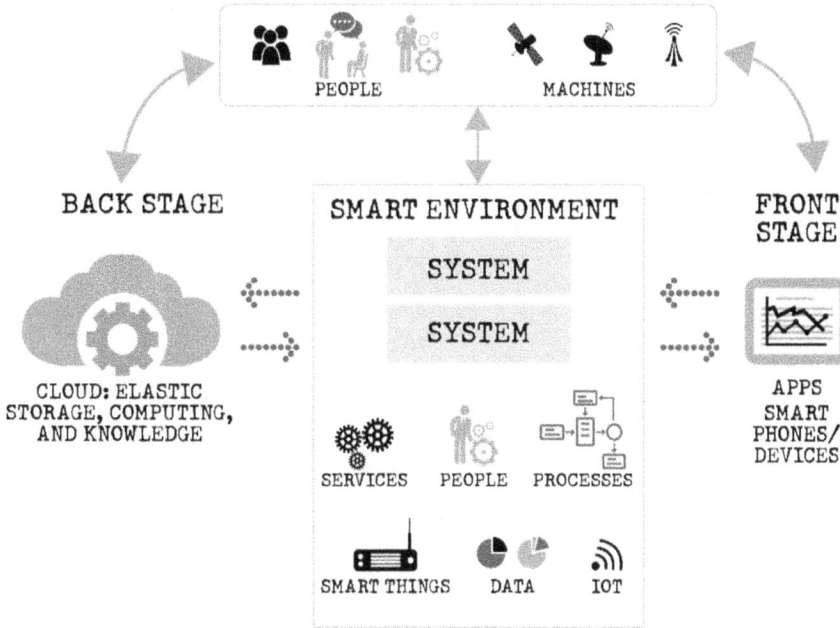

1.1 Smart Enterprise: System of Systems View

Smart Things

A Smart Thing is an electronic object, generally connected to the Internet or other networks through WiFi, 3G, or other protocols usually with a display, a small information store and with touch or voice-activated controls to interact.

People, Things, and Social Networking

Millions of people regularly participate in online social networks. The sensing of people constitutes a new application domain that broadens the traditional sensor network scope of environmental and infrastructure monitoring [9]. People become a key system component, enabling a variety of new application areas such as personal, social and community sensing. People become the carriers of sensing devices and both producers and consumers of events [11].

A people-centric sensing system imbues the individuals it serves in a symbiotic relationship with itself [12]. People-centric sensing enables a different approach to sensing, learning, visualizing and data sharing, not only about ourselves but also about the world we live in. These sensors can reach into regions where static sensors cannot and make them useful for applications that occasionally require sensing [14, 17,18]. Application of these systems will revolutionize the context-aware computing [13], enabling every interaction and engagement to be contextually driven and thereby reducing the information overload. In *personal sensing*, the focus is on monitoring the self; and information is generated for the sole consumption of the user and is generally not shared with others. In *social sensing*, information is shared within the group. Individuals who participate in these applications have a commonality of interests, forming a group [11]. The combination of social networks and intelligent things enables not only sharing and problem solving collaboratively, but also providing more accurate solutions to complex problems [20].

Cloud and Infinite Computing and Storage

The amount of information generated through Internet-based systems, users, devices, etc., as well as their interaction and collaboration require large computing and storing capacities due to the unprecedented amount of data. On the one hand, due to the advanced services delivered through the Cloud, the interactive collaboration and information generation can be at global large-scale systems. On the other hand, Cloud computing makes it possible to store and process very large amounts of data, known as "big data" and deliver insight as a service to end users. The shift from collective intelligence to inter-cooperative collective intelligence is being pushed by the integration of various paradigms and technologies into large-scale systems.

User Augmented Intelligence

The IoT is really about human augmentation. The applications are profoundly different when you have sensors and data driving the decision-making. By connecting and sharing ideas, large numbers of people and/or machines can provide more accurate answers to complex problems than single individuals [20]. You can measure, test and change things dynamically. Real-time user contributed data is invaluable to address community-level problems and provide a universal access to information, contributing to the emergence of innovative services [18]. Context is the metadata that describes the conditions to which sensors are exposed, affecting both data and sensors' ability to perform sensing operations. IoTs and User Augmented Intelligence make the data contextually rich and enable us to see where things are. There is a complex interplay of humans, interfaces and machines.

Smart Labels

Emergence of Smart labels enables new product-centric ways of machine-to-machine communication and human–machine interaction across an entire product lifecycle. The new generations of smart labels integrated in physical products also include sensor capabilities and hence facilitate applications that go over and beyond the pure identification function of RFID marking. From production through to disposal and recycling of tangible objects, it now becomes possible to capture and utilize up-to-date item level product data. Embedding sensors, communication and computing capabilities into physical products enables them to seamlessly gather and use information throughout their entire lifecycle. By capturing and interpreting user actions and ambient conditions, smart products with a data shadow stored in their embedded digital product memory are able to perceive and control their environment, to analyze their observations and to communicate with other objects and human users about their lifelog data [13].

Processes

A business process is a collection of structured and related steps or activities. Once a process is in place, its performance needs to be managed on an ongoing basis, in terms of Key Performance Insights (KPIs) that relate to customer needs and company requirements, needs to be compared to the targets for KPIs. Such KPIs can be based on customer expectations, competitor benchmarks, enterprise needs, and other sources [6].

In a fully-connected enterprise, society or nation, deep process insights enable them to proactively identify and respond better to periods of rapid change. In the past, businesses relied on market and customer segmentation to guide their sales and customer acquisition strategies. Through operational excellence, an enterprise can create high-performance processes, which operate with much lower costs, faster speeds, greater accuracy, reduced assets, and enhanced flexibility. Through mapping and optimizing the customer interactions with the key processes, an enterprise can ensure that its processes deliver on their promise and operate consistently at the level to which they are capable. These operational benefits of consistency, cost, speed, quality, and service translate into lower operating costs and improved customer satisfaction, which in turn drive improved enterprise performance [7].

Data

Data streams from these new devices need to be recognized by their affinities of place, time, or correlation to be incorporated into the original application's information landscapes or neighborhoods. Information neighborhoods created through data stream affinities will present opportunities for selecting and combining small data flows from many different kinds of end devices, not all of which are even part of a specific application. This allows smart systems or environment to become smarter and smarter over time, as ever more sensors or sensing mechanisms are enabled. The interoperability of data, both analog and digital, plays an important part in the context of collaborating enterprise systems. It not only facilitates the basic exchange of data but also the comprehensibility in terms of its representation as well as its handling on an organizational level.

The Edge: Operating System for a Smart Enterprise

The most fundamental technology requirement for smart enterprise or smart society is a digital platform of integrated data and processes. Large successful companies often operate in silos, each with their own systems, data definitions, and business processes. Generating a common view of customers or products can be very difficult. Without the common view, advanced approaches to customer engagement or process optimization cannot occur. The difficulty of operating without a platform becomes greater as companies engage in multi-channel operations. Many companies, for example, cannot link customers' activity in stores or bank branches to their activity on the web or mobile.

In developing this new architecture for the Internet of Things, key lessons have been drawn from the development of the traditional Internet and other transformational technologies to provide some basic guiding principles:

- the architecture is created from simple concepts that build into complex systems using the analog provided by natural phenomena,
- an open, scalable, flexible and secure infrastructure for the Internet of Things and People,
- systems must be designed to fail gracefully: seeking not to eliminate errors, but to accommodate them,
- guarantee that an attack does not affect the remainder nodes in the network and thus preserves data integrity and freshness
- user-centric, customizable Woots applications including interaction possibilities for the benefit of society,
- graduated degrees of networking functionality and complexity are applied only where and when needed,
- all functional components should be prepared to do asynchronous calculations and synchronization needs to be planned accordingly, and
- meaning and context may be extracted from data in real time.

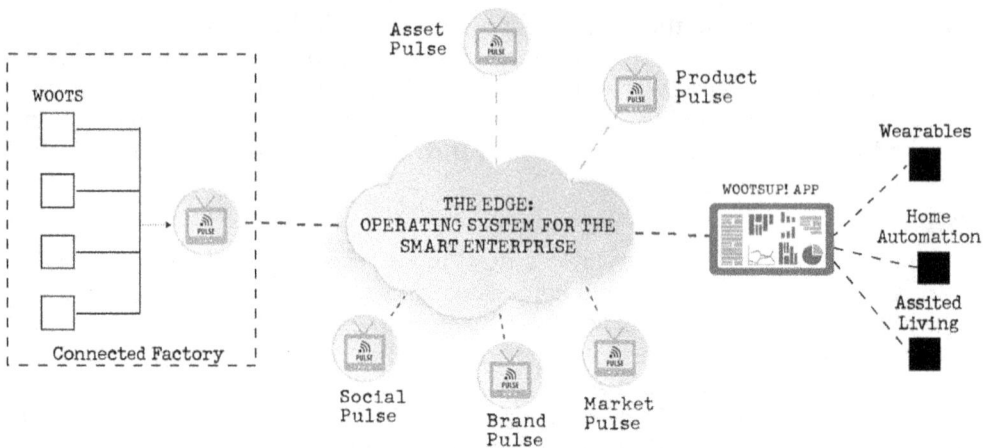

Asset Pulse
Product Pulse
Wearables
WOOTS
Connected Factory
THE EDGE: OPERATING SYSTEM FOR THE SMART ENTERPRISE
WOOTSUP! APP
Home Automation
Assited Living
Social Pulse
Brand Pulse
Market Pulse

1.2 Woots and Edge Service: Reference Architecture

Woots – Smart Things that think, act, learn, and talk

In our proposed approach, we recommend to move the application logic from the embedded devices to the Cloud. This approach enables the reuse of deployed devices for different applications without changing the firmware. On the device side, the approach is based on the implementation of thin servers, embedded web servers which do not host any application logic and which only provide interfaces to elementary functionalities such as sensor/actuator access and configuration of device parameters to interact with the physical world. The thin server's interfaces are RESTful APIs mainly implemented [16].

Woots Implementation Models

WOOTS CONCEPTUAL ARCHITECTURE	Woots Pulse Deployed in Routers and Aggregator Boxes	WOOTSUP! IPhone and Android App	WOOTSUP! IPhone and Android App+ Woots Sensor	
PULSE	JAVA VM TO RUN IN ROUTERS	IOS/ANDROID OS	WOOTS OS	
	PULSE	PULSE	PULSE	
TASK ROUTER/ PROCESS MANAGER	TASK ROUTER/ PROCESS MANAGER	TASK ROUTER/ PROCESS MANAGER	TASK ROUTER/ PROCESS MANAGER	Realized as a software
CO-OPERATIVE MACHINE LEARNING	CO-OPERATIVE MACHINE LEARNING	CO-OPERATIVE MACHINE LEARNING	CO-OPERATIVE MEACHINE LEARNING	
SEMANTIC DIGITAL MEMORY	SEMANTIC DIGITAL MEMORY	SEMANTIC DIGITAL MEMORY	WOOTS OS	Realized as a embedded hardware
			SEMANTIC DIGITAL MEMORY	
SENSING AND SIGNALING	SENSING AND SIGNALING	SENSING AND SIGNALING	SENSING AND SIGNALING	

(c)2014-2015 Quantiply Corp.

1.3 Woots Conceptual Architecture

Web of Open Things (Woots) are everyday "Things" with significant intelligence, a specific identity, address and presence on the Internet; and capabilities to self-organize and communicate with other things with or without human intervention. To make sense of the flow of information, activities, and rich interaction experience,

Woots architecture realizes a cloud-based semantic digital memory (SDM) to provide context awareness, autonomy, business process intelligence and reactivity. A semantic digital memory (SDM) embedded into Woots stores a digital diary of an individual physical object in a persistent way and makes this information available to other devices, applications, and its environment.

Semantic Digital Memory

The semantic digital memory (SDM) physically and conceptually associates product digital information in an application-independent way. As an individual digital memory for a physical product, a SDM provides a comprehensive collection of product-related information, including a meaningful record of a product's history and use over time. Valuable data originate from real-world events detected within an instrumented environment and by smart items with integrated sensors. In addition to fully automated machine-to-machine communication, specific interactions with a current user may also lead to information updates inside the given SDM. The directly-associated SDM provides a valuable knowledge source that can be exploited by specific applications to realize novel kinds of context-anticipatory services.

By capturing and interpreting activity streams, triggers and user actions, such SDM enhanced products have digital fingerprints and are able to perceive and control their environment, to analyze their observations and to communicate with other smart objects and human users about their Lifelog[1] data. By embedding sensors, communication and computing capabilities into physical products enables them to seamlessly gather and use information throughout their entire lifecycle [13].

Cooperative Machine Learning

To achieve active learning, unsupervised learning approaches are used. It aims to categorize events when there is no prior knowledge of such events and activity stream. One approach is for learning events based on encounter frequency and duration, excluding less frequent ones, as it is impossible to store all possible patterns in the local stores, while adapting the classifier to identify these events. This solution achieves scalability for modeling a personal context, without relying on user triggered re-trainings, thus simplifying the learning problem.

The Pulse: Adding Networking and Semantic Brain for Optimal Local performance

At the edge of the network are the simple end devices, Woots or Woots-enabled. They transmit or receive small amounts of data either wirelessly over any number of protocols or directly connected to a Pulse gateway. These edge devices simply "speak" their small amounts of data or listen for data directed toward them.

Pulse is a software component that will sense and aggregate data feeds from sensors, both physical as well logical sensors; and overlay them with the enterprise digital genome to help C-level executives to better engage with their customer, deliver new innovations, products and services, addressing the needs and desires of their customers, creating a delightful customer experience.

The protocol intelligence resides within the Pulse. The Pulse listens for data originating from any device. Pulse nodes decide how to broadcast these transmissions to other Pulse nodes or to the higher-level *EDGE* Service. In order to scale to the immense size of the Internet of Things, these Pulse nodes must be capable of a great deal of discovery and self-organization. They will recognize other Pulse nodes

---

[1] https://en.wikipedia.org/wiki/Lifelog

within range, set up simple routing tables of adjacencies, and discover likely paths to the appropriate integrators.

One of the important capabilities of Pulse nodes is being able to prune and optimize broadcasts. Data passing from and to end devices may be combined with other traffic and forwarded in the general direction of their transmission. Pulse nodes are perhaps the closest functional elements to the traditional idea of peer-to-peer networking, but they provide networking on behalf of end devices and integrator functions at levels above and below themselves. Any of the standard networking protocols can be used, and Pulse nodes will perform important translation functions between different networks.

The self-describing classification inherent in the structure of the Pulse data streams is designed to publish/subscribe relationships possible across applications, vendors, locations, and time. These self-describing classifications will identify characteristics that allow data subscribers to distinguish between all manner of sensors, actuators, and other smart things or devices. The power of self-classified data streams is the fundamental driver of realizing the EDGE service.

The EDGE Operating System

We introduce a new concept called Enterprise Digital Genome (EDGE). The EDGE architecture is aimed at the ubiquitous and seamless interaction among client applications and smart spaces providing real world services. In order to deliver the scale-out architecture, we defined a reference architecture as shown in fig 1.4. The lowest layer address the connectivity and sensing with the Woots and other smart environments. Then Gather, Analyze, Predict, and Optimize layers provide sophisticated data fusion and machine learning algorithms. The top most layers Create and Engage provide micro-services delivery framework enabling rapid delivery of new EDGE enabled applications.

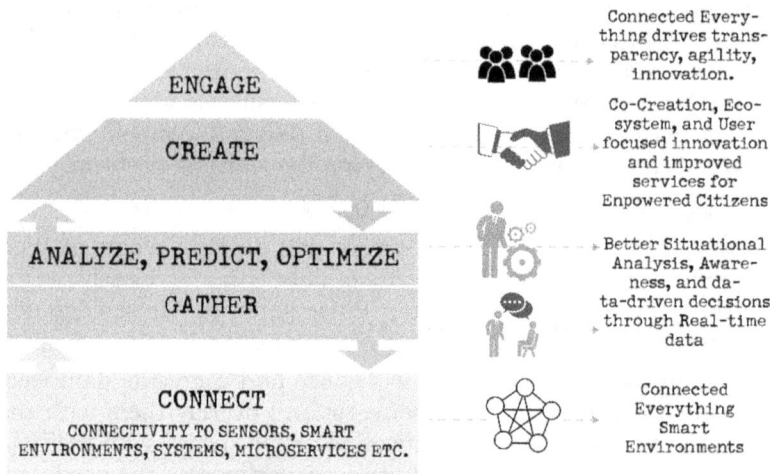

ENGAGE

CREATE

ANALYZE, PREDICT, OPTIMIZE

GATHER

CONNECT

CONNECTIVITY TO SENSORS, SMART
ENVIRONMENTS, SYSTEMS, MICROSERVICES ETC.

Connected Everything drives transparency, agility, innovation.

Co-Creation, Ecosystem, and User focused innovation and improved services for Enpowered Citizens

Better Situational Analysis, Awareness, and data-driven decisions through Real-time data

Connected Everything Smart Environments

©2014-2015 QUANTIFLY CORP.

1.4 EDGE Service: Building Blocks

The Digital Genome is based on all digital traces we leave on the Internet in some form that is publicly accessible; data that was initially gathered directly or indirectly by user input or passively gathered by other sensors employed by the end users. The Digital Genome is computed using the sound mathematical and machine learning techniques. But it uses the real world data to solve real-world problems.

To realize the EDGE, enterprises need to pull data from many traditional data sources including CRM, ERP, commerce, relational databases, data warehouses and other data sources. These sources yield demographic information, point of sale transaction details, loyalty card data, customer survey results etc. This includes data from IXL, ACXIOM, Dun & Bradstreet, Nielson etc. Combining and enriching this information would yield very interesting attributes to construct the Customer Genome and Product Genomes. Data sources from Facebook, Twitter, Pinterest and Yelp gives us additional dimensions into customer and product related data. The EDGE service assembled from number of systems as outlined in the following figure 1.5.

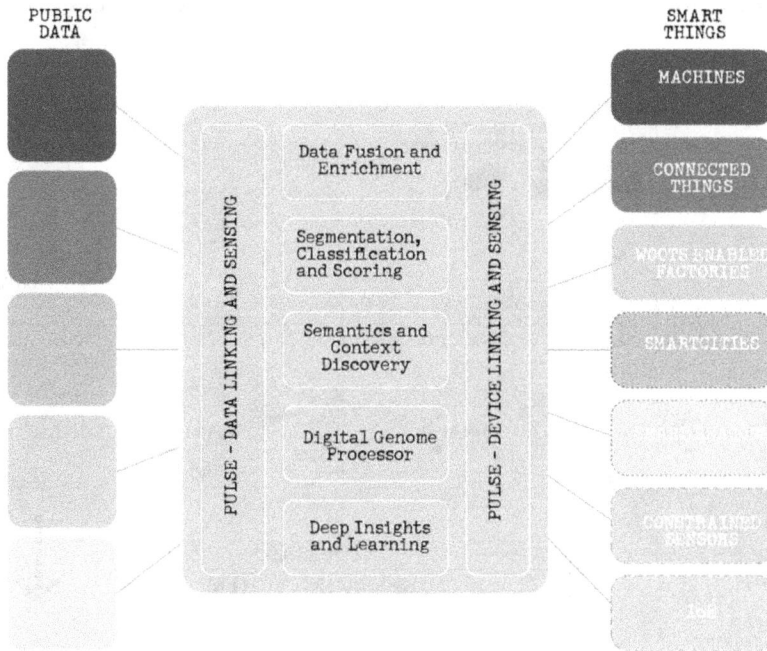

1.5 EDGE Service: Functional Architecture

The Digital Genome approach allows enterprises to see through a new lens and they can read the facts, trends, and patterns in a different way and shift our focus toward bias for action, anticipatory thinking and away from forecasting. With enterprise digital genome, enterprises can develop a deeper understanding of individual customer needs, preferences, and lifestyles. They can also streamline and manage inventory, product promotions and distribution. In addition, EDGE can be used to convert insights into actions, developing and delivering contextualized and personalized information that suit a specific customer need. EDGE is designed to provide a holistic view of the enterprise and its stakeholder's interaction with the enterprise. EDGE also delivers the infrastructure necessary to ensure the fast execution of resulting tasks.

The Edge: Collecting, Integrating, Analyzing, Predicting, Acting, Optimizing

The EDGE implements number of machine learning algorithms and automated reasoning services to power the behavior of Woots. The detailed explanation of concepts unique to the EDGE needs another chapter to explain and hence outside the scope of this chapter. These techniques include, but not limited to:

- Clustering
- Classification and Regression techniques
- Case-Based Reasoning
- Case-Based Recommender Systems
- Graph-Based Reasoning and Network Analysis
- Bayesian Learning

Following figure shows the interactions and inner-workings of Woots and the Edge service:

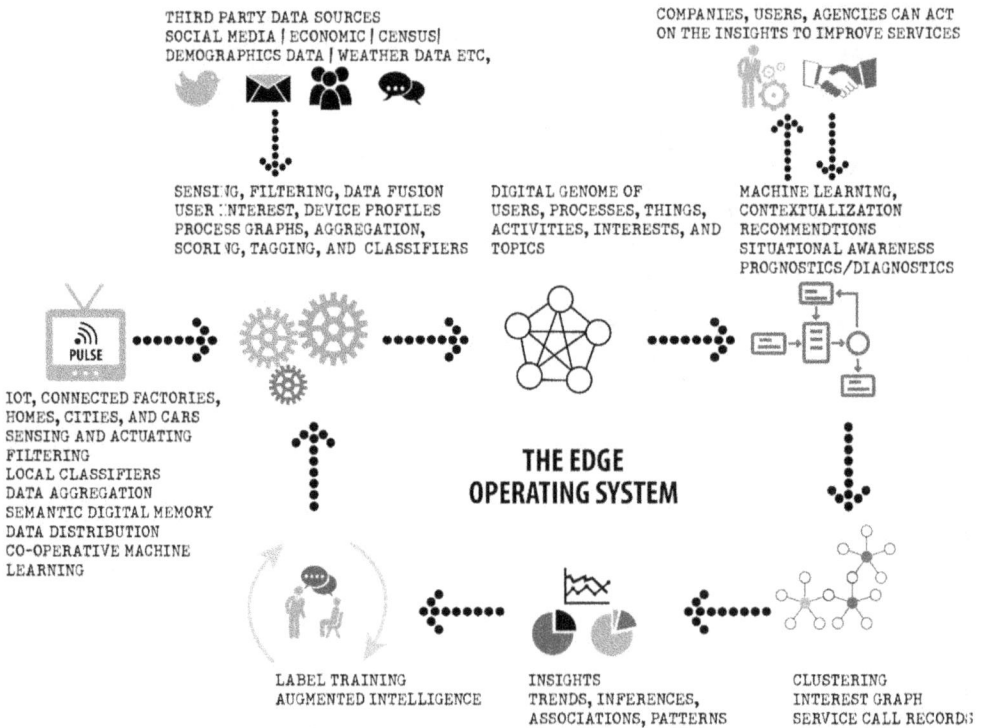

©2014-2015 QUANTIPLY CORPORATION.

1.6 EDGE Service: Machine Learning Interactions

WOOTS APPLICATION USE CASES

Use Case for Manufacturing

Flexible, scalable, smart manufacturing requires a seamless flow of information between all the parties involved, including the very machinery responsible for carving out and assembling products. Previously, without the necessary level of connectivity and ubiquitous computing, smart manufacturing was all but impossible. Today, the Industrial Internet is creating the very foundation needed to make smart manufacturing possible by bringing together brilliant machines, analytics, and scalable software platforms to enable nearly instant person-to-person, person-to-machine, and machine-to-machine communication. Following scenario describes the application of Woots and EDGE to establish real-time, machine learning-based feedback loops that drive business value with no bottlenecks. Alex Rugo in this scenario is a tech-savvy innovator who implemented Woots-powered elastic production facility that enables him to change operations in real-time to maximize productivity efficiency and agility.

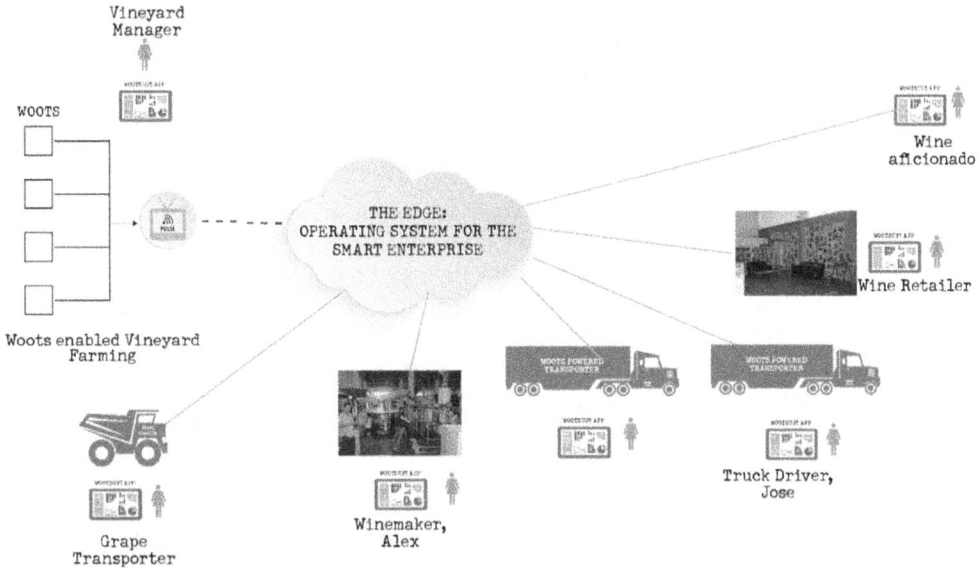

1.7 Woots and EDGE enabled Smart Production and Distribution

Alex Rugo is a fine winemaker. Alex is well known for his fine wine craft and his attention to detail in taking care of making, storing, and transporting the best wines in the world to his highly sensitive, high-net worth collectors, prestigious high-end retail stores and restaurants. Alex invested heavily in anticipatory business process intelligence, supply chain and logistics management software. Recently he deployed Woots and EDGE to provide the Lifelog of his fine wine to his select few wine collectors. Alex partnered with number of wineries in Italy, France, and California to extend his production capacity by using Woots-powered manufacturing planning systems.

José Fernández is a fine wine distributor transporting premium wine to large retail stores. After loading the wine cases on his truck, José plugs-in a Wootsup app to sense temperature, light, and movement of cases. While José is driving his truck, he gets hungry and decides to stop and have lunch. He parks the truck at a resting spot, turns off the engine and goes into a nearby restaurant. Since it is a very hot day, the temperature inside the truck starts to rise. When the temperature reaches a predefined critical level inside one of the load carriers, Woots installed inside the load carrier notices this and sends an emergency signal to José's Wootsup App on his phone.

On the Wootsup's display, José can now see that the Wine in the load carrier is in danger due to a high temperature. He therefore turns the air conditioning back on using his Wootsup App. The Wootsup App also keeps track of any alert messages it receives from the load carriers and saves this message history for future inspection in a way that cannot be altered. When the truck reaches the retail store for delivery, the Woots history stored on SDM is transferred to the store's enterprise system automatically as Wootsup App is pre-authorized into the enterprise ERP system and the sensors authenticate themselves as not having been tampered with.

The measurements from history data are used to estimate the quality of the Wine. Depending on the humidity and temperature of the environment, the estimated future quality of the Wine is determined and prices are reduced, even before a perceivable degradation of quality occurs. By applying this data-driven quality control and combining it with dynamic pricing, the store can ensure that the goods are sold before quality degradation is likely to occur. Alex is notified of this information.

This Saturday, Jim Aficionado decides to walk into local fine wine store. His mobile shopping application points him to a special offer of special Wines of his interest. He immediately thinks of his friend, Surendra, who loves French Wine and would appreciate them as a gift from Jim. Just as he approaches the shelf with the French Wines, he sees their price going down by 30%. Happy about the price reduction, he immediately picks a case of a Bordeaux wine and continues his shopping.

From a business and industry perspective, the scene demonstrates two important retail-related concepts: dynamic pricing and quality control of Wines. Dynamic pricing as a real-time tool for price optimization strategies has always been crucial for profit maximization. In contrast to the state of the art, dynamic pricing in the use case featured is not performed based on static information such as best-before end dates in the transaction data of the backend Enterprise-Resource- Planning (ERP) system, but is based on real-time IoT data gathered from a sensor infrastructure.

Conclusions

Enabling Woots, either embedded or software defined, for everyday objects and other related technologies enable new product-centric ways of machine-to-machine communication and human–machine interaction across an entire physical product lifecycle. Semantic Digital memories (SDM) associate evolving digital information with things (Smart Things) in an application-independent manner. Such digital memories are designed to support information exchange and reuse across environments and specific applications.

The EDGE approach paves the way for novel kinds of product-related applications and services. Practical application of the EDGE framework for the successful realization of a rich set of advanced system prototypes demonstrates the high potential of the innovative concept. The overall framework also includes a generalized architecture conception for the required technical infrastructure and middleware components. While digital transformation started with enabling digital strategy to connect customers with the brand, now with the advances in mobility, cloud, and data analytics, it is now enabling enterprises to achieve digital transformation excellence where every business element is digitally connected and managed like a biological system. The EDGE enables new types of innovation and creativity by decoding and mapping the Enterprise Digital Genome. The EDGE is a value-driven approach to business process excellence that can result in dynamic operations of an enterprise. EDGE enables business outcomes by linking business strategy with people and technology based execution, at pace with certainty. The resulting next generation enterprise is ready for long-term success since it can adjust to the volatile business environment.

References

1. Dr. Jacques Bughin and Dr. James Manyika: Internet Matters. Essays in Digital Transformation, McKinsey Global Institute (MGI), 2012

2. Mulligan, G.: The Internet of Things: Here Now and Coming Soon. IEEE Internet Computing 14(1), 35–36 (2010)

3. M. Weiser, The computer for the Twenty-First Century. Sci. Am. 265(3), 94–104 (1991)

4. Weiser, M., Gold, R., Brown, J.: The origins of ubiquitous computing research at PARC in the late 1980s. IBM Syst. J. 38(4), 693–696 (1999)

5. Cook, D., Das, S.: Smart Environments: Technology, Protocols and Applications. Wiley, London (2004)

6. Michael Hammer, What is Business Process Management? In: Handbook on Business Process Management 1, International Handbooks on Information Systems, Second Edition, DOI 10.1007/978-3-642-45100-3_1, © Springer-Verlag Berlin Heidelberg 2015

7. T.H. Davenport, Process Management for Knowledge Work, In: Handbook on Business Process Management 1, International Handbooks on Information Systems, Second Edition, DOI 10.1007/978-3-642-45100-3_1, © Springer-Verlag Berlin Heidelberg 2015

8. Iván Corredor Pérez and Ana M. Bernardos Barbolla, Exploring Major Architectural Aspects of the Web of Things, Internet of Things, Smart Sensors, Measurement and Instrumentation 9, DOI: 10.1007/978-3-319-04223-7_2, © Springer International Publishing Switzerland 2014

9. Ackoff, R.L.: Towards a system of systems concepts. Management Science 17(11), 661–671 (1971)

10. Senge, P.M. (1990). The Fifth Discipline: The Art and Practice of the Learning Organization. (1st ed.). New York: Doubleday/Currency.

11. Artur Arsénio, Hugo Serra, Rui Francisco, Fernando Nabais, João Andrade, Eduardo Serrano: Internet of Intelligent Things: Bringing Artificial Intelligence into Things and Communication Networks, Springer Berlin Heidelber(2014), http://dx.doi.org/10.1007/978-3-642-35016-0_1

12. A. Campbell, S. Eisenman, N. Lane, E. Miluzzo, R. Peterson, H. Lu, X. Zheng, M. Musolesi, K. Fodor, G.S. Ahn, The rise of people-centric sensing. Internet Comput. IEEE 12(4), 12–21 (2008)

13. Wolfgang Wahlster: The Semantic Product Memory: An Interactive Black Box for Smart Objects, Cognitive Technologies, DOI 10.1007/978-3-642-37377-0_1, © Springer-Verlag Berlin Heidelberg 2013

14. N. Lane, E. Miluzzo, H. Lu, D. Peebles, T. Choudhury, A. Campbell, D. College, Adhoc and sensor networks: a survey of mobile phone sensing. IEEE Commun.0 Mag. 140–150 (2010)

15. D. Zhang, B. Guo, B. Li, Z. Yu, Extracting social and community intelligence from digital footprints: an emerging research area. Ubiquitous Intell. Comput. 4–18 (2010)

16. Kovatsch, M., Mayer, S., Ostermaier, B.: Moving application logic from the firmware to the cloud: towards the thin server architecture for the internet of things. In: 6th International Conference on Innovative Mobile and Internet Services in Ubiquitous Computing (IMIS 2012), July 2012

17. H. Lu, W. Pan, N. Lane, T. Choudhury, A. Campbell, SoundSense: scalable sound sensing for people-centric applications on mobile phones, in Proceedings of the 7th International Conference on Mobile Systems, Applications, and Services (ACM, 2009), pp. 165–178

18. E. Miluzzo, N. Lane, K. Fodor, R. Peterson, H. Lu, M. Musolesi, S. Eisenman, X. Zheng, A. Campbell, Sensing meets mobile social networks: the

design, implementation and evaluation of the cenceme application, in Proceedings of the 6th ACM Conference on Embedded Network Sensor Systems (ACM, 2008), pp. 337–350

19. Weichhart, G., Feiner, T., Stary, C.: Implementing organizational interoperability the sudden approach. Computers in Industry 61(2), 152–160 (2010), http://www.sciencedirect.com/science/article/pii/S0166361509002048

20. L. Atzori, A. Iera, G. Morabito, M. Nitti, The social internet of things (SIoT)—When social networks meet the internet of things: concept, architecture and network characterization. Comput. Netw. 56(16), 3594–3608, 14 Nov (2012)

21. Sujith Samuel Mathew, Yacine Atif , Quan Z. Sheng, and Zakaria Maamar: The Web of Things – Challenges and Enabling Technologies, Internet of Things & Inter-cooperative Comput. Technol., SCI 460, pp. 1–23., DOI: 10.1007/978-3-642-34952-2_1 © Springer-Verlag Berlin Heidelberg 2013

Cognitive BPM

Peter Fingar, USA

Artificial Intelligence is likely to change our civilization as much as or more than any technology that's come before, even writing.

—Miles Brundage and Joanna Bryson, Future Tense

The smart machine era will be the most disruptive in the history of IT.
— Gartner "The Disruptive Era of Smart Machines is Upon Us."

This is a new era of computing—cognitive computing.

—Virginia Rometty, CEO, IBM

The era of cognitive systems is dawning and building on today's computer programming era. All machines, for now, require programming, and by definition programming does not allow for alternate scenarios that have not been programmed. To allow alternating outcomes would require going up a level, creating a *self-learning* Artificial Intelligence (AI). Via *biomimicry and neuroscience,* Cognitive Computing does this, taking computing concepts to a whole new level. Once-futuristic capabilities are becoming mainstream.

Organizations have a lot to learn about the impact of cognitive computing, so we we'll open with an Albert Einstein quote, "Once you stop learning, you start dying."

Tabulating Era 1900 — Programming Era 1950 — Cognitive Era 2011

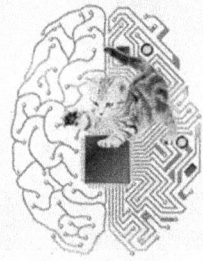

Cognitive computing, the AI redux, has arrived and all is changed, changed utterly.

But wait, AI has been around since John McCarthy coined the term in 1956. Traditional machine learning techniques, including classic neural networks, need to be supervised by humans so they can learn. Although AI has been around since the 1950s, experiencing springs and winters (expert systems and LISP machines came and went) something new, really new, is happening. It's called "deep learning." *Deep learning* is an approach to have the system learn on its own, without intervention. Get ready for Cognitive BPM, or else. It is already impacting the other big game-changers: *Smart Process Apps, Gamification,* and *Prescriptive Analytics* driven by the Internet of Things.

When we associate names with current computer technology, no doubt "Steve Jobs" or "Bill Gates" comes to mind. But the new name will likely be a guy from the University of Toronto, the hotbed of deep learning scientists. Meet Geoffrey Everest Hinton, great-great-grandson of George Boole, the guy who gave us the mathematics that underpins computers.

Hinton is a British-born computer scientist and psychologist, most noted for his work on artificial neural networks. He is now working for Google part time, joining AI pioneer and futurist Ray Kurzweil, and Andrew Ng, the Stanford University professor who set up Google's neural network team in 2011. He is the co-inventor of the back propagation, the Boltzmann machine, and contrastive divergence training algorithms and is an important figure in the deep learning movement. Hinton's research has implications for areas such as speech recognition, computer vision and language understanding. Unlike past neural networks, newer ones can have many layers and are called "deep neural networks."

Deep Learning

Geoffrey
Hinton

Geoffrey Hinton: co-inventor of the backpropagation and contrastive divergence

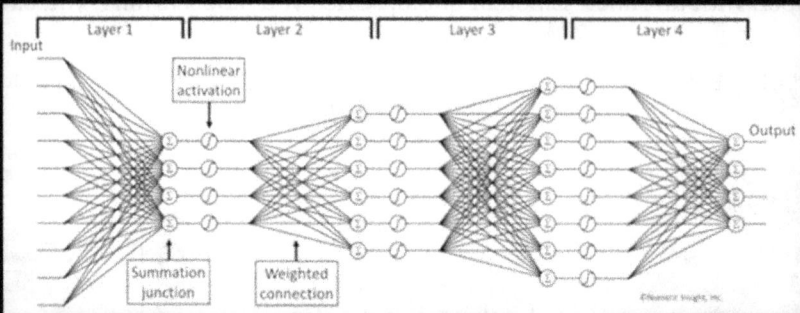

Biomimicry of the human cortex

Cognitive computing systems can understand the nuances of human language, process questions akin to the way people think, and quickly cull through vast amounts of data for relevant, evidence-based answers to their human users' needs. And very importantly, they learn from each interaction, to improve their performance and value to users over time.

Cognitive Computing uses hundreds of analytics that provide it with capabilities such as natural language processing, text analysis, and knowledge representation and reasoning to ...

- make sense of huge amounts of complex information in split seconds,
- rank answers based on evidence and confidence, and
- learn from its mistakes.

And, of course, this capability is deployed in the cloud and made available as a cognitive service:

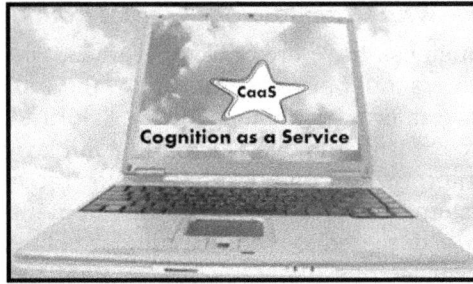

Cognitive computing will have an enormous impact on the use of data in solving real world problems and for process innovation. The impact on fields like healthcare, education, finance, legal (eDiscovery), manufacturing, logistics and retailing are where the power of technology has the chance to change entire industries. Some industries are likely to be negatively impacted by this type of technology and many people in these industries will resist change. What the people in these industries need to clearly understand is that with the pace of evolution in technology, change is going to happen and it has the potential to change quickly and exponentially. Understanding big data has everything to do with the process of discovery, advanced analytics and machine learning solutions that can help people in realizing that data is an asset and the data holds many of the answers to questions that improve industries.

In today's Digital Pangea (digital library) where the entire world and 'things' are interconnected, you can no longer just manage your enterprise, but must collaborate across the entire Value Chain. There won't be one cognitive system at your service, there will be many, many COGs (cognitive systems) serving all the companies and customers in your Business Network.

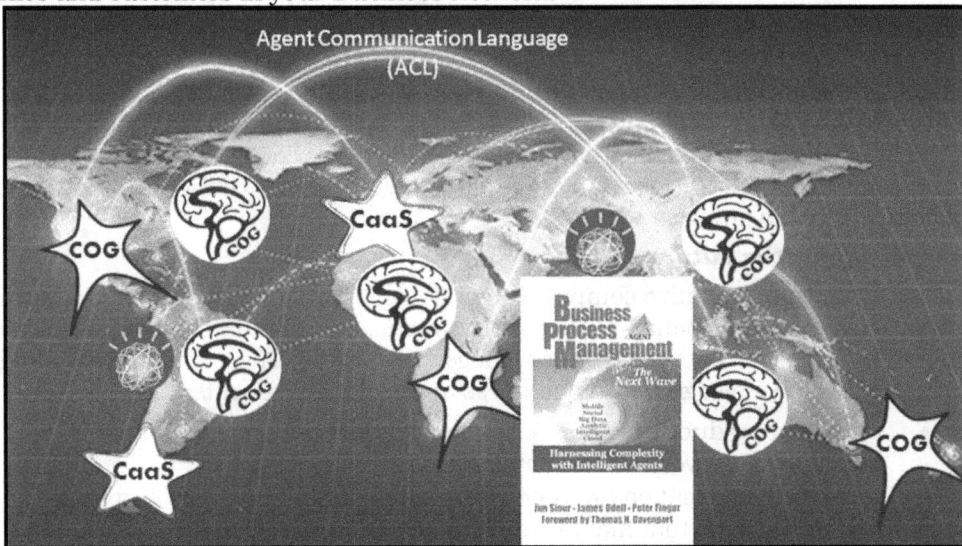

These special purpose COGs will interoperate via an Agent Communication Language (ACL) for multi-agent collaboration and problem solving. They will also communicate with humans via natural language processing (NLP).

These digital resources won't be limited to office workers in advanced economies.

Creative Destruction – What Came Before What's Coming Next[1]

The new realities of business have created imperatives for business information systems. Business systems must provide enterprise (and inter-enterprise) reach so that islands of disparate information can be integrated into a meaningful whole. They must be able to cope with the overwhelming complexity of distributed technology and an inter-enterprise information base. They must be open to survive a network-centric ecosystem. Rapid-applications development goes without saying, and applications must be designed to embrace constant change. Business systems must be cognitive, knowledge-based (not just information-based) if they are to cope with the incompleteness and ambiguity of real business processes and workflows. And they must be adaptive to meet the needs of the moment and bring productivity to an increasingly overwhelmed business user and self-service to our customers. That's what is being asked of IS today, a very tall order.

Both BPM technology and agent paradigms focus on addressing *change* and *complexity*. Next-generation intelligent agent technology, or Cognitive Computing, is the next logical step in moving the BPM technology paradigm forward and overcoming some of its shortcomings. Intelligent agent technologies have been around for quite a while but only now are they being repurposed for business in response to a rapidly changing world.

While the retail industry was slow to grasp the significance of the Internet—until it got *Amazoned*, we are currently witnessing a seismic shift in information technology. It's called the Cognitive Cloud, and cognitive computing is set to unleash a perfect storm in business. But unlike the retail industry that got Amazoned, the Cognitive Cloud will affect every industry and go beyond enabling a virtual company and on to multi-company virtual business networks and ecosystems. Complexity will grow exponentially, and tools and methods are desperately needed to build businesses that are complex adaptive systems capable of bringing order out of the chaos (*charodic* systems). That's precisely where Cognitive Computing comes in.

Business leaders know all about rapid change and increasing complexity, and some are now asking "Why can't software change *itself* to keep up with the changes in the business?" It is this business case that is bringing cognitive intelligent agent technology out of the research lab and military establishments and repurposing it for competitive advantage.

Competing for the Future

The importance of cognitive computing technology is widely recognized in several industries, especially defense, telecommunications, and manufacturing, as well as standards bodies such as the Object Management Group. These and other leading organizations have recognized the business and technical benefits:

- increased productivity of business computer users and self-service customers in a network-centric business;
- combined information and knowledge model of the business and information systems that makes rapid development in a complex environment a reality; and
- bandwidth efficiency so necessary in a network-centric computing environment.

---

[1] Adapted from: *Cognitive Computing* (www.mkpress.com/cc) and *Business Process Management: The Next Wave* (www.mkpress.com/aoBPM).

Not only do they recognize the benefits, some companies have already deployed cognitive computing technology as a competitive weapon. They convert web traffic into business relationships. They use smart technology to plug suppliers and customers into their core business systems. They profile their constituents and search for new patterns in their data warehouses to meet ever changing needs. Is your company ready to compete with them?

With careful planning and armed with a solid understanding of the current intelligent agent technologies, powerful business process management systems can be developed that exploit the Internet and distributed objects to gain strategic business advantage. Although the tasks of designing and building them are not trivial, information systems based on intelligent agent technology are inevitable. Harnessing this technology is a top priority for business and technology leaders. Companies can go it alone but those that face immediate mission-critical requirements will be well advised to seek outside assistance from those who have gone before.

To be more precise, companies should pounce on their BPMS providers and insist that they develop an agent-oriented BPMS (aoBPMS). AI technology can sound quite intimidating if you are unfamiliar with it, but process analysts and business architects are ultimately concerned with how to make processes better—and this new technology makes for better processes—so it's worth learning about.

I've included a Chapter Appendix: *Developing Enterprise Systems With Intelligent Agent Technology* to provide you with the concepts you need to discuss with your BPMS supplier(s) to be sure they are providing you with the capabilities you need for the cognitive computing era.

Cognitive computing startups are creating lots of new ways to assure that we can make future business processes more flexible and more responsive to employees and customers. One pioneering startup, *Cognitive Scale*, has implemented several vertical industry cognitive clouds for the travel, healthcare, retail, and financial services industries. Examples include consumers looking for inspired travel or shopping advice or healthcare providers looking to manage high-risk populations by combining clinical, social and lifecycle data. These industry-optimized clouds contain billions of curated data points and contextual facts and help accelerate the creation of industry specific cognitive business process analytics that deliver insights-as-a-service. The old-fashioned BPM business rules management systems (BRMS) will never be the same in light of distributed, cognitive, intelligence.

CONCLUSIONS

Based on many years of experience gained from large-scale agent-based projects, this chapter described an approach to using complex agent-based software systems. A holistic, *agent-oriented* view of design is advocated in the appendix to this chapter, and an appropriate lifecycle model is introduced. The discussion of implementation strategies identifies a number of technical issues. Currently, a mix-and-match software strategy has to be adopted, resulting in the need for well-defined systems architecture to maintain coherence in an aoBPMS.

Corporations will not take the step to agent-oriented BPM because they *can*, they will do so because they *must*. Now is the time to move from the current BPM methods that deliver excellent results for systems that underlie high-level BPMN models, to the ubiquity of business process management where processes are developed by unsophisticated programmers and business people using visual development tools. While this vision of simplicity is appealing, the underlying enterprise framework is extremely complex and requires intelligent agent technology to harness the complexity. With careful planning, sound software engineering and solid systems architecture, an intelligent greenhouse can be architected to grow the BPMS software of the future—now.

That's why it is time for *Intelligent Agent* technology, a technology that's been around for years, to take center stage in the world of business in general, and specifically in the world of BPM, for business processes are how work got done in the horse and buggy age and how work gets done in the emerging Cloud economy.

The *agent-oriented* BPM system (aoBPMS) with *choreography* (not old-fashioned process orchestration) will be at the heart of multi-agent systems that seek the common goals set by the aoBPMS.

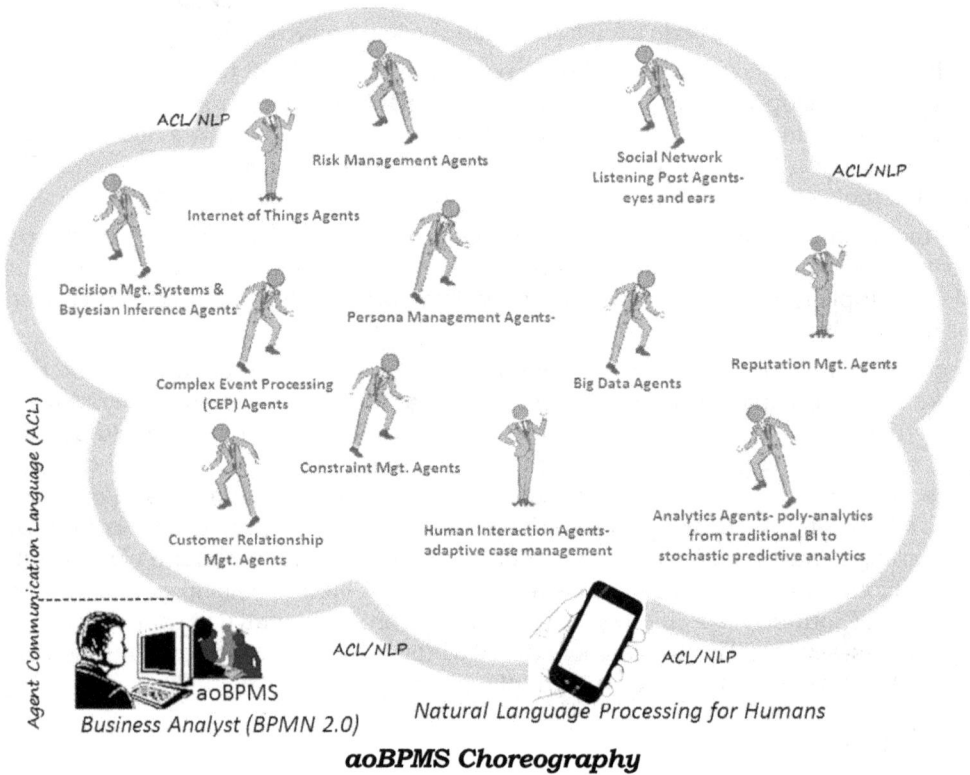

ACL/NLP

Risk Management Agents

Social Network
Listening Post Agents-
eyes and ears

ACL/NLP

Internet of Things Agents

Decision Mgt. Systems &
Bayesian Inference Agents

Persona Management Agents-

Reputation Mgt. Agents

Complex Event Processing
(CEP) Agents

Big Data Agents

Constraint Mgt. Agents

Agent Communication Language (ACL)

Customer Relationship
Mgt. Agents

Human Interaction Agents-
adaptive case management

Analytics Agents- poly-analytics
from traditional BI to
stochastic predictive analytics

ACL/NLP

aoBPMS
Business Analyst (BPMN 2.0)

Natural Language Processing for Humans

ACL/NLP

aoBPMS Choreography

Think this is a bunch of hype? Think it will be years and years before such systems affect the marketplace? Think it will take quantum computing to implement? Think again, for in many ways the future is already here; it's just not evenly distributed.

Here's a 2012 update on G.E. from the *New York Times*, "G.E. is America's largest industrial company. It makes the heavy-duty machinery that transports people, heats homes and powers factories, and lets doctors diagnose life-threatening diseases. G.E. resides in a different world from the consumer Internet. But the major technologies that animate Google and Facebook are also vital ingredients in the industrial Internet—tools from artificial intelligence, like machine-learning software, and vast streams of new data. In industry, the data flood comes mainly from smaller, more powerful and cheaper sensors on the equipment.

"Smarter machines, for example, can alert their human handlers when they will need maintenance, before a breakdown. It is the equivalent of preventive and personalized care for equipment, with less downtime and more output. These technologies are really there now, in a way that is practical and economic,' said Mark M. Little, G.E.'s senior vice president for global research. 'G.E.'s embrace of the *industrial Internet* is a long-term strategy. But if its optimism proves justified, the impact could be felt across the economy.'"

G.E. has opened a new research center in Silicon Valley. More from the *New York Times* (November 23, 2012): "When Sharoda Paul finished a postdoctoral fellowship last year at the Palo Alto Research Center, she did what most of her peers do; considered a job at a big Silicon Valley company, in her case, Google. But instead, Ms. Paul, a 31-year-old expert in social computing, went to work for General Electric. Ms. Paul is one of more than 250 engineers recruited in the last year and a half to G.E.'s new software center here, in the East Bay of San Francisco. The company plans to increase that work force of computer scientists and software developers to 400, and to invest $1 billion in the center by 2015. The buildup is part of G.E's big bet on what it calls the 'industrial Internet,' bringing digital intelligence to the physical world of industry as never before. The concept of Internet-connected machines that collect data and communicate, often called the "Internet of Things," has been around for years. Information technology companies, too, are pursuing this emerging field. I.B.M. has its 'Smarter Planet' projects, while Cisco champions the 'Internet of Everything.' But G.E.'s effort, analysts say, shows that Internet-era technology is ready to sweep through the industrial economy much as the consumer Internet has transformed media, communications and advertising over the last decade."

"At Mount Sinai, G.E. has worked on optimization and modeling software that enables admitting officers to see beds and patient movements throughout the hospital, to help them more efficiently match patients and beds. Beyond that, modeling software is beginning to make predictions about likely patient admission and discharge numbers over the next several hours, based on historical patterns at the hospital and other circumstances —say, in flu season. The software, which Mount Sinai has been trying out in recent months, acts as an intelligent assistant to admitting officers. 'It essentially says, 'Hold off, your instinct is to give this bed to that guy, but there might be a better choice,' Mr. Keathley explained. At a hospital like Mount Sinai, G.E. estimates that the optimization and modeling technologies can translate into roughly 10,000 more patients treated a year, and $120 million in savings and additional revenue over several years."[2]

In 2014. the Industrial Internet Consortium (IIC) [3] was founded to bring together the organizations and technologies necessary to accelerate growth of the Industrial Internet by identifying, assembling and promoting best practices. Membership includes small and large technology innovators, vertical market leaders, researchers, universities and governments.

Although the capability to sense and control the physical world has been in use in manufacturing industries for quite some time, ant-sized radios could help connect *trillions* of devices to the IoT. That can take us to a whole new world beyond the

---

[2]   http://www.nytimes.com/2012/11/24/technology/internet/ge-looks-to-industry-for-the-next-digital-disruption.html?hpw&_r=0

[3] http://www.iiconsortium.org

process industries and on to every industry and our everyday life. A team of researchers from Stanford University and the University of California, Berkeley, has created prototype radio-on-a-chip communications devices that are powered by ambient radio waves. Comprising receiving and transmitting antennas and a central processor, the completely self-contained ant-sized devices are very cheap (pennies) to manufacture, and don't require batteries to run. Highlighting its low energy consumption, the researchers say that a AAA battery--if it were hooked up--would keep it running for more than a century.

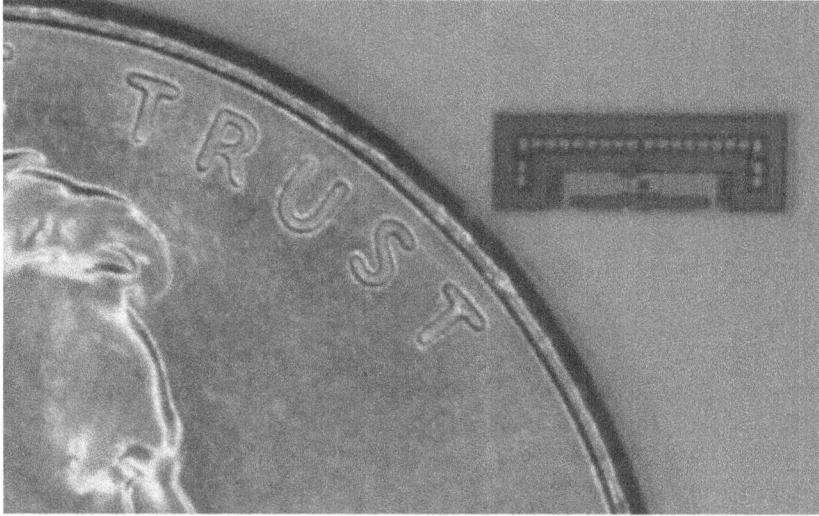

Prototype ant-sized, radio-on-a-chip communications devices

While the much-talked about IoT is the next technology transition when devices will allow us to sense and control the physical world, it's also part of something even bigger; the *Cognitive Internet of Everything* (CIoE). The Internet of Everything is the networked connection of *people, process, data,* and *things.* Its benefit is derived from the compound impact of these connections and the value it creates as not just "things," but "everything" (people, process and data) comes online. Machines will talk to machines and humans and *vice versa.*

As noted BPM expert, Jim Sinur[4], wrote in his blog, "In advanced situations resources can collaborate in a machine-to-machine (M2M) fashion, a human-to-human fashion (H2H), a human-to-machine fashion (H2M) or a machine-to-human fashion (M2H) all of these styles can interact with each other to accomplish business outcomes. The type and amount of intelligent business operations that can be created by the combination of process and the Internet of Things is now being expanded to the Internet of Everything."

The IT analyst firm, Gartner, describes the *Internet of Everything* as comprising:

- Internet of Information – the traditional World Wide Web
- Internet of Systems – network of business and consumer applications
- Internet of People – network of relationships in social networks
- Internet of Places – commercial and public places as Internet nodes
- Internet of Things – connected physical devices with sensors
- Internet of Virtual Entities – "intelligent" digital entities

---

[4] See also iBPMS: Intelligent BPM Systems (Future Strategies Inc).
http://futstrat.com/books/iBPMS_Handbook.php

H2M, M2H? In a *Time* magazine article, "Never Offline," the author writes, "What might post-humanity be like? The paradox of a wearable device is that it both gives you control and takes it away at the same time. Consider the smart wristwatch's fitness applications. They capture all data that your body generates, your heart and activity and so on, gathers it up and stores and returns it to you in a form you can use. Once the development community gets through apping it, there's no telling what else it might gather. This will change your experience of your body. The wristwatch made the idea of not knowing what time it was seem bizarre; in five years it might seem bizarre not to know how many calories you've eaten today, or what your resting heart rate is."

And, of course, this changes how you do business with consumers; how you individually customize your products and services to meet the ever-changing, specific, needs of your customers. It takes little imagination to apply these concepts to manufacturing, logistics, and supply chains; in short, across industries and types of businesses.

BPM pioneer, Setrag Khoshafian[5], noted, "The coordination and execution of connected devices will need a context. They will also need collaboration to achieve specific goals. The increasingly intelligent things, together with human participants, need to have their tasks orchestrated to achieve business objectives. Furthermore, the intelligence that is mined from Big Data needs to be made actionable – again in the context of specific business solutions. Enter 'Process of Everything.'"

I chose the kind of simple case study from G.E./ Mount Sinai to illustrate that the move to agent-oriented BPM isn't a future big bang, ERP conversion or Orwellian event. This isn't Star Wars stuff and in no way implies complicated systems or some esoteric stuff from some research lab. We are talking about practical cognitive computing. It works.

---

[5] See chapter: "Digital Prescriptive Maintenance" by Khosafian and Rostetter

So, don't panic when you hear the term aoBPM. Don't take on all the rules nor all the possible types of analytics or try to build an all-encompassing agent infrastructure. Focus on a given process where multi-agent systems agents can make a difference, as did Mount Sinai when choosing to take on just its admission process. Such beginnings can grow into a bright future in today's world of unexpected change and total global competition.

Cognitive BPM isn't a "flavor of the month," it's a whole new era. What can be done with cognitive BPM will be done, and it won't be just **BPM Everywhere**, it will be *Cognitive BPM Everywhere*. The only question is "Will you be the doer or the one done in?"

What to do? What to do?

- Get informed and stay informed by participating in the standards groups listed above or similar groups for your industry. Check out the speakers at the Rome conference and other specialists and read their reports[6].

- Form a team to track the expanding literature on cognitive computing as there's a lot coming down the pipe. It's also a good idea to set a Web search "alert:" "Cognitive Computing." Add the Cognitive Computing component to your BPM Center of Excellence (CoE).

- No matter where you are on the BPM maturity curve, pounce on your IT and BPMS service providers and build strategies with them, for this stuff will be done. Traditional booksellers and retailers shied away from that once scary technology, the Internet —until they got Amazoned! Don't get Cog'ed by a new competitor from nowhere who "gets it" today.

- Collaborate or send some of your employees to school. Enrollment is now open for cognitive computing courses at Carnegie Mellon University, New York University (NYU), The Ohio State University, Rensselaer Polytechnic Institute (RPI), University of California, Berkeley, University of Michigan and the University of Texas in Austin.[7]

CHAPTER APPENDIX:

Developing Enterprise Systems with Intelligent Agent Technology

Although you as a business analyst or architect are not necessarily a software developer, here are some of the key points you should be prepared to talk to your BPMS providers about, just so you can determine if they "get it."

Going one step beyond distributed object technology, cognitive computing is poised to transform the way we model the enterprise, build information systems and manage business processes.

Information systems based on intelligent agent technology are inevitable, even though the tasks of conceiving, designing and building them are not trivial. As we turn our attention to these tasks, we will benefit from keeping the fundamental question in mind, "How can we conceive, design, and build adaptive, multi-enterprise-scale information systems and business processes?" Intelligent agent technology is an enabler of such systems, but is not an end unto itself. When combined with the maturing disciplines of object technology and BPM methods, their synergy, embodied in *agent-oriented BPM* (aoBPM), can take us to a new level in the search

---

[6] Stay up to date at www.cognitivetrends.com

[7] See: http://cognitive-science.info/community/experts

for the prize of managing complex business ecosystems and multi-company business networks.

The approach to building agent-based systems can be characterized in terms of three distinct, but related, topics:

1. *A full-lifecycle solution development process* that explicitly addresses domain modeling—the effort spent in domain and problem understanding can be leveraged to guide and accelerate information systems development.

2. *Ontology-based domain models*—fully understanding the domain is essential to understanding the problems in the domain. The richness of domain models determines reuse and flexibility.

3. *Architecture*—agents must follow a consistent architectural approach so they can interoperate with each other.

After a brief introduction to the agent-oriented lifecycle, we focus our attention on the heart of the matter, domain modeling and architecture.

A full-lifecycle solution development process

The agent-oriented lifecycle model should be iterative and incremental. Decades of experience taught us that agent orientation will enrich contemporary OO and BPM approaches by providing an *active* modeling paradigm and better analysis models that enable reuse. As shown below, our agent-oriented domain modeling and architectural frameworks can be integrated with best practice software engineering lifecycles, leveraging the contributions of artificial intelligence (AI) and object-oriented software engineering. We thus preserve considerable intellectual capital while taking the next step in development methods for truly intelligent and adaptive information systems. Radical new methods will not be accepted as corporations are in this not to advance computer science, but to advance their business.

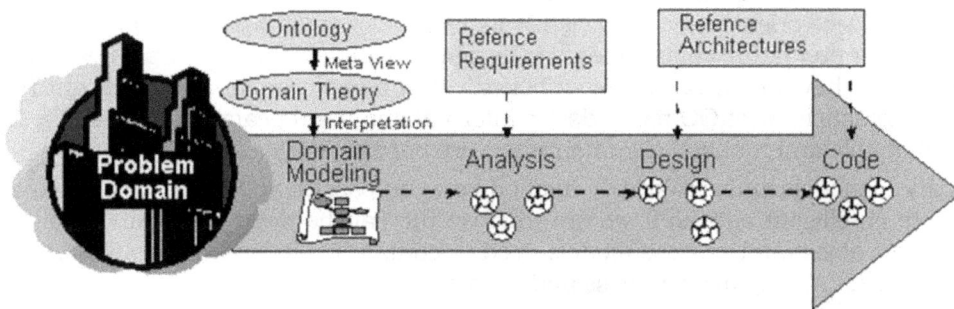

Agent-oriented Lifecycle

The approach to building agent-based solutions emphasizes the importance of domain modeling as a critical initial step in producing business technology solutions. There are at least three distinct approaches to domain modeling: business process management (BPM), object-oriented (OO), and artificial intelligence (AI) which the underpinning of intelligent agent technology.

All three approaches are model-based and offer techniques for describing problem domains. As shown below, the three approaches offer differing perspectives of the problem domain. The convergence of OO, BPM, and AI methods results in a significant breakthrough in building models of the enterprise that are capable of end-to-end integration of business analysis and software systems. Although the fusion of these disciplines is not yet complete to the point of standardization, pioneering companies have recognized the competitive advantage and launched major agent-oriented development initiatives.

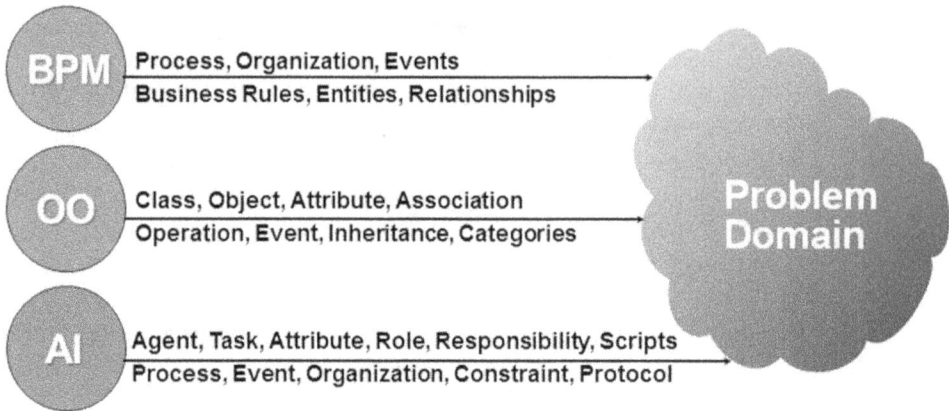

BPM | Process, Organization, Events
Business Rules, Entities, Relationships

OO | Class, Object, Attribute, Association
Operation, Event, Inheritance, Categories

AI | Agent, Task, Attribute, Role, Responsibility, Scripts
Process, Event, Organization, Constraint, Protocol

Problem Domain

BPM, OO and IA Perspectives on Business Domain Modeling

Traditional BPM methods are expressive and easily (often, naively) understood for describing business process and organization. But traditional BPM produces separate models of data, processes and organization that soon become unmanageable. The models are difficult to integrate, validate or leverage for the development of software systems. Information is captured using informal techniques even though more formal notations such as BPMN are deployed, and incomplete lifecycle models lack a clear implementation path .

Underlying high-level process models, object-oriented methods are well suited to software engineering and have potential for reuse. They are, however, not inherently business oriented, not sufficiently expressive of most problem domains, and often foster premature commitments to design and implementation strategies. Consequently, they do not capture a sufficiently rich domain model for significant reuse. In practice, most OO methods are informal and not repeatable. Traceability is questionable and robust design heuristics are hard to find.

Business models must make a distinction between passive and *active, goal-seeking* objects (intelligent agents) if we are to close the gap between model and reality. Business object and process models need to contain behavioral declarations, role definitions, ontological awareness and constraint axioms.

Intelligent agent technology can be leveraged to enhance enterprise modeling as well as offering new techniques for developing intelligent applications and smart technical infrastructure services. An agent-oriented perspective allows us to develop rich and expressive models of the enterprise as the foundation for adaptive, reusable business software.

What's new under the sun? Object-orientation and artificial intelligence have been around for decades. And, many informally describe "BPM" as new clothes on industrial systems engineering. It is the melding of these disciplines into a unified approach to enterprise modeling that represents the breakthrough. Blending the strengths and sifting out the weakness of each discipline, agent-oriented BPM can take us one great step forward. aoBPM is a full life-cycle proposition, not just a programming or implementation issue. The secret to aoBPM's success is to apply agent technology up front as a *domain modeling metaphor* while using the maturity of object-oriented methods to provide the infrastructure lacking in the artificial intelligence world. The figure below shows that agent-based domain modeling produces the business object model in terms of ontologies, and uses ideas and techniques from traditional business analysis (Process Modeling/BPMN), OO (UML), and AI (Agents and Rules). While devoid of implementation details, the business object model is agent-based and is used to support user task analysis, requirements modeling, and the specification and design of the software object model.

The flow of activities in the figure would be somewhat different if we were working in a green field. In the real world of business, green fields are rare, and the figure reflects the use of preexisting BPM and OO analysis models.

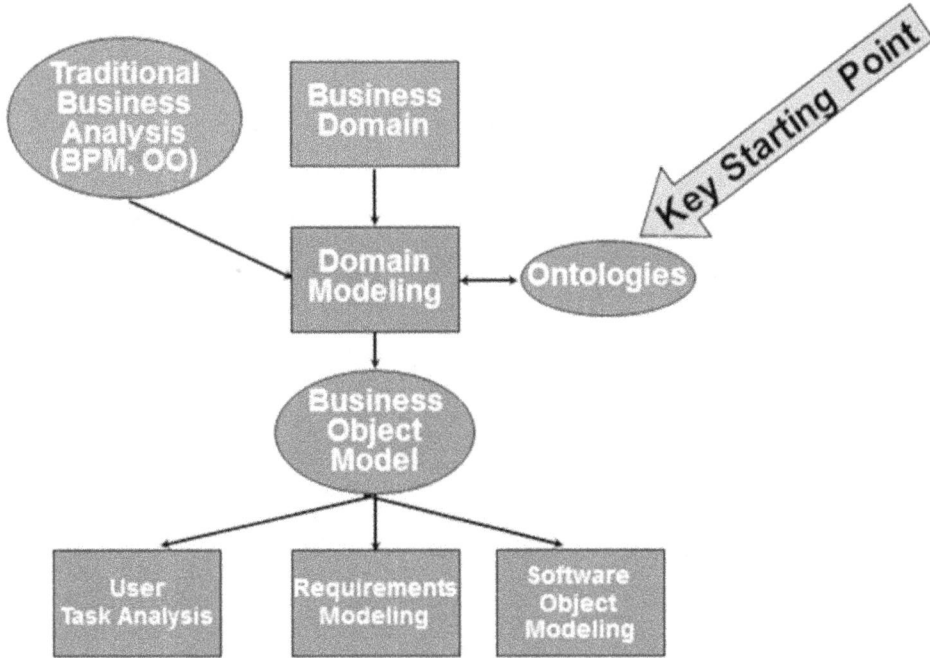

Combined BPM, OO, IA Domain Modeling Process

A domain model is commonly defined as a representation of entities, their attributes, their behaviors, and the processes that bind them together within a domain—nothing new to the experienced business analyst. What is new and highly beneficial is to define the information in a domain model in terms of ontologies and then to use these to construct business object models.

What is an *ontology?* Tom Gruber of Stanford University provides the short answer, "An ontology is an explicit specification of a conceptualization." He explains, "A body of formally represented knowledge is based on *conceptualization*: the objects, concepts, and other entities that are assumed to exist in some area of interest and the relationships that hold among them."

An ontology defines the basic terms and relations comprising the vocabulary of a topic area, as well as the rules for combining terms and relations to define extensions to the vocabulary. All domain models embody an ontology—albeit mostly implicitly. An agent-oriented approach to defining business objects emphasizes the use of explicit ontologies as implementation-neutral representations of knowledge that can then be mechanically translated into different target modeling tools.

An ontology can be expressed in a variety of ways, for example: informally (Natural Language, Graphical Notations), semi-formally (for example, Ontolingua), formally (first order logic languages such as Knowledge Interchange Format [KIF]). The *de facto* language for encoding ontologies is Stanford University's *Ontolingua,* a portable language for writing ontologies. Ontolingua is a LISP-like language that is based on KIF. Because KIF provides for the representation of knowledge about the representation of knowledge, storing business knowledge in KIF opens up many opportunities for delivering reuse and validation at the knowledge level.

Digital Prescriptive Maintenance

Disrupting Manufacturing Value Streams through Internet of Things (IoT), Big Data, and Dynamic Case Management

Dr. Setrag Khoshafian and Carolyn Rostetter, Pegasystems Inc., USA

INTRODUCTION

Digitization is disrupting manufacturing by using innovative approaches and solutions involving agile business processes that optimize end-to-end manufacturing value chains. This paper focuses on a novel approach to "Total Productive Maintenance (TPM) [1]" processes that leverages three essential digitization forces: Internet of Things, Big Data analytics, and of course, Dynamic Case Management[1].

The holistic approach to maintenance is now augmented with Things that are increasingly intelligent and responsive. Traditional maintenance tends to be "reactive." This is the worst case scenario for maintenance: reacting to failures in equipment or devices, after the fact. Connected devices and IoT are changing the dynamics of conventional TPM. Devices are now incorporating intelligent software that is becoming a key enabler for diagnostics and maintenance.

Prescriptive maintenance goes beyond the realm of descriptive, preventive [2], and predictive [3]. Descriptive focuses on what happened in the past. Preventive maintenance empowers operators to carry out continuous maintenance.

Predictive analytics discover potential options for the future. Prescriptive leverages all these approaches and capabilities. The realm of what *should* happen and the execution of optimized maintenance strategies is precisely the realm of prescriptive maintenance. With prescriptive maintenance devices, in collaboration with operators, are pro-active participants in their own maintenance.

There are several trends coming together to disrupt manufacturing: especially maintenance. These include the main forces of digitization (Social, Mobile, and Cloud), Internet of Things, and Big Data analytics [4]. Increasingly, Big Data is becoming "Thing" Data - with connected devices in manufacturing value chains generating enormous amounts of information. Potentially, sensors on edge devices can continuously record their behavior and status. These event data is filtered and aggregated in Big Data repositories managed through NoSQL databases. Big Data analytics is then used to prescribe maintenance tasks that get executed in the context of dynamic cases. Mining and discovery from Big Data allows pro-active diagnostics and fixes that often preclude incident events that require expensive maintenance processes.

Dynamic Case Management [5] is perhaps the most important pillar supporting prescriptive maintenance. DCM is perfect fit for Digital Prescriptive Maintenance (DPM). The maintenance tasks involve pre-determined repetitive process fragments. Maintenance needs to also support unplanned and ad-hoc tasks. The end-to-end maintenance case is quite complex and involves several types of workers,

---

[1] Also known as Adaptive Case Management. http://adaptivecasemanagement.org

organizations, and tasks. Therefore the fit of DCM includes a number of key capabilities: digitization of value chain stages for end-to-end maintenance; planned and ad-hoc tasks that execute in the context of maintenance processes within a case hierarchy; decision management that leverages various types of business rules and predictive models to determine the next best action for maintenance; as well as just-in-time integration with enterprise applications.

The focus of this paper is this new digitization of maintenance that is prescriptive, especially through DCM. The paper will also highlight a number of use cases from key industries that are leveraging IoT (aka "Industrial Internet," "Internet of Everything," and "Machine to Machine" [6]). The disruptive digitization approach to maintenance from descriptive, to predictive, to prescriptive with digitized decisions, cases, and IoT applies to any industry. Industries include aerospace, defense, automotive, energy and utilities, agriculture, mining, and consumer products, such as home appliances, lighting, thermostats, televisions, healthcare devices, and wearables.

FROM TOTAL PRODUCTION TO DIGITAL PRESCRIPTIVE

Total Productive Maintenance (TPM) is an important phase in the overall end-to-end product manufacturing lifecycle. TPM has its roots in the Toyota Production System [7], and historically it has focused on improving Overall Equipment Effectiveness (OEE) in the plant. OEE is a common calculation of Performance X Availability X Quality, and the work cells in every plant focus on making that number better. Traditionally, Total Productive Maintenance is holistic and inclusive: manufacturers and operators collaborating to maintain devices or equipment. The objective of TPM is to create a self-directed team environment to engage employees in preventing equipment break-downs, which ultimately leads to improvements in product quality and the ability to meet commitments to customers.

Embedded sensors, software, controllers, and connectivity are creating a digital revolution in manufacturing and aftermarket services, such as warranty and repair. Breakthroughs in networking, edge and fog computing, cloud technology, faster CPU's, cheaper memory, energy efficiency and miniaturization are all converging to create low-cost processing power and data storage everywhere. Essentially there are now computers in machines, gadgets, wearable devices and smart Things that are streaming data about their operations, performance and conditions. Things will be generating more data than people or applications. Translating all of that data into insights and intelligent decisions is the key to effective analytics.

The business rules, business logic, Big Data analytics and algorithms are all important aspects of maintenance optimization that spans "Descriptive," "Preventive," "Predictive," and most importantly "Prescriptive." DPM focuses on operationalizing what *should* be done while leveraging various types of digital technologies.

In this paper we use Digital Prescriptive Maintenance (DPM) to mean:

- Total Productive Maintenance +
- Descriptive, Preventive, and Predictive Analytics of Equipment data for Maintenance +
- Automated end to end processes with IoT sensors and Dynamic Case Management within intelligent Business Process Management (iBPM [8]).
  - We have called this "Process of Everything" [9]: the orchestration of dynamic end-to-end dynamic cases involving people, applications, trading partners *and* Things as participants.

The evolution from traditional TPM is a dramatic shift from simply minimizing machine down-time to a more proactive approach that uses data to predict future events and diagnose potential problems before they occur. With DPM machines will predict potential failures and autonomously trigger maintenance – all with minimal human intervention. Dynamic Case Management is used to automatically create a maintenance case with tasks that can be assigned to Things or people. If possible the equipment maintenance or repair can be done remotely by software. In situations that require a technician to be dispatched, they can arrive with advance information about the problem and the right parts and tools to fix it the first time. The case is tracked from beginning to end to ensure the appropriate resolution. The case data can be audited and mined for subsequent knowledge management. For example, the root causes and conditions that contributed to the case event can be analyzed (predictive analytics) to prioritize the next best actions to trouble-shoot the problem, diagnose the underlying issues, and identify the most likely solution. Machines become self-learning and over time can take care of themselves and reduce rework and manual efforts.

Advances in technology have created an over-abundance of "Thing" data from machines, sensors, robots, etc. Smart connected devices are flooding the system with data. Manufacturers have an obligation to mine, leverage the detected patterns, and act (prescriptive) to avoid potential failures that could sometimes have serious consequences for people, the environment, and equipment. Without prescriptive maintenance, we are paying an increasingly high price for inefficiencies due to the waste and lack of coordination between things, people, processes, data, and technology.

The ability to collect and analyze the structured data feeds from machines and other sources, along with the ability to combine semi-structured and unstructured data (e.g. images, audio, and video) into the mix, is transforming the future of manufacturing and after-sales service. Another important aspect of DCM for DPM is the flexibility in having structured, semi-structured, as well as ad-hoc tasks in the context of end-to-end cases created by people or Things.

Case management gives everyone in the value chain the visibility into the stages and steps of the process from end-to-end. The analytics and data visualizations on the performance of the process provide a virtual cycle of continuous improvement. Case tracking and resolution data will point managers and operators to additional opportunities to eliminate bottlenecks, streamline and simplify. The biggest benefit is that the process is no longer static or dependent on reactive outside interventions to drive improvements. The optimization of the process is dynamic and built-in to the system. The sum of the parts is now greater than the whole: manufacturers are simultaneously improving cycle times, quality, productivity and the customer experience, which in turn reduces costs and risks, thereby yielding tangible bottom-line results.

DYNAMIC CASE MANAGEMENT FOR DIGITAL PRESCRIPTIVE MAINTENANCE

Prescriptive Digital Maintenance is transforming and disrupting manufacturing processes. Dynamic Case Management is *the* core capability that allows DPM operationalize what *should* be done to optimize maintenance. The value proposition of dynamic case management can be summarized as follows:

- *Dynamic yet Holistic and Organized Automation:* Maintenance is all about organizing and executing *tasks* that are typically work orders executed by different participants. These participants include in-house operators, contractors, as well as skilled engineering experts from the manufacturer or supplier. With DCM the maintenance case involving multiple workers, operators, departments, and applications. The tasks and content is coordinated and automated by the underlying DCM maintenance solution. In an overall value and supply chain, each department and team can focus on a subcase contributing to the overall objective of the parent maintenance case. The DCM is essential for the prescriptive (what should be done) orchestration of all planned maintenance, ad-hoc maintenance, and as well as maintenance that reflect changes in manufacturing processes.

- *Social, Collaborative, and Flexible:* DPM involves content, documentation (including text, images, and video) as well as continuous collaboration to achieve the objectives. Dynamic Case Management allows documents and content for maintenance be aggregated and referenced in the context of a case. Furthermore, DPM case workers and managers can leverage discussion streams, synchronous exchanges or chats, knowledge wikis, and opinion blogs —all within the context of the dynamic case and its objectives. The case stays alive and continuously improves with innovative idea exchanges, while knowledge about the product and service gets aggregated for either reference or analysis down the value stream. Flexibility is key. Exceptions happen. There are scheduled maintenance processes that can be controlled and automated through DCM. There are also ad-hoc tasks that maintenance technicians and managers can dynamically assign in the context of a maintenance case.

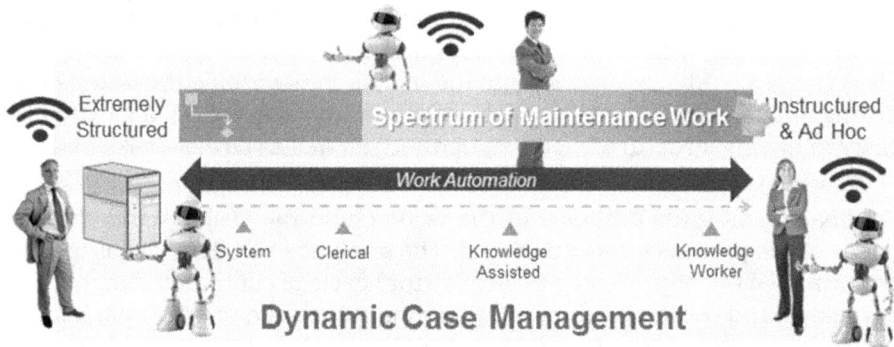

Figure 1: Maintenance Knowledge Work

- *Engaging Knowledge Workers and Knowledge-Assisted Workers:* The Knowledge workers [10] are the engineers and the cognitive maintenance subject matter equipment experts and often the authors of standard operating policies and procedures for maintenance. Traditionally they are siloed and do not engage in operational processes. That is changing with dynamic case management, and this very important category of knowledge workers is becoming increasingly more engaged in operationalized cases. An even more important category of workers who are supported through dynamic case management are the knowledge-assisted maintenance workers [11]. This most common category of worker leverages the decisioning, business rules, and situational/contextual execution of interactions in particular to help them complete their specific, contextual work within the case hierarchy.

What is a Case?

A case is the coordination and collaboration of multiple parties or participants that process different tasks for a specific business objective. The tasks are organized in a case hierarchy (subcases).

There will be a lot of collaboration among various case engineers, field workers, office workers and increasingly IoT or robotic workers to resolve the case. While processing these tasks, a case will have content, often from multiple enterprise information systems or content management repositories.

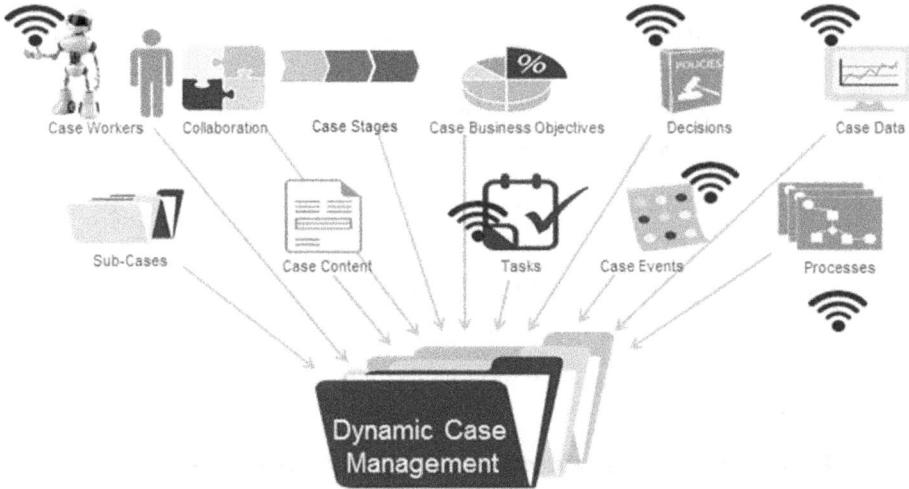

Figure 2: The Anatomy of a Dynamic Case

Some of the tasks will be planned in predetermined process flows, and some tasks will be unplanned. Cases are therefore dynamic, adding or changing any of their elements, and responding to and generating events.

A dynamic case (instance) in DPM it can be:

- *The device or equipment being maintained*: thus a dynamic case instance can be associated with the maintained device for its life time. There will typically be many subcases and related case instances associated with this case. Thus all documentation, history, events as well as maintenance, warranty, and upgrade cases will be either embedded or associated with the main device case.
- *A specific planned maintenance case*: this could be actually a subcase of the device case or a separate case that is related to it. There will be multiple planned maintenance case instances in the lifetime of the device. In addition to planned tasks there could be ad-hoc tasks (vs. entire exception cases) in the context of planned maintenance.
- *Un-planned and Exception Cases*: invariably there will be exceptional situations and unplanned incidents. Thus exception subcases will be generated with some semi-structure. There will be templates for handling the exception work and also provisions for ad-hoc tasks in the context of the exception case.
- *Related Cases*: The maintenance cases will often be related to or instantiate other cases. In maintenance one of the most important cases that will be instantiated for either planned or unplanned exception cases is the

warranty case. This case will check the warranty policies and accordingly adjust the maintenance costs and re-imbursements on the value chain (e.g. reimbursing dealers).

The following illustrates a Vehicle Maintenance case and some of its subcases. The maintenance illustrated here includes Tire, Oil change maintenance, and Anti-Brake System (ABS). There will be tasks, task workers and subcases for each one of these (and other) components in a vehicle.

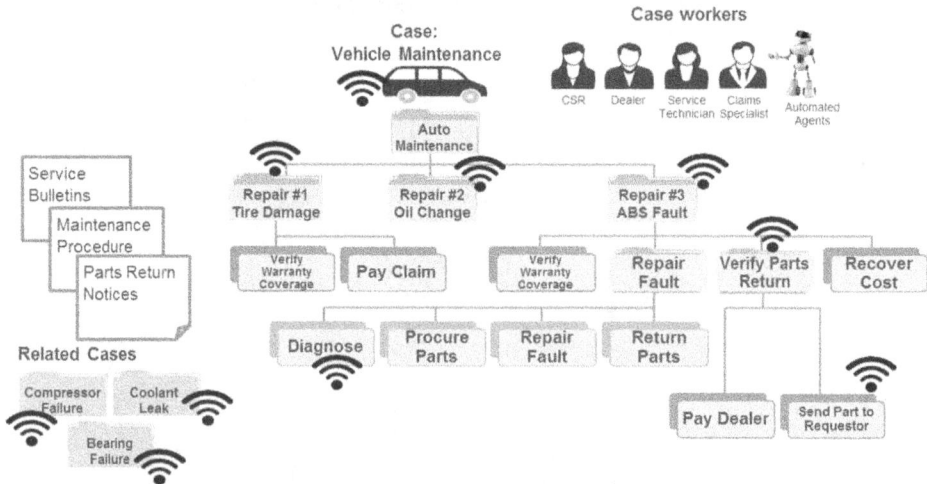

Figure 3: Vehicle Maintenance Dynamic Case Hierarchy

Rules and Analytics in DCM for DPM

Business Rules implement business decisioning logic and business policies. Rules drive the dynamic cases in DPM solutions. There are many categories and types of business rules such as decision trees, decision tables, constraints, and expressions. Business Rules are declarative. This means the focus on business rules is on externalizing the business logic, as close to the business as possible, without worrying about execution time, execution method, or execution order. There are many sources of operating procedure policies that end up in business rules, including policy manuals, the "heads" of experts or knowledge workers, and legacy applications. Examples of business rules that could be authored include: Expressions (e.g. for various calculations - volume, aggregate pressure, etc.), Decision Trees (IF – THEN), Decision Tables, Constraints (e.g. for actions when upper or lower bounds are violated).

Rules can also be discovered (aka "mined") from data: be that transactional, event data, data-warehouses, or increasingly Big Data repositories. The sources and types of data are heterogeneous. The on-demand or continuous sensor feeds of device status and event feeds are a tremendous source of data for maintenance. Predictive modeling techniques can be used to discover device performance patterns and then invoke or operationalize the discovered models in the context of DPM solutions. Predictive analytics can potentially unlock maintenance optimization strategies hidden in vast amounts of digital information: i.e. extract the "knowledge." Furthermore, the iBPM platform enables the insight that is discovered to become actionable in DPM.

An important category of business logic that is especially important with intelligent Things is *event rules*. The ability to correlate and respond to events, subscribe to an event or state changes, and handle the events by any device category is an essential building block in DPM. Temporal rules include service levels at either the dynamic case or task granule. Complex events can be correlated within temporal windows. DPM solutions (including the Robots or Things in maintenance processes) can be *adaptive*: they can continuously learn and adapt from the events or the behavior of the device or its components. Leveraging the business rules and achieving this continuous real-time analysis for actionable decisions provides tremendous advantages for the maintenance value chain. The aforementioned business rules and analytics capabilities allow organizations achieve preventive maintenance: detecting potential problems or degradation of equipment performance before its occurrence. Through analytics and business rules, the tolerance thresholds can be observed and dynamically maintained in control.

The following illustrates the intelligent "nervous system" of the Vehicle Maintenance Case. Many types of rules capturing various policies will be involved in the overall end-to-end case management of the vehicle maintenance case. Some of these will be authored by experts or knowledge workers. Others will be discovered through predictive analytics. Adaptive analytics will also be leveraged to learn dynamically from the maintenance histories and behaviors of vehicles. These will guide the next best preventive or maintenance actions for any of the vehicles parts or components.

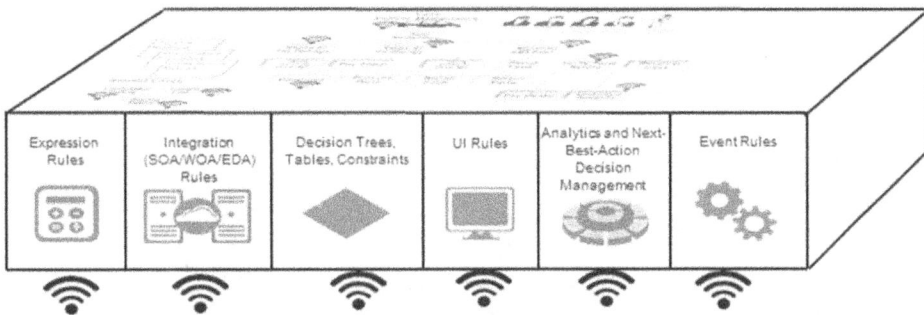

Figure 4: Business Rules and Analytics for DPM

PROCESS OF EVERYTHING: THE THREE USE CASES FOR DIGITAL PRESCRIPTIVE MAINTENANCE

To be impactful, IoT technologies need to solve real problems that typically involve multiple collaborating activities that include people, systems, and 'Things'. In other words, IoT needs orchestration through automated intelligent processes or what we have called the 'Process of Everything' (PoE) [9]. There are four important use cases of IoT in PoE for DPM:

- ***Things as Participants in Processes within Dynamic Cases for DPM:*** Traditionally, the participants in BPM were humans (roles, skills, teams, etc.), systems (back-end applications or services), and business partners (for B2B processes). With IoT and the Process of Everything, Things (including Robots) are also participants in processes. Things – manufactured or manufacturing device – are becoming intelligent and self-governing. Maintenance dynamic cases will include the Thing category of participants. In DPM Things (e.g. Vehicle components) will start to diagnose and maintain themselves. Similarly Robots will become active performers of maintenance tasks.
- ***Dynamic Cases Instantiated from Thing events:*** One of the most pervasive use cases for Process of Everything in DPM is the instantiation of a

maintenance case when sensing (through IoT sensors) a failure or critical issue with the device. This happens for example when detecting high levels of CO; or problem with an axle; or elevated temperature levels; or abnormal reduction in oil level. The intelligent Thing autonomously senses and then either directly, or through a brokering layer, activates an *exception* case (as discussed earlier). This typically includes monitoring back-office and dispatching field technicians to respond and resolve the problem. Within the processes executing in the exception case there will be tasks and activities assigned to people as well as Things or Robots. The dynamic case for DPM orchestrates the people, the suppliers, the manufacturers as well as back-office operations such as warranty management.

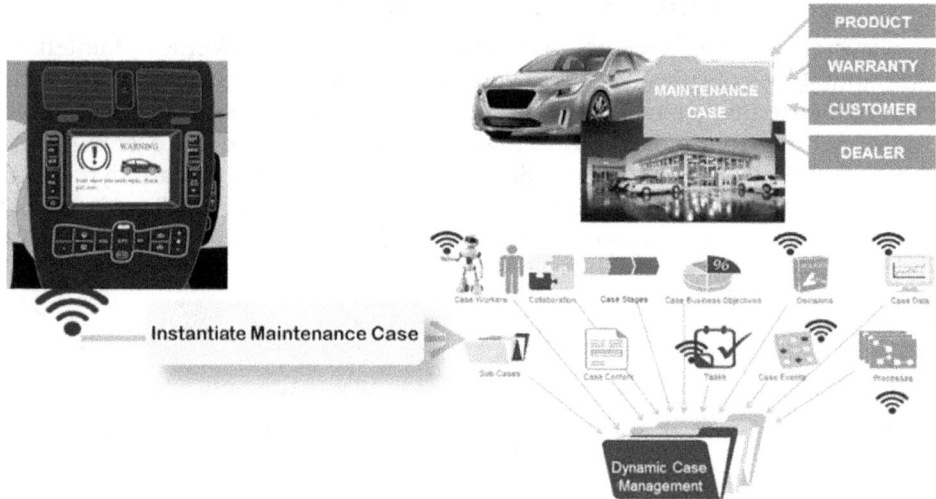

Figure 5: DPM Case instantiated from a sensed event

- *Complex event correlation in real-time for DPM.* The previous use case elucidated an adverse event or state that was sensed (potentially analyzed at the edge or the device) to instantiate a maintenance case. Often it is not just an individual event but a stream of events that could indicate a potential problem that need to be addressed through maintenance cases. Sometimes you need to detect patterns involving multiple events over a period of time. The correlation of these events in a temporal window is a common maintenance use case. The correlation needs to happen *real-time.* For example if two temperature peaks occurred within, say, 5 minutes it could indicate a serious problem that needs to be addressed with an exception case for maintenance. The event correlations will be digitized through decisioning rules and the prescriptive action will be handled through instantiating the maintenance case.

- *Predictive and Big Data analytics for DPM:* As noted above, devices are generating enormous amounts of information As more equipment and manufactured devices come on-line through connectivity (IoT), the amount of data they will generate will far exceed what human users of the Internet have been generating thus far. . Big Data will increasingly become Thing Data. Just having this raw data is not enough. This information could be mined and analyzed to better understand the device's behavioral characteristics and potential issues to maintain it intelligently. Unlike the previous scenario of real-time correlation of events, the data is aggregated over time and subsequently visualized and analyzed using predictive analytics models. Mining the event history of the Thing, predictive techniques sometime discover patterns or correlations that are unexpected or unusual. The discovered knowledge and predictive models are then digitized in DPM dynamic case solutions.

PoE and Digital Prescriptive Maintenance

Digital Prescriptive Maintenance leverages the iBPM platform with decision management in automated dynamic cases, involving IoT devices as participants. More specially, with DPM manufacturers will be provided the following capabilities:

- **Shop Floor Diagnostics:** Manufacturing Execution Systems (MES) [12] capture tremendous amounts of operational data that can be combined with data from the machines themselves, mobile devices, and the external environment. Mobile devices are allowing plant managers to monitor equipment and line efficiency through alerts, data visualizations, and real-time dashboards. For example, a global manufacturer is using iBPM to complement their standard ERP system and to improve their product quality and profitability. Product quality data is logged at every stage and step throughout the production process. The defect tracking is then correlated with the series of events and machine data, such as temperature, humidity, speed, and other conditions to determine root causes and contributing factors. A case can be created to monitor and report on any actions required to correct the defect and prevent it from happening again. This closed-loop feedback process allows the operators to make real-time adjustments to improve the first-pass yields and to reduce scrap and waste. The ability to trouble-shoot and diagnose in real-time gives a competitive advantage in an industry that is challenged with low margins.

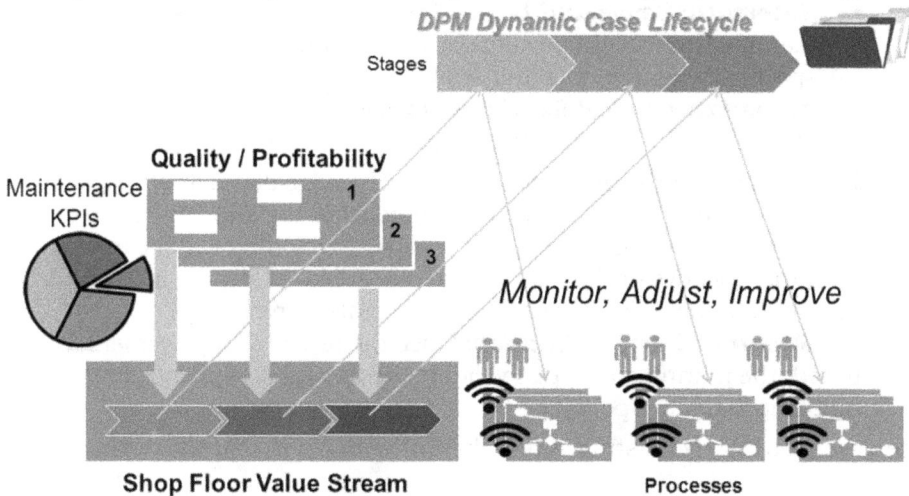

Figure 6: Shop Floor Value Streams using DPM Case Management

- **Supply Chain Analytics - A Plan For Every Part** [12]: IoT, Big Data, and Fast Data [13] are transforming traditional supply chain management from end-to-end. Top leaders in supply chain and logistics are accumulating and analyzing vast amounts of data, such as customer demand and the impact of external market trends and critical events. The supply chain today must leverage internal transactional data sources and external digital data sources – including both structured and unstructured data. These supply chain experts and data scientists are improving the ability to predict the future and to react to high-risk or disruptive events in the supply chain. By combining iBPM with Big Data, the advanced planning teams use workflow and case management to optimize inventory levels. They can run scenarios using predictive and adaptive models to ensure the right parts are available at the right times in the right places. If a major unexpected disruption such as a fire or flood occurs at a factory or at a supplier's site, the supply chain can respond in real-time to avoid shortages, move inventory to another location, or find an alternate source. Another global manufacturer is conducting a pilot to monitor data from social media, such and Twitter and Facebook. Analyzing customer sentiment and perceptions will be used to enhance the design and manufacture of future products and to enhance service after the sale.

The scope of use cases with IoT in DCM for Digital Prescriptive Maintenance is extensive. Here are some other examples for manufacturing and supply chain management:

- ***IoT Diagnostics:*** Things will either have on-board CPU and execution capabilities or be able to connect (e.g. via Bluetooth) to a device that has on-board execution for the device or Thing via low power connectivity. DPM will support:
  - ***Automatic Updates of On-board Device Software:*** Manufactured edge devices often have sophisticated software that can be updated remotely by the manufacturer.
  - ***Automatic Sense and Data of Measures from Edge Device***: A manufacturer might need to gather data from the device or ping it for specific measurements and analysis.
  - ***Automatic Control for Maintenance:*** Devices can also be controlled remotely or through on board decisioning software.
- ***IoT Supply Chain and Parts Return:*** The edge device that needs to replace a defective device can be monitored from the supplier to the distributer or customer (e.g. via on board Global Positioning (GPS) capabilities). Also, the defective device that needs to be replaced can be monitored for its return to the supplier or the OEM manufacturer.
- ***IoT Repair or Parts Validation:*** Once the repair or replacement is completed, the manufacturer can validate the fix and compliance to the warranty management policy.

These use cases clearly illustrate a new disruptive dawn in manufacturing through DPM.

CONCLUSIONS

New trends in digitization are disrupting the manufacturing and industrial economy. A shift in business strategy is required to stay ahead of the curve. The old manufacturing practice of TPM is being replaced by DPM, which provides the capability to create faster, better, and more value for the customer – with reduced cost and improved quality. The new value paradigm demands a fresh look at supply chain and shop floor activities to include the Internet of Things especially through the Process of Everything. Manufacturers need the ability to quickly analyze real-time events and act upon discovered models from Big Data in the context of end-to-end dynamic cases. The resulting DPM orchestrates the creation of value for the customer *and* the manufacturer – in fact the entire value chain - where work is done by humans and machines (aka Things) collaboratively.

In conclusion, Digital Prescriptive Maintenance is bringing revolutionary changes to the manufacturing and high-tech industry. The capability to bring together Big Data, IoT, and Dynamic Case Management will propel the industry forward faster than anything we have experienced in our lifetime.

The next Industrial Revolution has already started; it's the disruptive digital revolution. To be an industry leader means to make the investments now and take the steps forward before the competition does. Simply analyzing what happened in the past is no longer good enough. Moving toward predictive and prescriptive insights is the key to success. Leading manufacturers will anticipate what might or will happen in the future and make the best possible decisions to deliver optimal performance. Processes need to be more integrated and less silo'd across the enterprise, and legacy ERP systems and custom applications are too costly and time-consuming to change. Smart manufacturers are creating innovative solutions that harmonize everything across the digital ecosystem – interconnecting business processes, systems, data, people, and things.

REFERENCES

[1] http://en.wikipedia.org/wiki/Total_productive_maintenance

[2] Levitt, J. (2011). *Complete Guide to Predictive and Preventive Maintenance.* New York, NY: Industrial Press Inc.

[3] Khoshafian, S. (2010). "Predictive BPM." Published in 2010 BPM and Workflow Handbook Published in association with the Workflow Management Coalition (WfMC). Edited by Layna Fischer. http://futstrat.com/books/handbook10.php

[4] Khoshafian, S. (2014a). "The Adaptive Digital Enterprise: Top 10 Trends." http://e.pega.com/10-enterprise-trends

[5] Khoshafian, S. (2014b). "Dynamic Case Management for the Modern Worker." http://www.pega.com/insights/articles/trend-6-dynamic-casemanagement-modern-worker

[6] Khoshafian, S. (2014c). "Rise of Things: IoT's role in Business Processes." http://www.informationweek.com/mobile/mobile-devices/rise-of-thingsiots-role-in-business-processes/a/d-id/1317010

[7] Toyota Production System. http://www.toyota-global.com/company/vision_philosophy/toyota-production_system

[8] Khoshafian, S. (2014d). iBPM: The Next Wave. Covers all the various digital transformative capabilities of intelligent BPM – including digitization and dynamic case management (chapter 9). http://e.pega.com/ibpms

[9] Khoshafian, S. & Schuerman, D. (2013). "Process of Everything." Published in iBPMS: Intelligent BPM Systems, Foreword Jim Sinur, edited by Layna Fischer. Lighthouse Point, Florida: Future Strategies, Inc., Book Division. http://www.futstrat.com/books/iBPMS_Handbook.php

[10] Davenport, Thomas H. (2005). Thinking for a Living. Boston, MA: Harvard Business School Press.

[11] Khoshafian, S. (2011). "Knowledge-Assisted Workers."
http://www.zdnet.com/article/knowledge-assisted-workers/

[12] Meyer, Heiko; Fuchs, Franz; Thiel, Klaus (2009). Manufacturing Execution Systems: Optimal Design, Planning, and Deployment. New York: McGraw Hill

[13] For more details see: http://www.lean.org/library/the_plan_for_every_part.doc and http://www.supplychainbrain.com/content/logisticstransportation/service-parts-management/single-article-page/article/why-you-should-plan-for-every-part-1/

[14] For a description of Big Data and Fast Data: http://en.wikipedia.org/wiki/Big_data and http://www.infoworld.com/article/2608040/big-data/fast-data--the-next-step-after-big-data.html

When Harry Met R2D2: Connecting Humans and Machines in the Flow of Work

Larry Hawes, Dow Brook Advisory Services, USA

A networked business is one whose value-producing assets are connected to each other and with those of other organizations. Most large organizations simultaneously support multiple types of business networks, including information, financial, supply, transportation, retail, services, content and social networks.

This chapter briefly describes two types of business networks of growing importance; enterprise social networks (ESNs) of individuals and the Internet of Things (Iot), which comprises of both "dumb" and intelligent devices. It then examines ways in which the two may converge (and are currently doing so) to produce Networks of Everything (NoE), in which humans and machines interact with one another to accomplish work. Key technology considerations for NoE, such as those needed to support discovery, integration, coordination and orchestration, are discussed throughout the chapter.

ENTERPRISE SOCIAL NETWORKS

Social networks are emergent, dynamic structures in which individuals are connected in relationships of varying strengths. Information and knowledge may be shared either broadly or in a more controlled manner within the network. Either way, the interactions between nodes (individuals) in the network are ad hoc and manually initiated; there is no business process management (BPM) component providing coordination or orchestration of activities.

In businesses, there has been an increased focus on identifying, expanding and supporting social networks since the middle of the last decade.[1] Powerful forces such as economic globalization; the rapid growth of the Internet and Web-based computing; and increased partnership, merger and acquisition activity have resulted in large enterprises seeking new ways to better connect their employees with each other.

The objective of enterprise social networking has always been to improve business performance by increasing the flow of information and knowledge within and between organizations. Expected and demonstrated benefits include faster opportunity recognition and vetting, more rapid problem solving and the wider spread of good practices. Generally speaking, large businesses invest in their ESNs to reduce operating costs and boost revenues.

---

[1] Telligent, a pioneering vendor of enterprise social software, was founded in mid-2004. The next year, UBM held its inaugural Collaborative Technologies (later renamed Enterprise 2.0) Conference. Andrew McAfee's seminal article, "Enterprise 2.0: The Dawn of Emergent Collaboration", was published in April, 2006 (McAfee, 2006).

THE INTERNET OF THINGS

The Internet of Things (IoT) is another type of business network that has recently garnered much attention, although the concept and proof points have existed for decades.[2] Unlike ESNs, the IoT is made up of machines (sensors, actuators, RFID tags, etc.) and software systems (primarily databases associated with ERP, MRP and other backend enterprise applications) that have been connected using Internet protocols. While ESNs act as conduits for information and knowledge, the IoT is a series of Internet paths through which raw data travels between network nodes.

The growth of the IoT is expected to be rapid. IT research firm Gartner, Inc. estimates that there will be approximately 26 billion connected nodes in the IoT by 2020.[3] Clearly, there will be too many devices in-network to be able to hardwire connections and control of the data flowing between them. The movement of business process events and related data produced or recorded by machines in the IoT will need to be dynamically coordinated and orchestrated. These activities will most likely follow the broad principles and some of the techniques that currently underpin Software Defined Networking.

Academic researchers have proposed that the Service-Oriented Architecture (SOA) model of inter-node connection and communication could be applied to the IoT (Pintus, 2010). They and many software vendors see promise in using SOAP-based Web services standards (HTTP, SOAP, XML, WSDL, BPEL and others) to connect machines in the IoT and route data between them and connected databases.

This is comforting news to those of us in the BPM world, as we are already very familiar with SOA technologies. However, their prescription for the coordination and orchestration of IoT activity assumes that all nodes are known to each other. As Pintus et al note, "...the discovery of [Web services] via UDDI is not suitable for sensors or devices because [it does] not [have] context information (e.g. where a sensor is placed)." Therefore, another model is needed for IoT node discovery.

In addition, SOAP-based Web services standards do not accommodate ad hoc creation of applications that require interface with multiple networked resources (Atzori, 2013). So another architectural model is needed to enable that scenario, when it exists.

THE SOCIAL INTERNET OF THINGS

Several academic researchers have proposed creating a Social Internet of Things (SIoT), which would use social networking architectural principles and technologies to connect machines with each other in a highly-scalable manner. The most recent SIoT research suggests that the model could also enable machine-to-human connections.[4] In these academic papers, researchers advocate extending the "follow" or "friend" model found in ESNs to connect IoT nodes in trusted relationships. They

---

[2] Gil Press' blog post, "A Very Short History of the Internet of Things", on Forbes.com provides a useful and entertaining overview.
http://www.forbes.com/sites/gilpress/2014/06/18/a-very-short-history-of-the-internet-of-things/

[3] Read the complete Gartner press release at https://www.gartner.com/newsroom/id/2636073

[4] See (Ortiz, 2014) for a thorough review of SIoT academic research and its identified challenges and open issues.

also advocate using RESTful interfaces to connect to IoT data and information sources, as does most enterprise social software.

In fact, enterprise social software has already validated these researchers' visions, by demonstrating the ability to form limited relationships between people and machine- or application-produced data and information. In many ESNs, individuals can "follow" specific files and folders of documents (including those related to a discrete project) and be notified in an activity stream when a revision or addition is made. They may also be notified when another individual makes a comment on the followed document, even if they have not formally established an online relationship with that person.

Dorothy Grey added folder 20 - Release Notes to project ProjectDocs

Moments ago

John Smith added document 19 - Technical Design Document to project ProjectDocs

1 minute ago

David Moore modified document 16 - Functional Design Document from project ProjectDocs

- Current Revision was changed to '1.5'
- Revision Author(s) was changed to 'David Moore'
- Revision Date was changed to '02/03/2013'
- Revision Notes was changed

4 minutes ago

Figure 1: Notification of changes to project documents and folders

This model becomes very interesting in the case of a compound document whose components are automatically self-assembled (by definition) based on explicit relationships with other documents, as well as codified rules and policies. At this point, the document has become an intelligent thing that can aid an individual in the completion of his or her work.

Enterprise social networking provides another proof point for the possibility of M2H networks built on the SIoT model. Some ESNs feature the ability for applications to publish event-related notifications into an activity stream. For example, if Sally changes the status of a sales opportunity in her company's customer relationship management application, it can push a notification to the ESN's activity stream of her manager, Bob (if the two systems have been integrated and he has "followed" the specific sales opportunity on which she is working).

Demo User upgraded ABC Manufacturing from a Lead to an Opportunity. Posted 2 minutes ago. Comment Delete

> **Bob Smith** Finally! That's great news, well done. Posted 1 minute ago. Delete

> **Demo User** Yeah, there's a good opportunity there. Looking forward to working through the requirements on-site next week. Posted a few moments ago. Delete

Figure 2: Notification of status change in a sales opportunity

THE NEXT EVOLUTIONARY STEP FOR SIoT

The benefit of receiving these types of notifications in an ESN's activity stream is that the recipient can easily and quickly share them with others. By communicating and collaborating around system-generated events and information, individuals can gather additional data, information and knowledge needed to quickly make decisions and take appropriate actions.

The academic SIoT model assumes that machines will notify humans of changes to information and process states, but that the recipients will have to leave the activity stream to take a consequential action. In application, the SIoT would create even more business value if it enabled people to act directly from within the activity stream by interacting with the notification.

Again, we have existing validation points for this notion in ESNs. Currently, embedded experiences (as actionable notifications are frequently called) are limited to simple approval processes. For example, some enterprise social software enables managers to approve their direct reports' vacation time requests from within the activity stream.

For this to happen, the Human Resources (HR) system must be integrated with the ESN and an approval workflow must be built into the HR system. When those conditions are satisfied, an employee can submit a vacation request to the HR system, whose workflow will push a notification to the ESN activity stream of the predefined approver. That manager can hit an "approve" button that is embedded in the activity stream notification or choose the "deny" button if he or she objects to the request. When one of the buttons is selected, the workflow sends a message to the HR system, which changes the status of the request to record the manager's decision and notifies the requestor.

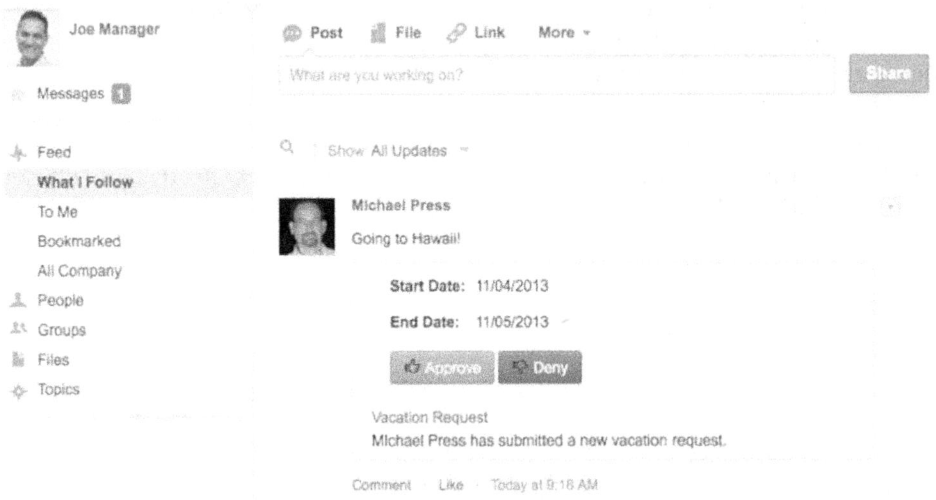

Figure 3: Vacation request approval via embedded experience in a notification received in an activity stream

Similar embedded experiences are available in ESNs for content, procurement and other approvals required to execute business activities. While they are rudimentary now, embedded experiences offer a workable alternative to email notifications and begin to deliver on the promise of SIoT-based machine-to-human interaction.

A final enterprise social networking advancement, which was recently announced, will further deliver on the SIoT vision. IBM Corporation will soon offer the option to include its Watson cognitive assistant as a full-fledged member of an ESN built on IBM Connections. Individuals will be able to find, "friend" and interact with a cloud-based instance of IBM Watson, from within the Connections activity stream, to get information that will help them make better decisions. When commercially available, this technology will make peer relationships between machines and humans are not only possible, but reality.

NETWORKS OF EVERYTHING

While the SIoT model is very promising in its ability to support multiple types of peer relationships between people and machines (H2H, M2M, M2H), it does have limitations. Enterprise social networking software currently does not include capabilities for coordinating and orchestrating activities between network nodes, whether they be human or machine. This is logical, because ESNs are designed and deployed to support emergent, ad hoc connection and communication. ESNs (and, by extension, SIoTs) are intentionally built to support the kind of work that can't be automated or controlled by traditional enterprise systems that encapsulate fairly rigid business processes.

It appears that what will really be needed to successfully connect humans and machines in a single network architecture, and create Networks of Everything (NoE), will be a combination of elements from traditional BPM , enterprise social networking and other technologies. Fortunately, these already exist. They are known by various names, but are most frequently called *adaptive case management* and *digital experience management.*

Adaptive Case Management

Adaptive case management (ACM) is a broad collection of enterprise technologies and other digital resources that let any knowledge worker simultaneously create and act on a business process. The overarching goal of ACM is to enable dynamic decision-making by providing relevant information at the right time in a prescripted process or by helping an individual (or machine) to quickly find it in an ad hoc manner.

ACM does this by surrounding a fundamental business transaction, opportunity or challenge – the case – with a set of capabilities that support effective and efficient decision-making and action-taking, as depicted below.

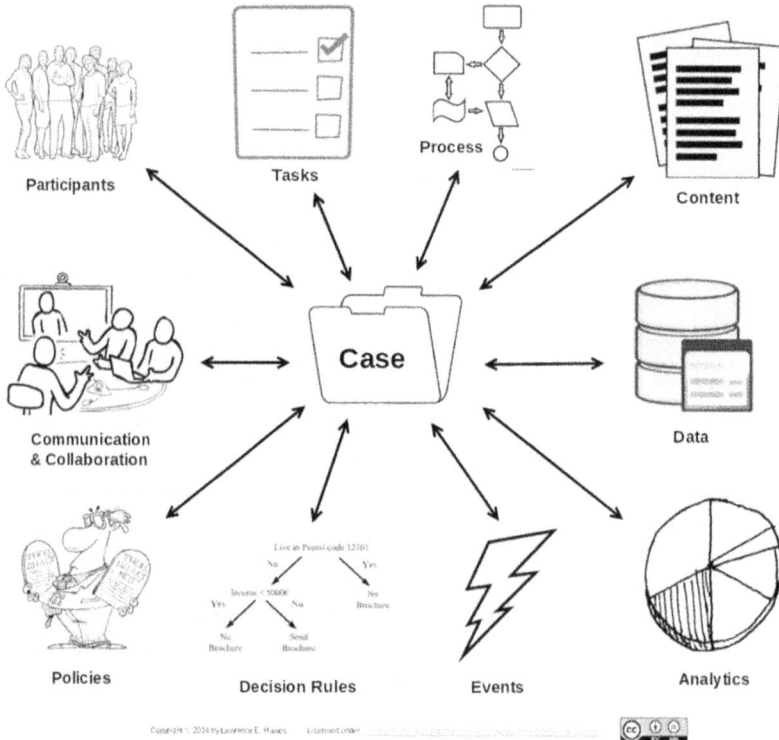

Participants — **Tasks** — **Process** — **Content**

Communication & Collaboration — **Case** — **Data**

Policies — **Decision Rules** — **Events** — **Analytics**

Figure 4: Adaptive case management framework

ACM is an ideal framework in which to manage tasks and get work done, because it has the right blend of structure and emergence. Traditional BPM and other process technologies are too inflexible, while enterprise social software and other communication tools lack sufficient structure and information work context. ACM lets knowledge workers (or machines) choose which activity sequence, tools and information sources to use to best complete tasks and meet project milestones, as well as to satisfy the overall objective of a specific business process.

ACM is an excellent conceptual framework and set of supporting technologies for NoE, because it already includes both human and machine participants and enables both structured and emergent work in the context of a single case. However, the ability to dynamically and automatically alter a business process based on real-time, predictive analysis of historical data generated by machines and humans is not yet fully-developed in ACM. To add this intelligent process capability, we must look to digital experience management technologies.

Digital Experience Management

Digital experience management (DEM) is the set of principles, methodologies and technologies around personalizing and optimizing online interactions   between network members. It is very similar to Web experience management, but embraces other networking technologies, including Bluetooth, WiFi and cellular. DEM is also comparable to customer experience management, but is not solely focused on ecommerce; DEM also encompasses other types of interacting participants, such as employees, business partners and nearly any sort of intelligent machine.

DEM relies heavily on analysis of historical and real-time data to dynamically tailor information presented during an interaction, as well as the actual flow of the interaction. Predefined policies and rules are also used to shape and guide interactions. In some cases, predictive modeling may be done or simulations may be run to determine what additional information is needed or which potential sequence of activities represents the optimal interaction process. In short, DEM provides the process intelligence that is currently missing from ACM, but required in Networks of Everything.

Google's Navigation Ecosystem as Network of Everything Exemplar

The navigation ecosystem that Google is currently assembling is a great example of how all of the elements discussed so far will come together in Networks of Everything. The Google ecosystem mixes humans and machines, physical and virtual assets, historical and real-time data, simulations, and predefined and emergent processes to optimize peoples' driving experiences by reaching their destinations as efficiently as possible.

Google's navigation ecosystem currently consists of Google Maps, its satellite-based mapping and navigation system and Waze, a community-driven system that Google acquired in June, 2013. Both components provide GPS-based services including turn-by-turn voice navigation, real-time traffic information and other location-specific traffic alerts. However, Waze also crowdsources information about accidents, traffic jams, police speed traps from drivers interacting with the service on their smartphones. In addition, Waze anonymously collects location and speed of movement data from the sensors embedded in those drivers' smartphones. All of this data is stored in a database, analyzed and used to recommend optimal driving routes from Point A to Point B on-the-fly.[5]

Waze is expanding Google's navigation ecosystem in another way too. By partnering with major cities, Waze has added new sources of traffic information to its database.[6] The City of Boston is providing information to Waze, in advance, on expected road closures due to annual events like the Boston Marathon or extraordinary ones like a parade after one of the Hub's sports teams wins a championship.[7]

The relationship flows the other way as well. Boston's Traffic Management Center is using historical data from Waze to augment information available from its own cameras mounted at hundreds of intersections to make decisions about traffic signal timing adjustments. Perhaps in the future those traffic signals will be integrated with the Waze network, so their timings can be altered based on real-time traffic data.

As (Bonchek, 2013) astutely noted, "Google Maps is a data network, while Waze is a social network...of cars, phones and people." By integrating Maps and Waze,

---

[5] See the Wikipedia article on Waze at https://en.wikipedia.org/wiki/Waze

[6] Read the related press release at http://www.prnewswire.com/news-releases/waze-launches-connected-citizens-program-debuts-inaugural-w10-277867931.html

[7] Press release available at http://www.cityofboston.gov/news/Default.aspx?id=18994

Google can create a fledgling Network of Everything. This synergy between network and participant types is precisely what the NoE is all about and what makes it so powerful.

Speaking of cars, the Google navigation ecosystem is becoming even more powerful and valuable with the pending addition of its own driverless car. The Google Self-Driving Car project has been underway since before 2010 and has produced prototype electric vehicles that have been tested on public streets and highways.[8]

The current Google vehicle is equipped with eight different types of sensors, which are used to detect objects (e.g. other cars, bikes, pedestrians) around which it must navigate, to read road signs and to send and receive location data to and from GPS satellites.[9] The car also uses Google Maps information in real-time to navigate to a specified destination.

The Google Self-Driving Car will be an integral participant in the company's navigation ecosystem, both producing and consuming data in real-time. Some of the data it produces will be consumed by humans logged in to the Waze application; some will be used by things such as other cars and traffic lights. When combined with Google Maps, Waze and government-owned databases, sensors and infrastructure, the driverless car will be the centerpiece of the Google NoE dedicated to navigation.

CONCLUSIONS

As demonstrated by the example of the Google navigation ecosystem, Networks of Everything are very real today in the consumer world, if not yet in the business domain. We have at our disposal many of the guiding principles and working technologies needed to create NoE. BPM and ESN are key components now; ACM and DEM will be indispensable moving forward.

Our work is far from done, however. To build valuable, large-scale NoE, we need to make some architectural decisions and to create interoperability standards, where they are missing.

(Atzori, 2013) chronicles the choice between SOAP and REST architecture styles in building NoE (or Web of Things, as they label it). Web-based transactional systems that include workflow and BPM components have tended to be built using SOA principles and technologies. ESNs (and most consumer Web applications) typically use the RESTful style of integration with other computing resources and do not use workflow or BPM to coordinate or orchestrate activities.

It is possible that NoE will incorporate both architectural styles. BPM and SOA may be used for reoccurring, relatively predictable work patterns, while ESN and REST will be employed for less predictable patterns and one-off integrations. ACM offers examples of current practice in which this mixed-architecture is leveraged.

Another developmental area for business-oriented NoE is social interoperability standards. Some exist and have been deployed, however their success has not been

---

[8] This blog post is how Google announced the Self-Driving Car project to the world: http://googleblog.blogspot.com/2010/10/what-were-driving-at.html

[9] For a succinct, clear overview of how Google's self-driving car works, see http://www.pcpro.co.uk/features/390085/how-do-googles-self-driving-cars-work

overwhelming.[10] Others, such as standards for digital identity and profiles have not yet been agreed upon or are in the early stages of being addressed.

Without these standards, it will be very difficult, if not impossible, to create NoE that leverage, in part, the SIoT model and enterprise social networking technologies. Without a consistent, accepted method of identifying people and machines in an online environment, it will be difficult for them to find, enter into relationships and communicate or collaborate with each other. Similarly, the lack of a common profile format and vocabulary will hinder the ability of humans and machines to understand each other's purpose and available expertise. This will further limit their ability to connect and collaborate with one another.

One thing is certain about the future of NoE. We are now at the very early stages of understanding how they may be designed, built, and used to connect humans and machines in the flow of work. We will learn much by trial and error and by persevering over time.

REFERENCES

(Atzori, 2013) Luigi Atzori, Davide Carboni and Antonio Iera. "Smart Things in the Social Loop: Paradigms, Technologies, and Potentials". Ad Hoc Networks, Vol. 18, July 2014. Elsevier, 2014, pp. 121-132.

(Bonchek, 2013) Mark Bonchek and Sangeet Paul Choudary. "The Age of Social Products". Harvard Business Review. October 14, 2013. Online at http://hbr.org/2013/10/the-age-of-social-products/

(McAfee, 2006) Andrew P. McAfee. "Enterprise 2.0: The Dawn of Emergent Collaboration". MIT Sloan Management Review, Spring 2006.

(Ortiz, 2014) Antonio M. Ortiz, Dina Hussein, Soochang Park, Son N. Han and Noel Crespi. "The Cluster Between Internet of Things and Social Networks: Review and Research Challenges". IEEE Internet of Things Journal, Vol. 1, No. 3, June 2014, pp. 206-215.

(Pintus, 2010) Antonio Pintus, Davide Carboni, Andrea Piras and Alessandro Giordano. "Connecting Smart Things through Web Services Orchestrations". Current Trends in Web Engineering, Lecture Notes in Computer Science, Vol. 6385. Springer, 2010, pp. 431-441.

---

[10] The OpenSocial Foundation's containerization standard and API set have been abandoned by its chief early proponent, Google. However, OpenSocial is still deployed in major enterprise social software offerings, including Jive Software and IBM Connections. The OpenSocial Foundation itself recently ceased independent operation, folding its work into the World Wide Web Consortium (W3C).

The activity streams standard for interoperability between activity streams of various ESNs has seen even more limited adoption. The W3C's Social Web Group is currently working on Activity Streams 2.0, which will both simplify and expand its JSON vocabulary and may incorporate elements of Schema.org's vocabulary as well.

Wearable Workflow, The Internet Of Things, and The Maker Movement

Charles Webster, MD, MSIE, MSIS

The following is adapted from a keynote I gave to the 2015 Health Systems Process Improvement Conference. My subject was about the great potential of wearable technology and the Internet of Things to improve healthcare workflow, and first steps to realize that potential. My audience was predominately made up of Industrial Engineers (my MSIE) and related professionals in healthcare. However, this chapter is directed toward those in the Business Process Management and Case Management software industry, interested in *selling products and services in healthcare and health IT*.

Note that much of the workflow technology I describe is already familiar to workflow technologists. Keep in mind my audience is a cross-section of healthcare process improvement and health IT professionals. I encouraged attendees, over 400, to tweet during my presentation. I had Google Glass set up so I could see tweets mentioning me, while I was speaking, to sort of demo what I meant by "wearable workflow." In fact, during my remarks you'll notice me occasionally thanking specific people for their tweets.

THE KEYNOTE

Thank you for attending this keynote! I'm honored. When I looked up past keynoters, I saw captains of healthcare industry and experts on healthcare process improvement. I'm a programmer and an engineer. I write code and build things. I hope my perspective may be of some use and interest. By the way, as noted on my slides, please tweet me at @wareFLO (no W at the end) on the conference hashtag during my presentation. I'll hear the ding on Google Glass. I might retweet you, or reply, or not, depending on momentum or distraction and so forth.

Here's the roadmap to what I will talk about.
- What do I mean by "Wearable Workflow"?
- What is the relationship between wearable technology and the Internet Of Things?
- Is Google Glass (and the smartglass concept) dead or alive?
- How can WT/IoT benefit, and benefit from, healthcare process improvement professionals

THE VERY IDEA OF "WEARABLE WORKFLOW"...

I tweet a lot, from @wareFLO on Twitter. So a lot of my slides are actually screenshots of past tweets. Here is my informal definition of workflow, one I offer to non-workflow professionals:

> "Workflow is a series of tasks, consuming resources (costs) and achieving goals (benefits)."

I like this definition of workflow because I was a pre-med accountancy major. Workflow occurs in an economic context. When cost-benefit ratio changes, workflow often needs to change too. But then, when speaking with health IT folks, I go on to say that all of these – tasks, resources, goals – need to be modeled and executed, or at least automatically or semi-automatically consulted, during workflow execution. That's why, for over two decades, I've been an evangelist for workflow tech in healthcare. By workflow tech I'm referring to workflow management systems, business process management, and, more recently, adaptive case management software systems.

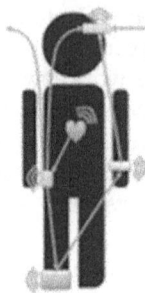

Mr. "Wearable Workflow"

A series of tasks, consuming attention, achieving personal & professional goals, facilitated by wearable tech.
(personified!)

I'm not above using cute stick figures to attract attention. You may recall Reddy Kilowatt, a stick figure made of lightning bolts, personifying electricity.

Mr. Wearable Workflow is a series of tasks consuming attention, achieving personal and professional goals, facilitated by wearable technology. The cost is distraction from other tasks, and the cognitive effort required to use one or more wearables to achieve those goals. Note that we're talking about personal AND professional goals. We've got this interesting interaction between the consumer side and the enterprise side of wearable devices, potentially the ultimate *Bring-Your-Own-Device* issue.

I'd thought that I'd invented the phrase "Wearable Workflow." I did come up with it independently. Then one day, I idly searched for it on Google and found that about ten years ago tens of millions of Euros were spent on a program called **WearIT@Work.** It involved many countries and companies, some familiar names in the healthcare industry. Their case studies included healthcare. (Hey, thank you! I just heard a ding in Google Glass because someone is tweeting about this presentation!)

WearIT@Work aimed at eliminating the distinction between information processing to support tasks, and performing the tasks themselves. Instead of interrupting working on an engine or performing surgery to do something on a computer, relevant information is automatically available ambiently and peripherally during each step of a user's workflow. And any data that needs to be entered into the computer is automatically created in the computer as a result of user task workflow execution.

WearIT@Work researchers believed that wearable computing will lead to more straightforward user workflows, higher quality, and less waste. Of course these beliefs need to be tested and borne out. However, these sorts of wearable workflow platforms are highly instrumented, with lots of time-stamped data that can be used to measure progress toward these goals.

I'm not going to drill down into the technical details of WearIT@Work, but I do love this word they used: "Wearlet." Back in the 90s there were applets, little programs running in web browsers. Then there were portlets, out of which web portals into enterprise data are constructed. You can think of a wearlet as an abstract wearable, a kind of software wrapper around a wearable device or specific wearable functionality. A wearable workflow is a sequence of wearlets exchanging data and precipitating actions, such as vibrating, buzzing, or displaying bits of data at just the right time. The idea of wearlet is highly compatible with increasingly popular approaches to drawing workflows and assembling applications by dragging, dropping, and customizing visual icons. In fact, we'll see examples in just a bit.

Wearable workflow has three levels: Intra-device, inter-device, and enterprise.

The lowest level of wearable workflow occurs when you are interacting directly with a wearable such as the Pebble smartwatch or Jawbone activity tracker. These button-to-button micro-interactions, interspersed with data displayed on a screen or perhaps just a vibration, are *intra-device wearable workflow*. Since I'm speaking to an audience containing many industrial engineers, I'll note that traditional sources of industrial engineering expertise, such as human factors and workplace ergonomics, are relevant to creating usable wearable devices.

Then there is *inter-device wearable workflow*. For example, the Pebble, Apple, and Android watches all interact with their host phones. In some cases, you can think of a smartwatch app as an extension to the smartphone. When notifications arrive, decisions should be made where to display them, how much to display, and how to handle users' responses. If you see an email notification in your watch and pull out your phone, should it already be open to the email? If someone sends you a video, the notification for which you see on your wrist, should it be automatically queued to play on your phone? You can see the eventuality; tasks will skip from device-to-device, at the level of inter-device wearable workflow. Some of these decisions, of what to display where, and in what order, may be learned, by applying machine learning to the device data exhaust. But there's also a role of non-programmer analysts to essentially draw out, and tweak, these inter-device workflows on platforms for authoring and managing wearable workflow.

Then there is *enterprise wearable workflow*. For example, last year I helped build a prototype of a hospital environmental services task management app for Google Glass[1]. It allowed a hospital housekeeping supervisor keep track of which rooms had been cleaned, which staff had cleaned them, and which rooms remained to be cleaned. It worked using QR codes by floor elevators and rooms, and through communication with business process management software in the cloud. The supervisor could request that rooms be recleaned and share comments with the staff. The glassware even recognized employee faces and displayed their names and employment history.

Now here is the interesting thing: this wearable workflow application was created by drawing workflows. [Keep in mind I'm speaking to a healthcare process improvement audience, not a BPM-familiar audience.] It did not require a Java or C# programmer to drag, drop, connect, and configure visual icons (though traditional programmers were initially required to create the software components represented by those icons). This sort of business process management development approach is an example of what is called "low code" software development. Thus, it is particularly relevant to you, who routinely draw and analyze healthcare workflow.

Consider your smartring, with a tiny display that can tell you that you have five email messages waiting. Indeed, that is all it can do, given its small form factor. You raise your smartwatch into view, which recognizes your gesture, in context, and

---

[1] http://ehr.bz/glassbpm

automatically opens to the notification it thinks has the highest priority. Perhaps it relies on machine learning or fuzzy logic or some priority conditions you've set. You can read, dismiss, acknowledge, or send a custom reply you've previously set up ("I'll call you later," "Cool!", "Go Bears!") such as is possible with the new Pebble smartwatch actionable notifications. (Ding! I hear someone just tweeted about this presentation again. Thank you! I'm on a roll at the moment, but just as soon as I'm done speaking, I'll be sure to RT and reply!)

Every wave of information and communication technology into healthcare – social, mobile, analytics, cloud, and now wearable and Internet of Things – brings with it more and more sophisticated process-awareness (to use the academic phrase). Here is another example, reminiscent of the low-coded environmental services Glass app I previously discussed. What you see here[2] is a collection of icons connected in a workflow (highly reminiscent of what you'd see in many traditional workflow editors). In the lower left is a smart sock, which detects if its wearer has fallen over. As we proceed through the visual flows and logic toward the upper right, the application calls an automated emergency answering service. The service responds with a phone call; "Are you all right?" If the answer is no, or the call is unanswered, the workflow continues, sending a notification to the ambulance service, including a link to a map showing the location of the smart sock. Again, what's interesting for my purposes of advocating workflow tech in healthcare is that once the various adaptors are created — connecting to the sock, the answering service, and so forth — the final app was created by drawing workflow.

THE RELATIONSHIP BETWEEN WEARABLE TECHNOLOGY AND INTERNET OF THINGS

That was the section of my presentation about wearable workflow. Now we're going to talk about the relationship between wearable technology and the Internet of Things. This presentation could have been a litany of headlines and case studies about Google Glass, wearables, and the Internet of Things in healthcare. But as a programmer and engineer, what I want to understand is how stuff works under the hood. And what are the implications? So I'm going to drill down, briefly, into just one example of a wearable and Internet of Things startup. (I just heard a ding in Glass. Thank you for tweeting, Katie!)

This is a startup out of MIT. Getting medical staff to wash their hands before and after touching a patient is a really big deal in healthcare. The startup creates sensors to attach to anti-bacterial soap dispensers. These sensors can tell from movement and vibration when the dispenser is used and communicate with user-worn badges. The information is logged. Wireless beacons are scattered around. When you walk up to, or leave, a patient, the badge vibrates to remind you to wash your hands, if you have not. Down the hall is a base station and a dashboard to keep track of how well staff is complying with the hand hygiene initiative.

That is all well and good. But do you remember when I told you we were going to talk about the relationship between wearable technology and the Internet of Things? They're basically the same thing. A wearable is an Internet of Thing object that you wear. It's the interaction between these objects, some on your person and others in your environment, that will give healthcare process improvement a new set of tools to "see" workflow and, ultimately, intelligently influence workflow in real-time.

---

[2] Diagram will not be displayed, this presentation was shown to a live audience. The diagram is simply what you'd see in many traditional workflow editors

The second point this example illustrates is the tremendous amount of pivoting and generalizing going on in the wearable and Internet of Things arena. As soon as these sensors were in place, folks start thinking, "Hey, why don't we put them everywhere? We could gather data about patient wait times and treatment patterns. We could potentially spot all kinds of opportunities for healthcare workflow and process improvement. Why stop at that? We have this information in real-time. We know moment-by-moment where there are idle resources. Let's send notifications and move those resources around in response to spikes and surges in demand."

Now, if what I'm talking about isn't already an obvious example of pivoting and generalizing, from hand hygiene to a hospital workflow support system, then what I'm about to tell you will surely convince you. This startup started with a smart dog collar. They went from pet wearables to hand hygiene to a real-time hospital workflow system. And just got $15 million of investment.

How is this possible? Here's a button-sized microcontroller, coming out of Intel, called the Curie. It's got an accelerometer and gyroscope and communicates by Bluetooth. It's so small; it might actually conceivably be worn as a button. Or it could be in your pocket. Or dropped in potted plants at that hospital hallway intersection where patients keep taking the wrong turn. It could be sewn into a waiting room chair. Whether it's used as a wearable or Internet of Things depends completely on context, not the intrinsic characteristics of the technology itself. In both cases, it's a smart object.

A smart object has four kinds of capabilities: sensors, actuators, connectivity, and logic. Sensors sense vibration, temperature, light, and so on. Actuators vibrate, buzz, and show small amounts of data. Smart objects also have connectivity. There's local connectivity, such as interactions between soap dispensers and staff badges. That's inter-device wearable workflow. Then there is enterprise wearable workflow. Data flowing to the cloud, notifications flowing back. The data that flows up can be used to find bottlenecks and rework. It can be used in real-time to drive workflow using notifications sent back down to users, to actually influence their workflows in real-time. The fourth smart object capability is logic. It controls the interactions between sensors, actuators, and communication with the world. It's what you update, if you decide you don't want a smart dog color, but instead a smart soap dispenser.

You've heard the phrase "The Internet of Everything"? Wearables are the **Internet of You**. Because wearable tech is a subset of the Internet of Things (plus fashion!).

GLASS (AND SMARTGLASSES): DEAD OR ALIVE?

Now we come to the subject I know many of you have been waiting for. Is Google Glass dead or alive? Last year I came to this conference and gave a presentation about Glass and healthcare workflow. But I did something that I thought was pretty interesting and daring. I split the presentation in two twenty-two and one-half minute segments. I brought a large LCD monitor, large enough to be visible from even the back of the room. Everyone could see what appeared in the tiny head-mounted micro-display. During the first half of my presentation I rapidly covered how Glass works and where it fits into healthcare workflows. The second half was a bit like one of those stage hypnotist shows. I called for volunteers to come up and put Glass through its paces, with, maybe, 30 seconds of training. I've done over 500 of these two-minute personal demos. The only difference here was that about a hundred of your colleagues were looking on. Folks made lots of interesting mistakes (especially when it came to trying out the speech-to-text capability), resulting in good-natured laughter, since everyone could see what Glass actually transcribed.

My following comments are partly about Google Glass and partly about *smarteye* glasses in general. I don't have any inside knowledge about Google's future plans for Glass. However, I've used Glass since early 2013. I know a lot of the Glass pioneers, who, by the way, are also investigating competitors to Glass. And I can read and interpret tea leaves.

So, I will tell you about my experience with Glass. I'll tell you what I am hearing from these pioneers. And I'll go out on a speculative limb and make some predictions. [Mind you, if you are reading this several years after I've written these words, I hope you'll be charitable.] What Google does with Glass will be driven by a combination of complicated internal and external forces. I don't have special knowledge of those internal forces. But regardless of what Google does, I think *smartglasses* will indeed come into reality, especially in the healthcare enterprise.

I actually had to take a train to New York to visit Google to literally get "fitted" for Glass in a manner reminiscent of visiting an optometrist. I wore it every day, for about the four or five hours that its battery allowed. The day after I got Glass I was walking across Dupont Circle park in Washington, DC, under an overcast sky. I heard a ding, looked up, and a short email from my wife appeared, projected on the gray sky over the fountain, "Where was I?"

I replied, hands-free. Glass transcribed and sent my response. I'd replied to an email in almost less than a second, hands-free, without even breaking stride (setting aside for now, the debate about whether it is indeed good to be THAT digitally available via email). I was impressed! Hands-free email, Twitter, photography and videography are my favorite Glass capabilities.

I am a firm believer in the principle of the philosophy of science that you don't really understand a phenomenon unless you can reproduce it. If you're an engineer that means building something that does what you are trying to understand. I built a bunch of prototypes. This was a Glass Eye chart. Obviously it only worked for one eye. It was for developers to size their fonts when developing Glass apps, not for any clinical purpose. Though I did find it useful when giving a demonstration to folks, to make sure they could read even the smallest standard Glass fonts.

I also created this prototype of a Glass app for tracking tasks in a medical clinic. We've got Dr. Blue and Dr. Purple, and rooms N1 through N3, S1 through S3. Here's an exam waiting five minutes. The number of minutes change as time goes by. Dr. Blue is in room S3. That's what the little asterisk indicates, so he's busy in here. This is just showing everybody the current state of clinic workflow, moment to moment, which is a very valuable thing to do.

Glass or Glass-like systems (and there are emerging competitors) have enormous potential in improving the workflow and usability of many of our traditional, and perhaps traditionally disliked, electronic health records. Recently there were headlines about the Glass Explorer program ending. Half of the articles basically laughed at the "failure" of the product. I'd like to emphasize that Glass wasn't a product. It was a prototype. Google learned an incredible amount of information from a very public beta test. What do you do with a prototype? You throw it away.

I do wear Glass in my pocket a lot. I take it on and I take it off. When I first started wearing it nobody knew what it was. When people saw it sometimes they thought it was like a low vision assist device. Then for six months people would run across the street asking me, "Is that Glass?" Then there was a backlash in social media and in popular media revolving around perceptions, worries about privacy, esthetics, dorkiness, privilege.

Here, at this conference, I'm wearing it a lot because I'm expected to. I'm giving a keynote that touches on this device. In fact, I've already used it to record, upload, and tweet video interviews with some exhibitors and attendees. Also, I used it as I drove here, from DC; Glass has an incredibly usable GPS. A dashboard GPS takes five seconds for you to look at it and then to look back to the road. You've travelled enough distance that you have to reconstruct your mental picture of your environment, location, and trajectory. The same takes just a half a second with Glass.

I've never had a bad experience wearing Glass, but I've heard that people have. When someone comes up to me when I'm wearing Glass I take it off as a sign of respect. Old fashioned courtesy and etiquette works fine. Now, I will admit I used to wear a really ugly shirt, because it had a large enough pocket to stuff a giant battery. [Audience laughter at a picture of my ugly shirt, with a big battery in a big pocket...] I'd plug Glass into the battery and use it 18 hours a day. You know what? A big battery in the front pocket of an ugly shirt is just not going to be successful in the consumer realm. I understand that.

Right now, we're in the trough of disillusionment relative to Glass. I think in the next year or two we're going to climb out to the plateau of productivity. Why do I think so? Well the popular perception is that Glass is a wonderment of miniaturization. That's true as far as it goes. But it's a wonderment of miniaturization of off-the-shelf technology. When Glass came out in 2012 it was probably using 2010 circa technology. Various folks tore Glass apart, to price its components, to estimate how much Glass cost to manufacture. Some of the estimates were ridiculously low. Like this one for 80 bucks. In fact the most exotic Glass component is the little micro-display, three or five bucks. It's apparently been around for years in the industrial sector.

According to the guy who shepherded the creation of the Glass user experience, if Google could have gone to electronic component manufacturers and guaranteed them 100,000 in sales they could've miniaturized the components much further. He estimates the next version of Glass could be a five-fold diminishment in three-dimensional size.

If you dramatically reduce the price and size of Glass, you begin to remove some of the objections to Glass. Battery life is still a problem. But it's not just a problem for Glass. It's a problem for all wearables. And there's a tremendous amount of R&D and venture capital money going into figuring out how to increase the duration between charges. I've seen headlines about battery technologies that promise to provide twice the energy and duration. And I've seen headlines about new chips that are twice as efficient at using that energy.

Do I think the next version of Glass will last four times as long between charges? No, I don't think the success of these technologies will occur sufficiently fast. But in conjunction with the intelligent software to turn off the stuff that doesn't need to be turned on, I think we're going to see a substantial increase in the amount of time between charges.

Here's a vote of confidence in Glass: Intel, the largest chip company in the world, will be the basis of the next version of Glass. (Right now this chip is from Texas Instruments.) Intel is investing megabucks into the Internet of Things and into wearable technology. You may have heard of the Intel Edison. It's a Linux box, with a gigabyte of RAM, four gigabytes of storage, Bluetooth and WiFi connectivity, and it's the size of a postage stamp (just a little thicker). I don't know which Intel chip will power Glass. But whatever it is, I hope it's as hackable as the Edison. That is relevant to harnessing the Maker Movement, as I will discuss later.

Final thoughts about Glass, and smartglasses in general. Ideally, wouldn't it be great if smartglass technology could actually be built into your glasses? Believe it or not, computer displays embedded in eyeglass lenses are almost 20 years old. I don't know if Glass will be the first, but I think in just a year or two, we'll see smartglass tech actually embedded into eyeglass lens and frames. The micro-display will be in the lens. The electronic components will be small enough that most of the 3D volume of the eyeglass frame may actually be battery. If this sounds impossible, I'd like to note a headline I saw the other day, about actually 3D printing battery technology. Right now I'm wearing wire eyeglass frames. I may finally have to re-adopt the big nerdy plastic eyeglasses I lugged around during high school. (I was so temped to include my yearbook picture at the point in my slides, but I chickened out.).

I think Glass is going to be back. It may be rebranded. But regardless, at the very least, we'll see a wave of new smartglass wearable technologies in the next couple of years, and it's going to knock our smart socks off.

How Can Health Systems Engineering Benefit, and Benefit from, Wearable & IoT?

In this next section of my presentation, superficially, I might seem to be speaking to health systems engineering educators about designing a curriculum around wearable workflow. Doing so requires thinking about what the future will look like, five to ten years down the road. That should be valuable to anyone interested in wearable tech and the Internet of Things in healthcare.

Twenty years ago I designed the first undergraduate curriculum in medical informatics. We went from five students to 130 students in five years. Every single one got a job. In fact my original course descriptions from 20 years ago are still online some place. They've held up remarkably well. So I thought, what kind of curriculum would I design to help graduates leverage wearable workflow to improve healthcare processes?

Curriculum design is really about looking into the intermediate future and looking at your resources. Do you have a medical school or not? Do you have an engineering school or not? Do have a fashion school or not? You borrow courses from wherever you can, design new bridge courses, and plan for project capstone courses to synthesize knowledge together in the crucible of semi-real-world experience.

So, I'm going to show you the course descriptions of what I'd put together in a proposal to the Dean.

IE 401 Wearable Human Factors and Workplace Ergonomics

Survey of human sensory, motor, and cognitive abilities; healthcare workplace ergonomics; and patient fitness and monitoring opportunities relevant to the design and engineering of wearable hardware and software systems.

I'm not going to spend a lot of time discussing this course. It basically combines two areas traditionally associated with Industrial Engineering — human factors and workplace ergonomics — with wearable technology topics. I will point out what I think may be a useful organizing framework, the systematic exploration of three dimensions: anatomical location, sensory and effector modalities, and context of use. Up to this point I've focused on wearables and IoT as they relate to healthcare provider process improvement. However, these courses could be quite useful on the patient and consumer wearable and IoT side of the equation too. Especially, since patients are increasingly incorporated into a wide variety of health IT work-flows.

Regarding anatomical location, I've seen wearable directories with over a hundred categories of places where wearables are worn, including inside the body, as in implantables and ingestibles.

Regarding sensory and effector modalities: Sensors vibrate. They buzz and light up. Doing so consumes energy. What is the minimum appropriate signal, with respect to both human psychophysics and competing environmental noise? How can care staff and patient environments be designed to maximize the benefit of worn wearable and deployed Internet of Things technology?

IE 402 Data and Process Mining Wearable Data

Imagine what Frederick Taylor and Frank and Lillian Gilbreth could have done with time-stamped position and location data made possible today by wearable technology. Or with patient-generated health data. This course seriously explores this hypothesis.

Frederick Taylor and Frank and Lillian Gilbreth are famous work improvement gurus in Industrial Engineering. You may have seen the movie *Cheaper By The Dozen*, a humorous and heart-warming movie about efficiency experts running an large and fractious family household.

In my view, "Big Data" is giving way to what I sometimes call "Big Workflow." Folks don't just want data, they want action. How do we find the patterns that drive the automated and semi-automated steps that are necessary to provide value? I have a favorite subject, related to this: process mining. I gave a presentation three years ago at this conference about process mining time-stamped electronic health record data. Basically, three numbers, a time-stamp, an event name, and an ID tying together tasks into a workflow, can be used to generated evidence-based process maps. If you add some additional data, such as patient diagnoses and who interacted with the patient, you can begin to slice-and-dice process maps and ask (and answer) all kinds of process questions.

Three years ago I was like the guy who loses his keys and looks for them under the light post. The keys may be over there in the bush in the dark, but it doesn't do me any good because it's dark and I can't see. I was restricted to the time-stamped data in the electronic health record. There's certainly valuable information there. But what if you had so much more data, data that's literally coming out of the walls and off the wrists and the badges of staff and patients? That's the interaction between the Internet of Things and wearables, as they pass each other in the hallway. That interaction will give us a wealth of time-stamped wearable workflow data.

WEARABLE WORKFLOW AND THE INTERNET OF THINGS MEETS THE MAKER MOVEMENT

I've put the third, and final, course into its own separate section. It is the least traditional of the three courses (from an Industrial Engineering perspective) but it is also the most important, in my humble opinion.

IE 403 Designing and Prototyping Wearable Products

This hands-on lab course is a semester-long "hardware hackathon." You will learn to assemble and program inexpensive Arduino microcontrollers and modules, create and print 3D-models, and combine into prototype wearable products.

This course may raise some Industrial Engineering eyebrows! Back when I got my degree in IE, we didn't make stuff. In fact, some of the other engineering programs sort of viewed IE as really only part engineering and part management. And I was really envious of my Mechanical Engineering and Electrical Engineering friends, because they were working on cool artifacts. And sometimes, especially when working together, they created cool interactive artifacts. The ME would design the robot arm. The EE would design the electronics to control it. But today, due to the Maker Movement, any Joe or Josephine can build interactive stuff, via open source hardware and 3D printing. And, perhaps more important, with a large and supportive community.

I'm a big fan of hardware hackathons. In fact I'm going to one, two weeks from now, in Toronto. Hardware hackathons are an incredibly immersive experience, especially to young students. You don't have to be a software engineer. I looked at a bunch of IE curricula and everybody has at least one course in programming. You walk in the door on Friday. By Sunday you may have a robot that you can control with your smartphone. You may have a smartwatch that does fitness kinds of things. My favorite; this lady created a brooch and it had a facial recognition camera. Every time it saw her boyfriend it would show an animation of a smile and it would play a happy song. The visceral thrill of creating something physical, that interacts and behaves, is an incredibly positive and investing experience. Just the investment of the net, plus the physicality of building this stuff really draws folks' attention.

You get an idea. You "breadboard" it, by combining electronic components with inexpensive microcontrollers using boards with holes into which you stick wires. Then you got to make it a smaller version, without the breadboard, for a demo. Eventually you get to a version that you actually want use, or provide to someone so they can use and provide feedback. But you can't send that naked gadget into the real world. There are prying eyes. Grime and substances can cause short circuits. So you need some sort of device enclosure. That's where the 3D printing comes in. Of course, if it's a wearable it's got to be a little aesthetic.

You don't have to start from scratch. There's a variety of wearable platforms coming into existence. For example, this is a smart bracelet platform and you can basically plug in an LCD, plug in an accelerometer, plug in a gyroscope, plug in a Bluetooth transceiver, etc.

So, how does this third course relate to wearable workflow? Consider how Google Glass was prototyped. A prototype might be a hat on top of which is a tiny projector. Coat hangers extend to hold a sheet of paper on to which images are projected. That was one of the 150 prototypes of Glass. That was the R, for research, in R&D. The goal was to maximize learning. On the other hand, after you get to the most promising prototype, and decide to move forward, maximizing quality and efficiency, that's the D, for development, in R&D.

What if those prototypes weren't pieces of hardware? What if they were entire workflows? There's probably more concentrated knowledge, in this room, about healthcare process discovery and how to evolve workflow and how to figure out how to do it in such a way that it doesn't unduly challenge human tolerance for change. What if you had a data rich environment, where you had lots of time-stamped data and the tools to analyze it? And then, in a Tinker Toy-like fashion, what if you could construct the workflow application to gather information and push notifications?

What if you could iterate and improve? It's what you're already doing. It's just adding additional, new, and useful tools to do so.

[At this point I showed the audience a series of pictures of a specific project of my own, called Mr. RIMP (for Robot-In-My-Pocket). Mr. RIMP is a 3D-printed, interactive, customizable robot for entertaining pediatric patients. It combines many of the themes from this presentation. Mr. RIMP is always changing, since he's my experimental wearable workflow platform. But, he's easy to find on the Internet and Twitter, if you like to catch-up on his current state and recent adventures.]

We have come to the end of the road of my presentation. My goal was to stimulate flights of imagination about how wearable tech and the Internet of Things can be used to improve healthcare workflow. If I have done so, I will very smugly rest on my laurels. Thank you very much. If we have any time for questions or comments, I'm happy to entertain them.

<Applause> (I swear!)

PS. I operate (network, think, blog, tweet, etc.) at the intersection between the workflow technology and health IT industries. While the previous presentation was directed at health process improvement and health IT professionals and educators, many BPM and case management software professionals interested in healthcare, may themselves be given to flights of imagination. Every time a new wave of technologies arise, new and interesting combinations and applications also arise. This is especially true for wearable technology and the Internet of Things. I hope you'll consider how to leverage these new opportunities to bring more process-aware information systems to healthcare and health IT.

Process Oriented Architecture for Digital Transformation

Vinay Mummigatti, USA

Vinay Mummigatti, USA

INTRODUCTION

Digital technologies are transforming every industry while throwing up new opportunities and challenges every day. Global enterprises are confronted with the need to understand, adapt and capitalize on these trends.

There are four distinct digital trends that are touching every enterprise today viz. Internet of things (IOT), Social media, Big Data and Cloud. These are distinct trends but complementary to each other. The burgeoning technology revolution in the connected devices market accompanied by the social media revolution is driving newer demands on business strategies every day.

Amid this chaos, we find an increasing ripple effect of these trends across key value chains and processes. These processes touch all customer interactions across domains such as supply chain, manufacturing, operations, innovation and marketing. Firms that will outlive this chaos are the ones who will successfully leverage the digital trends to transform their business processes. But the massive scale and pace of this change is making the adaptation process very challenging. This paper focuses on connecting the digital trends and business process management concepts to deliver tangible transformation around experience, efficiency and growth.

THE BIG TRENDS – DRIVING THE NEED FOR DIGITAL TRANSFORMATION

Estimates from Cisco, Intel, GE and McKinsey predict that more than 25-50 Billion (predictions vary by each source) connected devices will be in use by 2020 and the value creation through IOT can vary between $15-20 trillion in the next decade. The growth of connected devices from 10Bn today to about 50Bn devices by 2020 is an exponential growth and indicative of many ripple effects across major industries. About 30% of the world's 7.2Bn population is using social media today and about 50% of the global population is using mobile phones[1].

The IOT and social media are distinct trends but are enabled by mobile internet penetration. The confluence of mobile internet and connected devices is creating exponential growth in data that is generated. IBM research states that from 800 petabytes of data stored in 2000, we will be storing about 35 zetabytes of data by 2020. ($1ZB = 10^6PB$). More than 80% of this data is unstructured and generated from interconnected devices, social media, web, search indexes, emails and documents. Ninety percent of the data today was created in the last couple of years, which demonstrates the pace at which we are generating data.

The recent introduction of IPv6 (Internet protocol version 6) eliminates a major barrier to adoption of IOT, as the currently-used IPv4 would soon be reaching a maximum limit on internet addresses that can be allocated to devices. Every device on the Internet is assigned an IP address for identification and location

---

[1] source Internetlivestats.com

definition. IPv6 uses a 128-bit address, allowing 2^{128}, or approximately 3.4×10^{38} addresses, or more than 7.9×10^{28} times as many as IPv4.

To make meaningful use of the IOT penetration and social media information exchange, we need to leverage big data concepts and technologies. This kind of data volume needs to be ubiquitously stored and made available for real time and batch processing. This is where cloud storage comes into play.

As IOT and social media trends create disruptions for enterprise, Big Data and cloud are becoming the enablers for enterprises to harvest the business value. The disruptions caused by these trends will impact the business processes and business models offered by every large firm. The demands of a connected customers in the Generation-X and Y groups makes it even more challenging as we need to provision goods, services and information in real time. These groups are characterized by being digitally savvy, always connected, real time action oriented and driven by a sense of community. It is a struggle for many firms to deal with the boundaries of digital transformation that will decide their sheer existence in the next 3-5 years. The below diagram provides a conceptual view of the opportunity that exists in front of us to connect the digital trends to the enterprise processes, thereby delivering a tangible outcome.

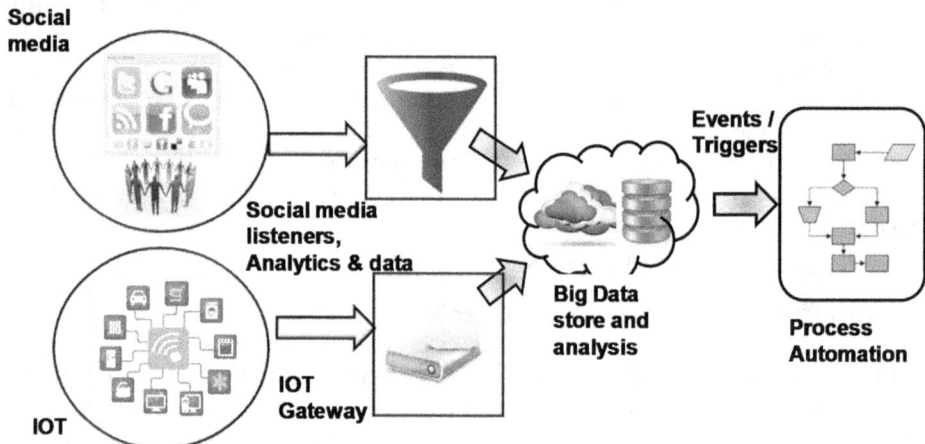

Figure 1: Digital trends impacting business processes

The sheer size of the value that will be created through these disruptive trends can give birth to many new firms that will thrive on the emerging connected world. This paper attempts to describe the key aspects of digital trends, their impacts on vertical industry processes, technology and business enablers. It is also an attempt to explain how the "Digital BPM" concepts are evolving and the business and technology considerations needed to capitalize on the digital revolution.

DEFINITIONS

Throughout this paper we will be discussing about the following terms and hence providing a basic definition will help in setting the right context.

1. **Internet of Things (IOT):** IOT refers to a network of dedicated physical devices that have the capability to sense and interact with the environment using the embedded technology. The IOT applications involve capturing data from "things." aggregating, analyzing that information over a network and the ability to take actions at device level or connected processes. The IOT also involves interplay of devices (may or may not have

unique IP address) and gateways/interfaces (with unique IP) that together perform a function to deliver value. IOT may include wearable devices, smart homes / cars, mobile devices, smart meters, any kind of motion or object tracking devices (with RFID), security devices and more.

2. **Social media:** Social media refers to the tools used by people to communicate, share ideas and exchange user generated content. The power of social media lies in empowering the users to create, share and consume information and content in line with their preferences. Social Media is characterized by the use of various kinds of tools including blogs, microblogs, social networks, location based networks, collaboration tools, multi-media, professional networking, social games and many others that are still evolving.

3. **Cloud technology:** "Cloud computing" refers to on-demand delivery of IT resources via internet to build and host applications that are available across channels and offer massive economies of scale, availability, elasticity and rapid provisioning. Cloud computing is a great enabler to the IOT and Social media trends. Cloud computing is a complex infrastructure of software, hardware, processing, and storage that is available as a service. The key characteristics of cloud which make it a disruptive enabler to IOT and social media trends are ubiquitous availability and unlimited scalability and extensible processing capacity.

4. **Big data:** Big Data refers to technologies and solutions that involve data that is too diverse, fast-changing or massive for conventional technologies, skills and infrastructure to address efficiently. Big data is characterized by the volume, velocity and variety of data that is too great to be handled by traditional RDBMS technologies. Both IOT and social media are keys to the burgeoning data that is generated across the web. Billions of devices are constantly streaming data that needs to be captured, stored and analyzed for taking actions. More than two billion people use social media and every interaction creates more data that needs to be stored and processed. This data explosion is what is causing enterprises to adopt "Big Data." Most of the data generated by IOT and social media are unstructured, which cannot be processed using traditional RDBMS concepts. Big data is characterized by data sets that deal in *large volumes* (from TB to ZB – Facebook ingests 500TB of new data every day), *high velocity* (from batch to streaming – billions of devices / sensors constantly generate new data that needs real time processing) and *wide variety* (from structured to unstructured - geospatial, images, videos, and unstructured text).

5. **BPM and Case Management:** Business Process Management stands for concepts and tools used to manage business processes in an enterprise. A BPM platform usually consists of the following components: *Modeling and Simulation, Workflow Engine, Systems Integration, Business Rules Engine and Business Activity Monitoring.* Traditional BPM implementations are suitable for static business processes with streamlined workflow that has finite start and end points. As we deal with more complex scenarios involving dynamic flows and collaboration across channels and unstructured content, we need to look at Case management platforms. Case Management involves case intake, setup, fulfillment and wrap-up as dynamic processes coordinate knowledge, context, actions

and correspondence. Monitoring and events driven actions become critical value added functionality in case management applications. The below diagram brings together these capabilities.

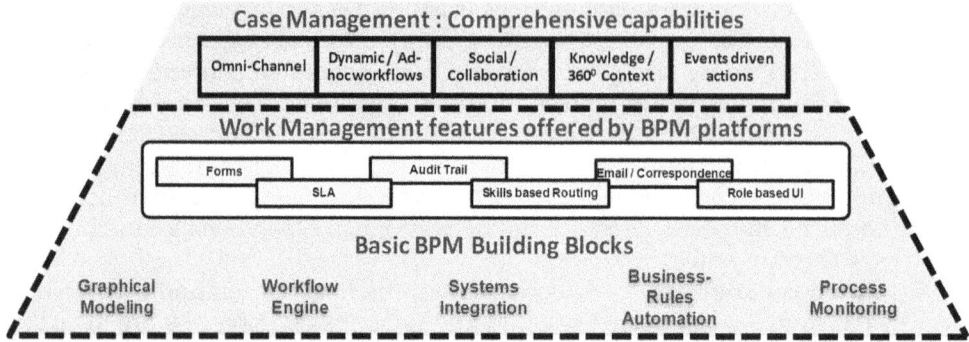

Figure 2: From BPM to Case Management – holistic capabilities

IS "BPM EVERYWHERE" = "DIGITAL BPM"

As we deal with the technology disruptions around major themes of IOT, social media, Big Data and cloud, enterprise economics is driven by four major entities – people, process, data and devices. This book is aptly titled as "BPM Everywhere" which connotes the ubiquity of business processes in a digital enterprise.

The broader meaning of "BPM Everywhere" is an ability to *Initiate, Manage, Report and Connect* processes across channels, geographies and systems. "Digital BPM" is characterized by process automation for connected customers and devices, generating data through their constant interactions across mobile, social and web. Between the two concepts of "BPM everywhere" and "Digital BPM." we see three "P's" of processes eg: pervasive, pertinent and perpetual, as core concepts:

1. **Pervasive:** Digital concepts of IOT and Social media constitute majority of interactions impacting every process. Hence to make any business process relevant and contextual to our customers through every step of key value chains, we need to integrate the IOT and social media to enterprise business processes. Our business processes need to be "omnipresent" – meaning availability across the enterprise, Cloud, web/mobile and connected devices. Only then we can capitalize on the full potential offered by IOT and be assured of holistic delivery of products and services. (Example: A monitoring device for elderly person or patient, will serve its fullest purpose when the process of dispatching emergency services is connected to the data coming from device signals and the process is coordinated with health providers to enable downstream actions.)

2. **Pertinent:** We need processes which can connect related events across all interactions driving real time and batch responses that will influence the critical outcomes. Ability to build the context through IOT and social media interactions is key to delivering the right process at the right time. This is only possible with the Big data that can collate data points across interactions and apply logic that will generate events to initiate business processes. (Example: A customer posting issues or complaints about products/services on social media and also contacting the call

center is an indicator of possible churn. Ability to trigger a service process proactively can mean not only saving a customer but also building long term loyalty).

3. **Perpetual:** To maintain continuous and uninterrupted value chain delivery across different spheres such as networked devices, channels, geographies and value chains, we need to be able to trigger and access the processes in real time across channels. We cannot be hindered by the restrictions of firewalls, scalability and accessibility. This is where the cloud hosting becomes an enabler as the physical boundaries are removed. (Example: maintaining large volumes of data around web searches, browsing patterns, e-commerce behaviors, location tracing can be key to detecting events which can feed processes for fraud management, market segmentation and intelligent offers)

The word "Digital BPM" takes a broader meaning in a digital enterprise where we need to manage People, Process, Data and Devices in a holistic manner. Below is a description of how these four entities come together in a "Digital BPM" world:

1. **People:** Connecting people not just for communication but doing transactions seamlessly as peer-to-peer, peer-to-groups and groups-to-groups (such as peer-to-peer payments, opinion sharing, crowd sourcing of ideas, education, services, financing, trading etc). Mobile internet and social media have become the biggest disruptors that have enabled people-to-people connections.
2. **Process:** Intra and Inter enterprise processes connected to people and Devices which can deliver the right information to the right person or Devices at the right time *(smart homes managing security, ordering supplies, automated maintenance, power and utilities management, temperature control while being connected to various retailers and services firms)*.
3. **Data:** People and Devices not only generate data but also consume the data/intelligence – hence we need to leverage the vast data generated to produce intelligence which can feed into processes or assist in decision making *(sentiment tracking and positioning, geo location tracking, purchasing patterns, online and offline behavior tracking, activity and health monitoring are some of the ways we can do micro-segmentation of our target market and position goods and services in a contextual manner that will translate into better logistics, production planning, cost reduction and return on marketing dollars)*.
4. **Devices:** Physical devices connected to the internet through embedded sensors and actuators to enable data gathering and intelligent decision making. Devices not only collect data but also perform functions without human interventions *(Wearables are changing many aspects of our personal life and digital commerce, but more so at industry level – energy and utilities management through smart meters, smart logistics with real time tracking are transforming whole industries)*.

TRANSFORMATION OPPORTUNITIES

What does the digital transformation bring to enterprises? Where do we see tangible benefits which will drive the ROI from digital transformation? The big opportunities are in the following areas:

1. **Asset utilization:** Provisioning of goods and services at the point of need, delivered optimally with minimal waste and predicting the consumption patterns can drive critical efficiencies in the "enquiry-to-offer." "Order-to-cash" and "service request-to-fulfillment" value chains.
2. **Customer experience:** The last mile in delivering goods and services is the most critical part of any customer journey maps and experience. Adapting to the IOT and social media trends and harvesting the radical benefits offered to transform the last mile, can mean exponential growth of revenues and market shares.
3. **Innovation:** Customer driven innovation and crowd sourcing are changing the R&D paradigm. Collaboration across geographies, enterprises and skills is helping find solutions to global challenges such as energy, clean water, pollution control, drug research etc. The elimination of time lag spread between data collection from R&D results, product launch and market perception of value realized is a major advantage offered by the digital revolution. The rapid time-to-market for goods and services with near real time feedback from consumers can mean radical improvement in revenue growth and cost efficiencies. Connecting the innovation engine of the enterprise to the customers, suppliers and partners can mean a paradigm shift in how a firm deploys its R&D budget.
4. **Agility** (supply chain, operations and logistics): A significant part of the cost structure in any firm is the supply chain, operations and logistics. There is significant wastage involved across human and material resources – mainly caused by lack of visibility and predictability due to systemic bottlenecks. Real time analysis of data feeds coming from IOT and social media can mean near real time response and continuous optimization of manpower, resources, logistics and inventory.
5. **Human Productivity:** Most of the bottlenecks in human productivity are due to lack of information and the intelligence needed to take actions. Inability to collaborate across knowledge workers is a major bottleneck across key value chains.

The transformation being driven by digital trends is making processes perpetual, pertinent and pervasive which is directly contributing to the opportunities listed above.

DIGITAL BPM EVOLUTION

BPM is not a new concept and we have the seen the evolution of BPM concepts and technologies from early 1990's. Mostly the early 90's focus was on industrial process automation around supply chains, assembly lines or HR/financial/ sales processes. The first decade of 21st century witnessed a shift to automation of customer service processes, knowledge/collaborative processes and innovation processes.

- In the Pre-2000 era, we saw silo processes that began and ended within a department (key focus was on system to system and human to system flows across ERP, MRP systems).
- From the year 2000 to now, we saw automation of end-to-end value chains (enquiry-to-order processes, order-to-fulfillment processes and problem-to-resolution service processes). Key functionality in focus was: Dynamic /Intelligent BPM – rules driven straight through processing, bringing together the 3 C's: Customer, Context and Content to deliver Dynamic Case Management.

- 2015 and beyond: The trends around digitalization portray the evolution of Digital BPM characterized by anytime, anywhere, ubiquitous processes driven by data (Machine-Machine and Machine-Person) and social interactions (Person-Person).

What differentiates "Digital BPM" from legacy BPM ?

1. Device driven: Billions of devices – mobile, wearable and everything with a sensor/algorithm/actuator/IP address can trigger or consume a Business Process.
2. Data driven: Peta and Zetabytes of unstructured and structured data that will drive algorithmic events tied into key processes
3. Social processes: The Gen Y (Born 1977-94) and early-Gen Z (1995 onwards) population is always connected to the internet and to their communities – and their interactions drive key business processes.
4. Multi-dimensional processes: The new paradigm of business processes will be to define processes that drive the value chains at multiple dimensions viz. device, gateway, enterprise and social/community levels.

The next section addresses the patterns for digital BPM that will take into account the evolving trends of BPM.

DIGITAL BPM PATTERNS

Digital BPM will have to address multitude of process patterns as we deal with following scenarios that depict the spread of processes between devices, gateways, enterprise/cloud and social networks. Each layer described in the table below indicates the level of complexity that needs to be accounted while designing solutions:

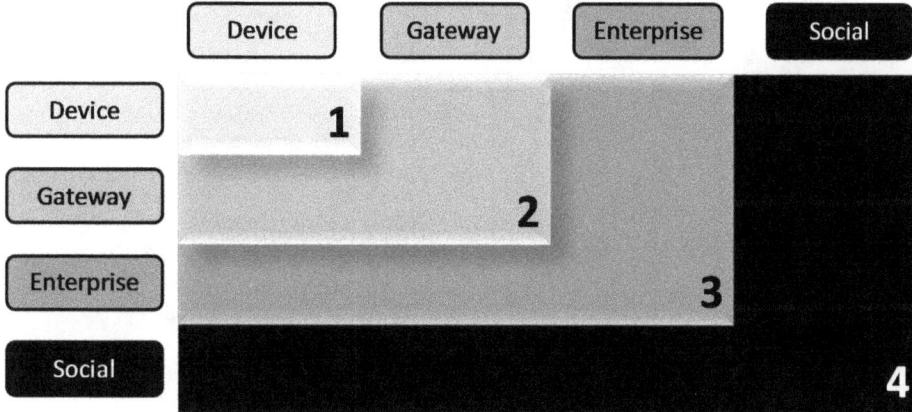

Figure 3: Process patterns for a digital enterprise

As we move from lower to higher numbers, the patterns are inclusive and hence incrementally complex.

1. **Device centric "Atomic" processes:** Processes which begin and end in each device or gateway (Wearable device communicating with a mobile phone). State and data is managed within the device or the gateway, and the gateway acts as a user interface.

Figure 4: Device centric "Atomic" processes

2. **Gateway centric "Composite" processes:** Multiple devices interacting through one or more gateways to manage processes. State is managed at device and gateway level. (Processes involving Peer-to-Peer interactions and collaboration, data sharing, location sharing)

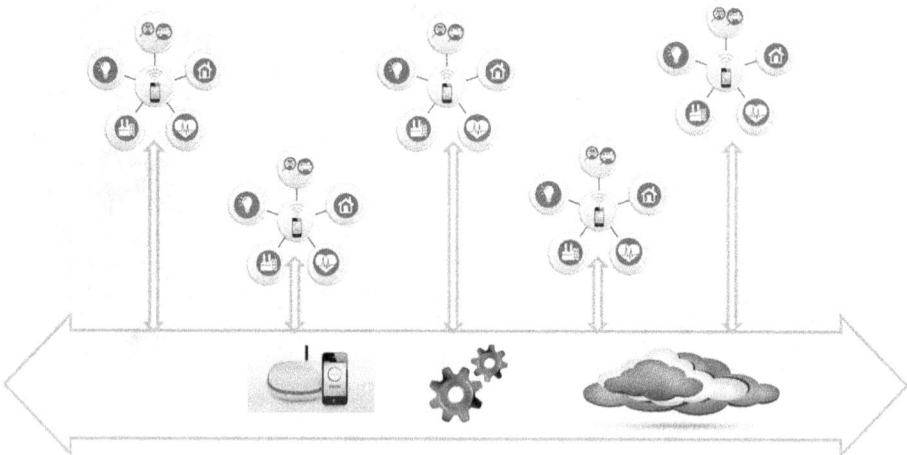

Figure 5: Gateway centric "Composite" processes

3. **Value chain centric "Enterprise Processes":** Inter-device and inter-gateway processes which connect to enterprise/ cloud hosted applications in real time or batch. (Integrated production assembly line – warehouse -distribution processes, complex logistics, transportation, power / energy flow control, smart offices)

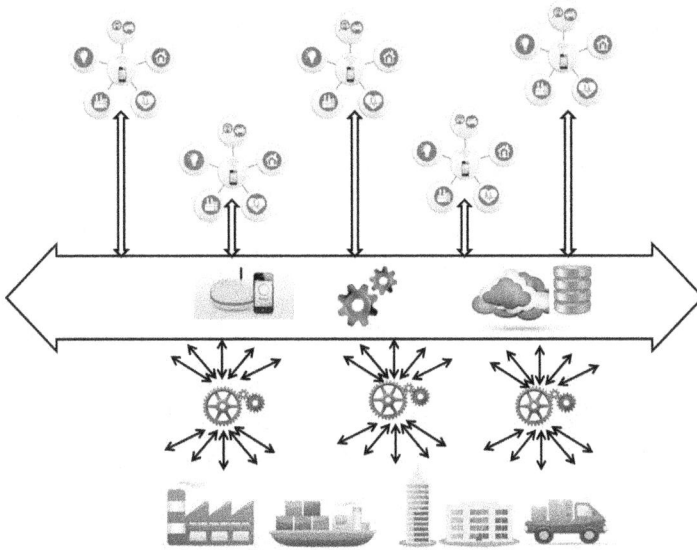

Figure 6: Value chain centric "Enterprise Processes"

4. **Cross value chain "Federated" processes:** Cross enterprise and cross social network processes which feed off of social and device interactions leveraging Cloud and enterprise hosted apps accessed over multiple channels.(Customer service, innovation, crowd sourcing applications)

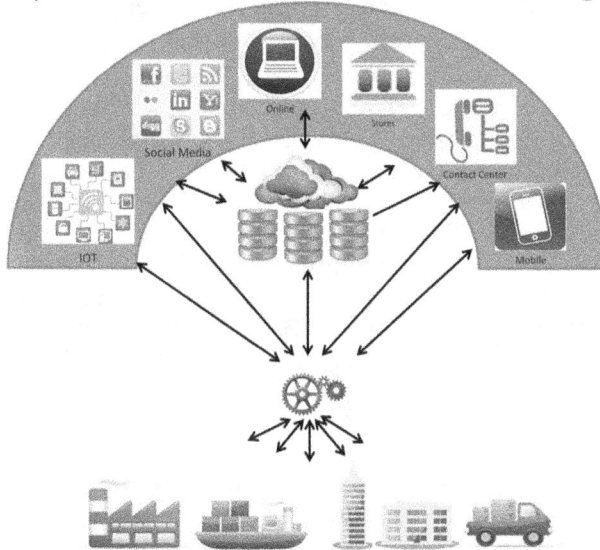

Figure 7: Cross value chain "Federated" processes

POTENTIAL FOR BUSINESS TRANSFORMATION ACROSS INDUSTRY VERTICALS

We will see significant impact of IOT and Social media trends across manufacturing, retail, financial services, healthcare and utilities industries. However the impacts across the value chains will vary by each industry. The below table provides a view of relative impacts by each industry.

Industry-> Value Chain	Manufacturing	Energy & Utilities	Retail & e-commerce	Financial Services	Healthcare and Pharma
Inbound / Outbound Logistics	▪▮▮▮	▪▮▮▮	▪▮▮▮	▪□□□	▪▮▮▮
Operations planning and management	▪▮▮▮	▪▮▮▮	▪▮▮▮	▪▮▮▮	▪▮▮▮
Campaign management & Lead generation	▪▮□□	▪□□□	▪▮▮▮	▪▮▮▮	▪▮▮□
Enquiry to offer	▪□□□	▪□□□	▪▮▮▮	▪▮▮▮	▪▮▮□
Order to Cash	▪▮□□	▪□□□	▪▮▮▮	▪□□□	▪▮▮□
Request / Problem to resolution	▪▮▮▮	▪▮▮▮	▪▮▮▮	▪▮▮▮	▪▮▮▮
Transaction monitoring, Fraud detection & risk management	▪□□□	▪▮□□	▪▮▮▮	▪▮▮▮	▪▮□□
Innovation	▪▮▮▮	▪□□□	▪▮▮▮	▪▮□□	▪▮▮▮

Figure 8: Relative scale of digital transformation opportunities by industry

Let us look at some use cases across the value chains in the verticals mentioned above. All the use cases listed below can be categorized in one or more of the five themes viz. asset utilization, customer experience, innovation, agility and human productivity, which we have described earlier.

1. Marketing, Sales, Service: The data generated from IOT and social media can help with targeting advertisements and product offers based on customer profile, location, behavior and community interactions. Cross channel customer analytics and predictive modeling can bring significant improvement in "CLV"- customer lifetime value (CLV indicates the present value of the future cash flows attributed to a customer relationship during their entire life time relationship with the company). Also we can define the optimal marketing mix model based on these data points which can get better ROI from the limited marketing dollars.

2. Smart distribution and logistics: The intelligence about customer behavior and patterns can help with predictive modeling of distribution logistics so we can move the right items to the right markets that can result in optimal inventory carrying costs, turnaround time for delivery, reduced wastage and avoiding "out of stock" scenarios. Recommendation engines can help with optimal pricing models, bundling of products/ offers, next best offers and tailored interactions.

3. Financial Services / Insurance / Healthcare: Patterns around Customer location, transactions and behavior can help detect fraud and proactive risk mitigation.

4. Resource optimization through remote tracking of physical and human resources in key industries such as mining, farming, shipping and logistics can bring significant asset utilization and profitability improvement including savings due to risk mitigation.

5. Smart meters can detect and communicate power consumption patterns at a customer level and various levels of aggregation which can help manage power distribution flows – leading to better utilization of power supply.

6. Device-enabled payments are taking on a different meaning as physical currency is giving way to mobile payments and crypto-currencies. As product and services firms are adopting digital payments, the opportunities to get a better share of customer's wallet are expanding.

7. Real-time customer and product monitoring can help enterprises detect product and service issues and proactively address them, thus helping improve the CLV (customer lifetime value).

8. Reduced waste by optimizing production and allocation of people / resources – based on real time feedback (customers, partners, supply chain and R&D)

9. Connected healthcare – real time patient monitoring, drug monitoring, drug effectiveness patterns, disease patterns – Impacting healthcare costs and innovation can reduce fraud and waste while improving overall healthcare economics.

10. IOT enabled Smart Cars, homes and Offices – are influencing how firms in the insurance, retailing, energy and security industries need to price their products and build value added offerings around distribution of their goods so as to maximize CLV.

These use cases are only a sample of opportunities that are emerging due to the confluence of IOT and social media. Entire industry value chains will need to be transformed to adopt the digital trends and adapt to the technology wave that is sweeping every aspect of our lives.

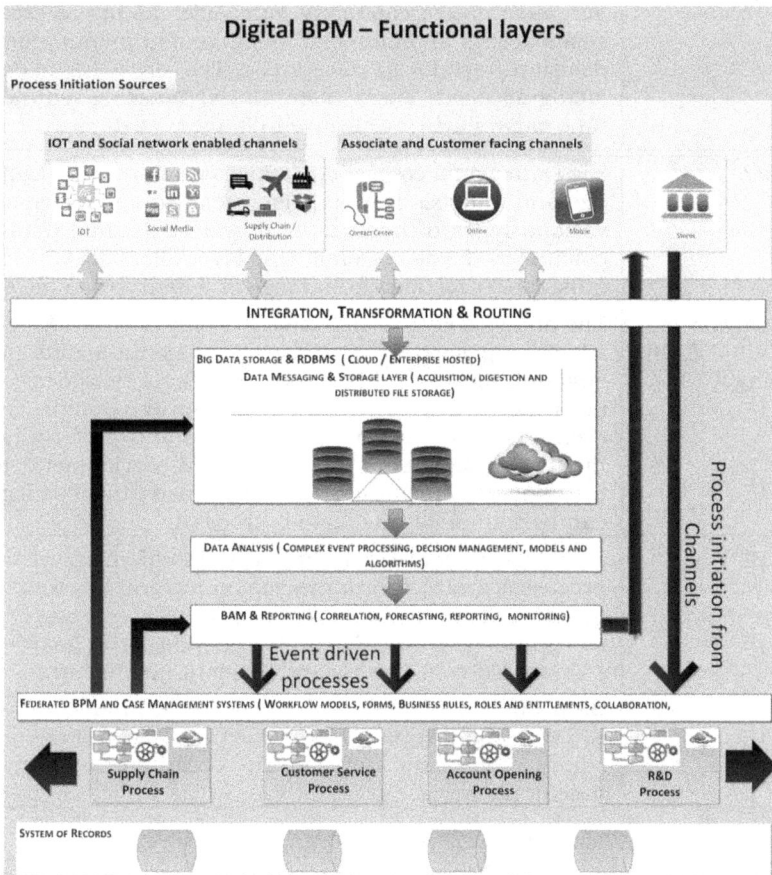

Figure 9: Digital BPM conceptual architecture

Based on the expansive use cases across major industry verticals, the prediction of achieving \$15-25 trillion of economic impact due to digital trends is not a far-fetched prediction.

PROCESS ORIENTED ARCHITECTURE PATTERN FOR THE DIGITAL ENTERPRISE

Earlier in this paper, we talked about four different patterns for digital BPM: Atomic, Composite, Enterprise and Federated processes. The solution architecture pattern for Digital BPM must address each of these process patterns. This section provides a high level overview of key components in a digital BPM solution and the interplay between them.

There are many finely grained logical layers in a Digital BPM solution. For the purpose of this paper, we are focusing on main layers which demonstrate the business value from a Digital BPM solution. These layers are not necessarily a representation of physical separation as many technologies can play one or more of these functions.

Each of the key layers of a digital BPM conceptual architecture is described below:

Solution layer	Core Capabilities
Process initiation sources	In a digital BPM architecture, we need to account for various sources which can trigger work. These could be human, machine or data sources. Processes might be triggered in real time or batch mode depending on the source. The process and case intake capability must offer ability to create new cases across all channels, using guided menus, forms and decision trees for all case types. The key value is customer facing associate enablement and eliminating redundant intake capabilities for all case fulfillment systems.
Big Data	Big Data would consist of Data acquisition, massaging, storage and analysis layers. It is crucial to apply formatting to various types of unstructured and structured data that is collated in the data stores. This layer offers scalable data acquisition, digestion and storage in a distributed file system.
Data Analysis and Complex Event Processing (CEP)	The analysis layer constitutes of Analysis and CEP engine—which help generate business intent from the data. Analysis engine leverages models and algorithms designed for business goals. CEP is an ability to capture notable business events across data sources, systems and perform transformation, aggregation, detection and enrichment to emit meaningful outcomes (based on defined business logic) that can be routed for any further processing.
BAM & BI	Business Activity Monitoring (BAM) helps monitor business processes and Key Performance Indicators. Key functionality includes Out of box integrations, ETL, events/ patterns recognition and correlation, forecasting, dash boarding, SLA / threshold based alerts and incident management.
	BAM offers real time and batch mode intelligence around KPI's by connecting with various data sources and applying rules/ correlation and pattern recognition to provide real time decisioning.

BPM & Case Management	BPM and Case Management are capabilities that are operationally aligned and address the process fulfillment activities. Traditional BPM applications handle more streamlined workflows where as evolving case management functions revolve around dynamic processes, operations centric work fulfillment and long running flows that need real time collaboration with content and correspondence. We might have multiple BPM and Case management applications that would be independently aligned to work teams and processes but performing similar functions around:
	• Process modeling, execution, monitoring, decisioning, collaboration and systems integration
	• SLA monitoring, correspondence, content management, audit trails and role based entitlements.
	• Our ability to track and connect processes/ cases that are being worked in different fulfillment systems and provide a 3600 view by case/ customer is key to digital BPM use cases. We also need a real time visibility to work status across Customer preferred channels and associates.

RECOMMENDATIONS

The concepts around Digital BPM and the business case demonstration are still evolving. Hence, we need an incremental approach to adopting and investing in the technology and infrastructure.

Some simple recommendations would be as below:

1. Focus on customer journey maps to identify key points of interactions between customers, IOT and Social Media. Also we can map the key value chains to use cases offered by IOT and social media interactions.

2. The technology space around digital BPM and IOT is still evolving. Hence, it would be worthwhile for enterprises and technology vendors to partner with industry thought leaders such as Google, Cisco, Intel, IBM, GE and others. Digital BPM would be a confluence of semiconductor, hardware and software, connectivity and various platform vendors around middleware, applications and data.

3. There are unknowns with respect to security, protocols and standards for IOT. Hence, it is recommended to watch for the evolving trends and keep pace with the developments before committing significant investments.

4. The business case for digital transformation is a factor of industry adoption of IOT and social media. Identifying the customer spend-patterns and opportunities to transform the interactions will drive the business case. On the industry supply chains, the intermediaries, partners and consultants will need to work together to develop end-to-end scenarios that will drive digital transformation.

CONCLUSION

We are on the cusp of a phenomenon that will change the shape of many industries and give birth to newer ones. The success of every enterprise depends on its adaptability to the digital trends. It is not merely about technology adoption but also the business models, product and service innovation that will drive the opportunities. As processes are underlying linkages to value chains that will continue to drive every business, digital BPM will gain huge importance in the transformation we will be witnessing.

The views expressed in this chapter are those of the author and do not necessarily represent the views of, and should not be attributed to, my employer or any other party.

REFERENCES

McKinsey Consulting research publications: "The Internet of Things: Sizing up the opportunity" published DECEMBER 2014 By Harald Bauer, Mark Patel, and Jan Veira

McKinsey Consulting research publications: "Disruptive technologies: Advances that will transform life, business, and the global economy" McKinsey Global Institute, May 2013 & " Disruptive technologies: Advances that will transform life, business, and the global economy" By James Manyika, Michael Chui, Jacques Bughin, Richard Dobbs, Peter Bisson, Alex Marrs, in May 2013

Gartner research publication "Toolkit: What Enterprise Architects Need to Know About IoT Technologies" Published: 27 October 2014 By Analyst(s): Mike J. Walker

INTEL: Presentation on IOT insights -2014 & LONDON ANALYST SUMMIT 2014 on The Internet of Things -The Next Evolution of Computing

IBM publication: Book on " Understanding Big data- analytics for enterprise class Hadoop and streaming data" by Chris Eaton, Dirk Deroos, Tom Deutsch, George Lapis and Paul Zikopoulos.

Cisco White papers on "Embracing the Internet of Everything to Capture Your Share of $14.4 Trillion" By Joseph Bradley Joel Barbier Doug Handler & "The Internet of Everything - (IoE) Value Index"

Managing BPM Toward the Singularity

Roy Altman, Memorial Sloan Kettering Cancer Center, USA

Roy Altman, Memorial Sloan Kettering Cancer Center, USA

WHAT IS "THE SINGULARITY?"

"The Singularity" describes when ordinary computers exceed the capacity of the human brain. "Moore's Law," which states that computing power increases at an exponential rate, has held constant since the dawn of the computer age. If one extrapolates forward, experts agree that the Singularity will be reached between 2030 and 2045. Once The Singularity is reached and exceeded, we will find answers to age-old debates, such as whether machines can have consciousness.

PREMISE OF THIS PAPER

Between the present and when The Singularity is reached, we will have increasingly powerful technologies available to us. We need to be able to manage these technologies effectively.

We are entering "the age leading up to the Age of Intelligent Machines." Big Data Analytics and Artificial Intelligence are already having a profound impact on business and society.

One can safely predict that the current trends will continue, and computers will get smarter and smaller. Digital devices will permeate everything we do and assist in every decision we make. The delineation between our digital and physical lives will continue to blur, as wearable devices will enable ubiquitous connection to the web. The nature of work is already changing, and technology will support a blurring of the lines between our work and private lives.

BPM's role has been to provide structure: initially for predictable processes and later for uncertain ones. The Internet of Everything, in which all devices and services are connected, still requires structure if it's to be utilized to its greatest extent. Given that some of the "things" will be advanced Big Data Analytics and Intelligent Agents, means that more than ever these resources need to be managed to achieve our goals. BPM will be more essential than ever to orchestrate resources while complexity is rapidly increasing. Essentially, the role of BPM will be to manage this complexity.

Traditionally, we manage the technology we have at hand. Most companies are late adopters of newer technology, preferring to mitigate the risk of early adoption before the market for that technology matures. Forward-thinking management is looking around the corner to plan to leverage leading-edge technology of the next three to five years (while mitigating risk). No doubt we will continue to be surprised and astounded by the technological advances over the next few decades, at a micro level. But since we *know* the general direction we're heading at a macro level, it only makes sense to plan to manage the powerful technologies of the next 5-30 years, with BPM being a central component of that plan.

How Near Is The Singularity?

The human brain is the most complex machine we know of. Computing power is usually measured in millions of instructions per second (MIPS). This measurement doesn't really relate to the human brain, because a computer does one thing at a time very fast and a brain does trillions of things at a time very slowly. This is because most computers are designed in what's called the Von Neumann architecture[1], named for the computing pioneer John Von Neumann. The Von Neumann architecture is designed to do one thing at a time very fast, with the ability to quickly switch between tasks[2] and remember where to proceed from when returning. The brain is a massively parallel architecture, whereby the billions of neurons and synapses can fire simultaneously. Von Neumann-architecture machines are good and deriving a finite answer very quickly. Parallel architectures are good at pattern recognition. Nonetheless, experts conclude that the activity of the neurons and synapse in the brain equate to between 100 million and 2.8 trillion MIPS. A large number, considering today's home computer is roughly 80 MIPS.

Moore's Law has stated that processor speed doubles roughly every 18 months. Computing speed is a function of how small you can build transistors, as their speed increases when they're closer together. This equation has held up throughout computing history, so far. There is a physical limit, however, when transistors are only a few atoms apart. Much of the increase has come from clever engineering, which will present challenges, but not necessarily roadblocks when the physical limit is near. However, we're nowhere near the physical limit. Extending the lines of Moore's Law will get us in the brain's MIPs range between 2030 and 2045, and there's still a lot of range for increasing power past that.

Calculating MIPS on a home computer misses the point, though. Today, computers are massively networked, so the power of a single computer doesn't represent the computing power available. Using the open-source software NEST, the scientists simulated a network consisting of 1.73 billion nerve cells connected by 10.4 trillion synapses. The process took 40 minutes to complete the simulation of 1 second of neuronal network activity in real, biological, time. Although the simulated network is huge, it only represents 1% of the neuronal network in the brain. Using a network of computers, The Singularity may be reached quicker than the estimates above.

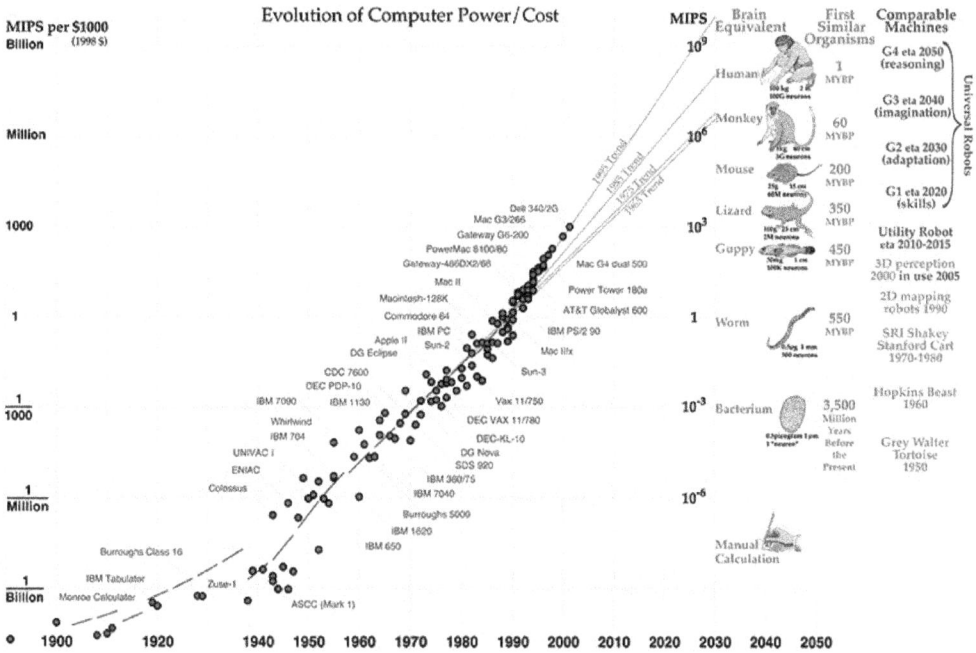

Figure 1: Evolution of Computer Power/Cost

WHAT WILL HAPPEN AT THE SINGULARITY?

When The Singularity is reached, nothing significantly different than the day before will occur. That is the nature of scientific revolutions; they tend to be evolutionary rather than revolutionary[3]. That's the point of this paper: between now and The Singularity (and beyond), we will have to manage increasingly powerful software. Let's start planning for that now, and seize the opportunity to leverage powerful technologies to solve our goals, rather than let the technology increase unplanned.

Just because we have computers with the technical capabilities of the human brain doesn't mean we can create an artificial mind. We don't understand the software of the brain. However, we can attempt to reverse-engineer the brain by recording the state of every neuron and placing it into computer memory. The Singularity actually represents a confluence of technologies, including non-invasive brain mapping. Today we can do MRI scans which can map large areas of the brain without having to dissect one. This technology will improve to the point where it can map the state of individual neurons. Neural networks have the ability to learn, so the artificial mind will have all of the memories of the source, but their experiences will diverge after the transfer. At that point, we will find out if consciousness can arise from the sum of its parts, or if human consciousness is something different.

A LOOK AT THE BRAIN

The brain is organized very differently than the architecture of conventional computers, which makes modeling the brain on the computer challenging.

- *Brain "circuits" (neurons) are very slow in comparison to digital circuits, but it's massively parallel:* on the order of one hundred trillion interneuronal connections, each with the potential of processing information simultaneously[4].

- *The brain combines analog and digital phenomena.* Although it is analog by nature, a neuron either fires or it doesn't. The firing of a neuron strengthens a connection, and the lack of firing weakens it. That's how we learn: by neurons firing to reinforce information that we want to preserve.
- *The brain can rewire itself.* The brain has a property called plasticity, which means it's constantly adapting to environmental changes or damages. The nervous system is self-organizing. Computers don't rewire themselves, but we're beginning to see "self-healing" software that can mimic this phenomenon.
- *The brain can contradict itself.* It is possible to hold conflicting beliefs simultaneously.
- *The brain uses emergent properties.* Intelligent behavior is an emergent property of the brain's highly complex, and seemingly chaotic, activity. It will be interesting to see if this emergent property can arise from man-made computers.

We are beginning to see more computers with massively parallel architectures, and software intent on modeling the way neurons behave.

WHERE WE ARE NOW

Current State of Operational Systems

We have had wonderful advances of technology that has made our lives better, but still many companies struggle to run payroll correctly. Operationally, many IT shops are dealing will common issues:

- *Processes:* many processes are broken, not consistently applied, poorly documented and understood, or just not followed. The Sierra-Cedar HR Systems Survey[5] has reported that the leading area that clients intend to spend time on is Business Process Improvement. This has topped the list the last three years.
- *Data:* access to data and reporting is often at a low state of maturity. Most companies can only provide basic reporting, not data visualizations, self-service or predictive analytics.
- *Integrations:* for the most part, "integrations" between systems are typically batch, flat-file interfaces; despite that web services are mature technologies. One reason that vendors often don't support modern integrations is that customers don't request them.
- *Siloed Organizations:* a single, hierarchical management structure only reinforces the siloed nature of organizations; there is duplication of processes for each reporting structure, and no coherent strategy for integrations. Management often doesn't take a holistic view of the highly matrixed relationships that determine how work actually gets done in an organization.

Many companies are struggling with the basic challenges and aren't prepared to integrate newer technologies into the mix.

Enterprise Software

Enterprise Software is in the throes of transition. Over the last couple of decades, companies would license Enterprise Resource Planning (ERP), Human Capital Management (HCM), Customer Relationship Management (CRM) or Financial software and customize it to adhere to their company's processes. However, the customizations made upgrades to the software more complex, so they occurred infrequently. Also, it was expensive to maintain the on premises software with dedicated IT teams.

Enter Cloud, or Software-as-a-Service (SaaS). Cloud is a deployment model: it means that neither your data nor the software is stored on premise, instead it is managed by the vendor. You don't know where your data is physically stored, nor do you need to care if you trust the vendor to keep it safe. Software-as-a-Service is a delivery model whereby use of the software is provided as a service, and client has a subscription for use. The architectures to support this means that every client is running the same iteration of the software, and all clients share a single, multi-tenant database. Because all clients are running the same code, it cannot be customized for the needs of a single client. It is therefore configurable, rather than customizable, whereby the configurations for each client are stored in the database, so that the software can react differently based on each client's needs, and still share the same code and database. Modern software has many very flexible configuration points. This means that the vendor can easily make updates to the software, which is then available to all clients. Since updates are quicker and easier, the vendor can make them available more frequently; so the vendor can innovate faster.

In certain industry sectors and cultures, companies have been reluctant to adopt cloud software out of concern that the vendor won't keep their data safe. However, more and more companies are concluding that these fears are unfounded and recognize the advantages to moving administrative applications to the cloud.

Managing Humans

Processes invariably involve humans, so software to manage those workers is critical to an organization's ability to function effectively. Human Resources (or Human Capital) Management software is a system of record for the workforce, and manages all of the transactions relating to workers (hiring, terminating, promoting, transferring, etc.). A recent category of software called Talent Management has emerged, which is specifically concerned with engaging the workers and optimizing their work. This includes functions such as Talent Acquisition, Performance, Compensation, Learning and Succession Planning.

Managing humans is complex in that they are expensive to recruit and hire, difficult to keep motivated, develop their careers, and retain them in the workforce. However, humans provide special skills that are difficult to automate; although that is changing.

Managing Processes – The State of BPM Software

BPM software is general-purpose (meaning not application-specific) software to manage the interactions between people and automated processes. It typically includes an integration engine to integrate the software agents and a flexible workflow engine to manage the human interactions in a process.

BPM software has been very successful in automating and more effectively managing complex yet predictable processes.

Enter Adaptive Case Management

Adaptive (or Dynamic) Case Management (ACM) recognizes that increasingly workers are knowledge workers – requiring special skills; whose work does not necessarily follow prescribed paths. The bulk of automated support thus far has been geared toward automating administrative tasks, rather than the more unpredictable and complex work knowledge workers engage in.

Adaptive Case Management is well-aligned with the trends toward more sophisticated software in that it addresses the needs of humans working the way humans do. Advanced automation often takes the form of an Intelligent Digital Assistants (IDA's), and ACM software is in line with this development in that it helps workers manage unpredictable tasks.

Mobile and Social

When the iPhone was launched in 2007, it ushered in a new age of mobile computing, and mankind never looked back. It has gotten to the point where people are inseparable from their devices. This is in line with Moore's Law stating that computing power will get faster, cheaper and smaller.

Social computing taps into a basic need of humanity to interact with others. It allows people to bridge physical space while at the same time polarizing people from interacting in the real world. Regardless, it's clear that social computing is eroding the division between our physical and digital lives.

Connected Devices

The Internet has given rise to a trend whereby devices can be connected and communicate with one another to share information relevant to the goal of each device. This is called "the Internet of things." An example is the Nest thermostat (the company has been acquired by Google), which becomes familiar with the patterns of your life to more effectively and efficiently heat your home.

The State of Artificial Intelligence

After early attempts fell short of expectation in the 1980's, artificial intelligence (AI) now pervades everyday life. The Siri voice recognition facility in the Apple iPhone usually understands what I'm saying, and often offers a useful response. GPS software quickly computes the best way to get from point A to point B. MS Word indicates usage errors in sentence construction. Google searches relevant results. Software is now being used to write earnings statements in business publications. Facial recognition software allows identification of people. Self-driving cars are well on their way to becoming mainstream.

Early attempts at AI were based on "Expert Systems," whereby the rules for decision-making were embedded in the process. What differentiates humans from machines is that humans are good at pattern recognition, whereas machines are good at fast computations. As stated earlier, the human brain is a massively parallel architecture, whereby design common computers are better geared for fast computation. For instance, it is an extremely complex task for a robot to navigate through a crowded room, such as Grand Central Station in New York, yet any self-respecting cat can do it with aplomb. Current and future AI is better, and will continue to improve, in tasks that require pattern-recognition. Google and others are making great strides with self-driving cars, a task heavily dependent on pattern recognition. Occupations that have traditionally fallen into the realm of knowledge-workers are in danger of being supplanted by machines. Highly-compensated fields like evaluating market trends may be among the casualties.

Big Data

Big Data, or advanced analytics techniques, have garnered much attention of late. Some definitions of Big Data require that the three "V's" must be satisfied:

- *Volume:* there must be a large volume of data ("large" is a relative term)
- *Velocity:* the data must be changing rapidly

- *Variety:* there must be several data sources

In the year 2000, mankind produced 15 exabytes of data (which is 15 billion gigabytes). In 2012, we produce 2.5 exabytes *per day*. Needless to say, the volume of data is increasing exponentially, which is a trend that is unlikely to reverse. Much of this is considered *unstructured data*, meaning that it isn't generated from systems used by organizations, but rather exists on the web. We can mine that information to produce correlations, or similarities between two occurrences. We can use statistical models to indicate strong correlations which are likely to be causal in nature. Using this, we can extend these models to make predictions about what is likely to occur, based on data analysis of what has occurred, and applied feedback mechanisms. Big Data analytics works by filtering out "noise" and recognizing patterns in vast amounts of information. It has already made an impact in targeted advertising, and is quickly making its way into the information strategies of leading companies.

The Role of BPM

BPM should play a significant role in managing increasingly sophisticated technologies. The role of BPM is to be a framework within which all other technologies will operate. As technologies become more geared toward the personal intelligent assistant concept, BPM and ACM will merge into a way to manage both structured and unstructured processes. We are entering an era of great complexity – among the available technologies and their impact on our lives. The concept of process *orchestration* will take on a new meaning as ACM/BPM becomes the framework for managing that complexity.

THE FUTURE OF WORK

We are heading in a direction where administrative work will continue to shrink, while knowledge work will be increasingly growing. Companies will "get their act together" and master operational systems with varying degrees of success, thereby achieving short-term strategies. *All* administrative systems will be in the cloud: the commoditization of infrastructure will be complete and there will only be sporadic vestiges of on premise systems, as the laggards hold out, apart from very application-specific systems developed in-house. As a result, areas that we now see as strategic will become operational and commoditized, and the focus of what is "strategic" will center on effectiveness rather than efficiency. We will be able to do things quickly and accurately, however we still need to decide what we want to accomplish.

BPM will follow suit and traditional BPM/ACM balance will increasingly shift toward the latter. More sophisticated Intelligent Assistants will augment the decisions of the knowledge worker, with the help of Big Data.

Social and collaboration tools will mean that we will increasingly become more connected from the confines of our home offices. Will coffee room gossip survive as it migrates to social media? The 9-5 workday will be a thing of the past. Our work and leisure lives will become intertwined, just as our virtual and physical worlds are merging.

The challenges will be as always, personalities, culture and politics, now with the added task of managing a plethora of increasingly intelligent and complex technologies.

As more types of jobs will be automated by intelligent agents, there will be a greater divide between the knowledge "haves" and "have not's." Even if we are able to raise the education level of our population, there exists the danger of pervasive, structural unemployment if we are not able to resolve this issue.

Where are we going – near-term, 5-15 years

What I consider to be the mid-term period will see rapid advances in technology. Big Data will grow to the point that every action and every decision we make will involve analytics. Predictive Analytics will become key to our decisions, and we will gain more insight into root causes through better data mining and analysis techniques. As a society we will have to make decisions as to the trade-off between personal privacy and connectivity and convenience. Work will become more virtual, as collaboration software will be better able to communicate non-verbal cues missing in emails, phone calls, and to an extent, video. More of our interactions will take place on social media (adding to the data that can be harvested for predictions).

Miniaturization will continue. Devices that we now carry in our pockets will be worn, perhaps on a shirt button. Google Glass, the famously unsuccessful attempt by Google at optic wearable device, was merely ahead of its time by a few years. Devices such as this will be ubiquitous, allowing us to superimpose generated digital information with that of the real world. With devices getting smaller, input methods will have to change. Voice recognition will continue to improve to the point where keyboards become unnecessary and impractical. Voice recognition technology will encompass semantic meaning rather than just syntactic understanding of an utterance, thereby enhancing the relevance of the response. Experts differ, but I think that implants will not catch on, as they are too invasive to install and update, so we will continue to use wearable devices.

Our devices will play the role of Intelligent Digital Assistant, and we won't leave home (literally or figuratively) without them. I'm unsure as to whether the Turing Test[6], whereby one can't discern between a digital or human intelligence, will be passed by then, but surely the interactions between human and device will become deeper. Imagine going through our lives with the equivalent of a genie on our shoulder filling in all the blanks of what we don't know? Still, humans are not just rational decision makers; emotion plays a large part of how we act and what we decide. Our IDA's will help us sort through the emotional side of our reasoning as well. This is not to say that we will become more rational decision makers, just that we will have the tools to augment what we know and are, for whatever ends we make of it. But since knowledge-workers add the most value by making decisions, and information supporting decision-making is readily available, people will spend a good deal of time making high-level decisions. There should be a great economic benefit from increased, and higher level automation, as productivity per (human) worker should soar.

MANAGING A HUMAN/SOFTWARE WORKFORCE

The workforce will consist of a mixture of humans and intelligent agents, each requiring their own considerations. While those most cantankerous of workers (humans), require a great deal of management to keep them engaged, compensated and productive, machines have fewer needs (apart from electricity). Since intelligent agents "learn" as humans do, one area of commonality is training. Robots need to be trained just as humans do. However, the way they learn will undoubtedly be different and will require different training strategies.

Robotics

Cognitive and spatial intelligence are two very distinct things. It is much easier to automate cognitive tasks, and non-moving technology will outstrip mobile robots. There are some applications that require robots that can move and manipulate their environments. There will continue to be advances in this field. Humana-form robots, as we're used to in Science Fiction movies, is probably further away.

- *Self-driving cars:* Google is making great advances with their self-driving car. Over the next 5-15 years, this technology will be commonplace. Human-driven cars will probably not disappear by then, but as people recognize the benefits of no accidents and no traffic jams, driverless cars will be rapidly adopted. Seniors and the disabled will be granted newfound mobility due to this technology.
- *Defense:* Many advances in AI come from Defense Advanced Research Projects Agency (DARPA) research, which has had many civilian applications. Drone airplanes are becoming commonplace already. Specially designed reconnaissance robots will rival cats in their ability to navigate terrain. Robotic soldiers are not long in coming. Currently, humans, who are responsible for making the kill decision, pilot drones remotely. By then, will we be ready as a society to have autonomous robots making kill decisions?
- *Home care:* Seniors and the disabled will be the big winners in this timeframe. Not only will self-driving cars afford a new mobility, but also domestic household robots can cook, clean and assist so as to enhance independence and quality of life.
- *Mining:* In general, robotics will be used for dangerous occupations. Mining or rescue operations are good applications.
- *Space exploration:* It seems obvious that robots will conduct space exploration. They lack the boredom that human explorers would be subject to in long journeys, and don't require life support. As AI becomes more human-like, it will make perfect sense that future space exploration be unmanned.

The Role of Humans

As machines increase in sophistication, more emphasis will be placed on the qualities that differentiate people from machines: expert thinking, interpersonal skills such as the ability to explain and persuade, creativity and applying common sense. Less emphasis will be placed on technical tasks, as they are easier to automate. In a sense, advanced automation democratizes the role of humans; a person coming from an underprivileged background is just as likely to have interpersonal skills and common sense than their privileged counterparts.

The arts offer an opportunity for differentiation. Artists perceive the world from a different perspective, interpreting the world abstractly. True creativity may be the final frontier of differentiation between humans and intelligent machines. Today, people bemoan that there aren't enough students studying STEM (Science, Technology, Engineering, Math) disciplines to meet the demand (particularly with representation of all demographics of the population). Perhaps the correct acronym should be STEAM (adding Art) for a more accurate depiction of our future needs.

Regardless, we can be assured that the needed skill sets will change over the coming decades, and today's students will be applying for jobs that currently don't exist. Futurist/author/inventor Ray Kurzweil (who now works for Google) predicts that the most in-demand job in the IT field in 20 years will be Personality Designers[7].

WHAT SHOULD WE BE DOING?

The Platform – Playground of the Future

One thing we do know about the future is that the basic protocols for machine-to-machine communication will not fundamentally change. While previous attempts at integration standards have been supplanted, XML, which has been around since 1998, is the fundamental building block to integrations going forward.

The "as-a-Service" paradigm extends to Platforms and Infrastructure as well as Software. We need to create a Platform-as-a-Service (Paas) that will be the key to leveraging advancing technologies in the decades to come. Such a platform's primary function should be to integrate the various and disparate digital agents that exist in the ecosystem of the 'Internet of Everything' and the enterprise. This platform would yield benefits today as well as being a platform for leveraging the future technologies. You can think of this platform as a "Playground of the Future," providing a framework for consuming technologies yet to come. Essentially, the challenge becomes one of managing a plethora of advanced technologies and how they interact in an ecosystem of more connected devices and intelligent agents.

Such a platform should offer the following services[8]:

- *Integration platform:* Integrations are key. The platform should support multiple API's, but particularly modern integrations based on XML and web services. The platform should have the ability to integrate both data and processes.
- *Data taxonomy:* All data should be identified as to the source and access rights. As the amount of data proliferates, this will be essential to managing large and disparate datasets, both structured and unstructured, and also key to improving data quality.
- *Common security model:* The platform should enforce a single common security model throughout the organization. Placing it on a platform reduces the need to replicate the security model in different places and ensures consistent application.
- *Multi-organizational model:* The management model is slowly shifting away from the single, hierarchical view of the enterprise to one with myriad connections, with a mix peer-to-peer network relationships along with mini-hierarchies, all dependent on the process or context. It is essential to manage these centrally to simplify the daunting task of maintaining the connections as well as the ability to re-use relationships wherever they are needed.
- *Orchestration services:* prescribed processes should execute as efficiently as possible, although they often involve software agents across multiple systems. These "traditional" BPM services should be integrated into the platform so as to manage processes across all participants.
- *Big Data Analytics:* Big Data is bigger than any one application, as it encompasses information from several sources, both structured and

unstructured. There should be a common analytics engine across the enterprise.

- *Adaptive Case Management:* ACM should be embedded within all processes available to the enterprise. There will be many intelligent resources available, but ACM will provide the framework by maintaining a goal orientation; keeping all resources focused on those goals.

THE SINGULARITY AND BEYOND – THE AGE OF INTELLIGENT MACHINES

Once The Singularity is reached, we will discover the nature of intelligence. Perhaps attempts at reverse engineering will be successful and we will be able to transfer the state of a human brain at a point in time to a computer. Will the machine demonstrate emergent intelligence? Or is intelligence something greater than the sum of its parts, and we will be left with an inert repository of neural states?

Our brains are biological organs that evolved over millions of years to be the centralized control of our bodies. Perhaps a disembodied brain would not function the same way. We are motivated because of our biology, and achieve what we do because we have wants and needs. Striving for survival is a powerful motivator. Would a machine without biology work the same way? If a computer received the neural states from a person at a point in time it would have all of the memories from that person up to that point. The machine would have memories of what it was like to have a body, much like an amputee remembers a missing limb. Perhaps that is enough to satisfy the brain's biological heritage.

Or maybe we'll figure out the software of the brain by then and create digital life forms other than by reverse engineering, that are different from humans in that they are not dependent on biology and derive their motivations from other sources?

One implication of the non-invasive scanning technology described earlier is that we'll then use thought control as an input device to computers; voice recognition will no longer be necessary. People will have to develop skills to control devices while protecting private thoughts. We may then be able to communicate with each other seemingly telepathically.

As mentioned before, The Singularity represents a confluence of technologies. Continued miniaturization will have profound impacts on health care. Nanobots will course through our blood streams, identifying cancer cells and zapping them before they have a chance to grow. Nanobots will be able to clean up the decay around cells associated with aging, so longevity technology will be available to those that are healthy enough (and wealthy enough, initially). As lifespans increase, we will naturally reproduce less, as historically populations have always self-regulated. The turnover of generations (death and new life) will happen slower, or perhaps disappear altogether. Before we opt in to this situation, we must consider the consequences of less generational turnover. How many of us want to live in a world where the only sure thing is taxes?

Humana-form Robot technology will come later, but the digital "brain" could be implanted in a robot and the body parts upgraded as the technology improves. Thus, humans can be fully immortal when they exist in purely digital/robotic form.

Ethical Implications

If digital intelligence is emergent, and we have digital sentient life forms, the notion of robots doing our bidding should be reexamined. If a machine can think and feel, does it have rights? Is dominion over sentient robots akin to slavery? Perhaps it would be more appropriate to think of them as our children or colleagues, rather than our servants?

If a person copies their brain into a computer, which "version" of that person is entitled to rights, such as ownership?

Should the computer version be considered the same person? If we replace an arm or leg, or even a heart with a prosthetic device, we still think of them as the same person. Why should it be different with a prosthetic brain?

Will they take over the World (...and is that a bad thing?)?

As computing power continues to increase, and digital life forms have access to all of the knowledge of humanity, it seems inevitable that they will quickly surpass our capabilities. Some people have suggested that once they can create other robots, there will be no longer any need for biological humans and we will be subjugated, or eliminated!

It seems obvious that if we have such concerns, we simply shouldn't build machines that are capable of subjugating us. We can modify the programming to prevent this from happening, much like Asimov's Three Laws of Robotics[9]:

1. A robot may not injure a human being or, through inaction, allow a human being to come to harm.
2. A robot must obey the orders given it by human beings, except where such orders would conflict with the First Law.
3. A robot must protect its own existence as long as such protection does not conflict with the First or Second Law.

Can we build intelligent machines that are not sentient, or once we build machines that can learn, will we have no control over how they process the knowledge they acquire?

When Watson famously beat the human champions on Jeopardy, Ken Jennings wrote along with his Final Jeopardy answer: "I for one welcome our new computer overlords." Perhaps sentient machines are the next evolutionary step for humanity. If Earth becomes uninhabitable due to climate change or wars, maybe robotics is the only way humanity can continue?

UTOPIA OR DYSTOPIA?

The "Brave New World" we are creating can result in a Utopian or Dystopian result (or, of course, a combination). The Utopian view, as exemplified in Star Trek, is that automation creates all the economic value we need, so people are free to pursue what enriches them, such as the arts or space exploration. The Dystopian view, as is commonly shown in Philip K. Dick novels, is where technology is in the hands of a few powerful people, and our very existence is for someone else's benefit. The future we create for ourselves depends on the decisions we make over the next few decades.

EPILOGUE

The purpose of this paper is not to draw conclusions about the technology of the near future, but to pose whether we are asking the right questions. With exponential advancement, very powerful technologies will be upon us very quickly. We need to manage them to achieve our goals, and avoid the undesirable outcomes that can result from corruption or neglect.

I'm fascinated by the notion that, as software designers, we can rearrange some electrons, and as a result, work gets easier, more value is produced, and maybe *we can create emergent life!* This is modern day alchemy: creating things of great value from basic ingredients. It is our sacred trust to use that power wisely and responsibly for the benefit of humanity.

REFERENCES AND NOTES

[1] – Von Neumann Architecture: computer architecture devised by computer pioneer John Von Neumann. Almost all conventional computers today use this architecture. http://en.wikipedia.org/wiki/Von_Neumann_architecture

[2] – Multitasking is a term originally applied to how a computer operating system quickly switches between tasks by placing the memory location of the last task on a stack, and then retrieving it from the stack when that task is resumed. Human brains, which have a massively parallel architecture, are notably bad at true multitasking. When a person claims they are "multitasking" it is more likely that they are "getting distracted."

[3] – (Kuhn 1962) Thomas Kuhn. The Structure of Scientific Revolutions, 1962. University of Chicago Press.

[4] – (Kurzweil 2005) Ray Kurzweil. The Singularity is Near, 2005. Viking.

[5] – Sierra-Cedar HR Systems Survey: http://www.sierra-cedar.com/research/annual-survey/

[6] – Turning Test: a test devised by Alan Turing to determine if an intelligence is human or artificial. http://en.wikipedia.org/wiki/Turing_test

[7] – (Kurzweil 1992) Ray Kurzweil. Age of Intelligent Machines, 1992. MIT Press.

[8] – (Altman 2013) Roy Altman. Creating an Integrated Platform for Process Intelligence. From Intelligent BPM, 2013. Future Strategies.

[9] – From Science Fiction writer Isaac Asimov's "Robots" series.

Standards and Techniques for Data-Driven, Decision-Centric Process Innovation

James Taylor, Decision Management Solutions, USA

INTRODUCTION

In an era of Big Data, organizations are applying analytics so they can become more data-driven: Cookie-cutter treatment of customers is being replaced with personalized, targeted communications and offers; pay and chase fraud recovery is giving way to the prevention of fraud before it gets into the system; and post-transaction risk monitoring is being replaced with dynamic, transaction-by-transaction risk-based pricing and management.

Process-centric organizations are also using data to analyze process performance and seek process-centric opportunities for becoming more data-driven. New data sources, better management of corporate data and the growing power of analytics are combining to create a new generation of data-driven, decision-centric processes.

Using data-driven decision-making to radically innovate their business processes, however, will mean adopting new standards and techniques. Proven approaches exist that allow organizations to discover the decisions in their processes. Adopting the new Decision Model and Notation (DMN) standard lets them clearly model this decision making, simplifying their process models and identifying clear and compelling analytic opportunities. Focusing on decisions and processes as peers creates innovative decision-centric processes with higher rates of straight through processing, more customer-centricity and improved operational effectiveness.

This chapter introduces operational decisions, discusses how to find them in a business process and shows how they can be modeled effectively in the new DMN standard. How to use these models to frame analytic requirements is covered as is the opportunity for process innovation created by changing the role of decisions in business processes.

THE RISE OF BIG DATA AND THE DATA-DRIVEN PROCESS

> Data-driven processes are going to be those that leverage Big Data and analytics to automate decisions.

Organizations today have more data that describes their business than ever before. Most organizations have been doing this long enough to acquire a detailed history of how their prospects, customers, suppliers, products, stores and supply chains are behaving. As the era of Big Data takes hold, this internal data is being supplemented by an explosion of new data sources. Social, mobile and Internet-of-Things (IoT) data sources are combining with newly open government data sources and web "exhaust" to enrich this history. Most organizations realize that future growth, even future survival, relies on leveraging this data and adopting analytics.

While it can seem that there are as many reasons for adopting analytics as there are organizations, the reality is that three key business needs are driving analytic adoption:

- A need to report on what happened in the organization.

- A need to monitor what is happening in the organization now.
- A need to make data-driven decisions.

Organizations are shifting their focus as Big Data takes hold, moving from reporting and monitoring to using analytics to make better decisions. The results of a recent survey [Taylor 2015], for instance, are shown in Figure 1, below. Three quarters of respondents are focused on reporting or monitoring today and are evenly split between the two. But in 12-24 months almost eighty percent of respondents are focusing on decision-making instead.

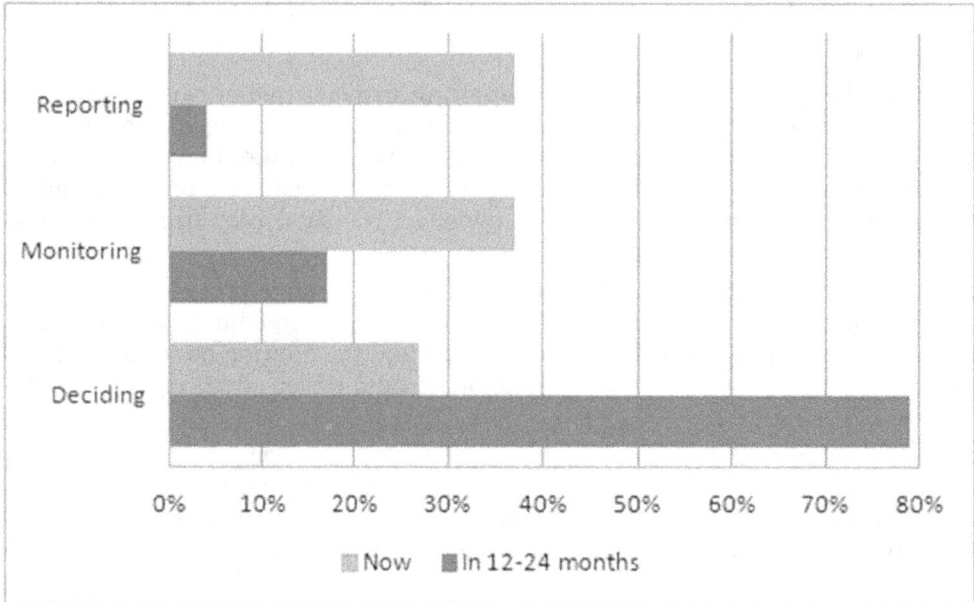

Figure 1: Analytics for Decision-Making

Applying Big Data Analytics to business processes, then, is not going to be about embedding reports in processes or about monitoring those processes. Data-driven processes are going to be those that use Big Data and analytics to make **decisions**.

THE CENTRAL ROLE OF OPERATIONAL DECISIONS

In a recent study [Decision Management Solutions 2013], companies that tightly integrate predictive analytics into operational systems are more than twice as likely to report a transformative impact from predictive analytics as any others. These operational systems automate operational decisions, often about customers, that are made over and over. The value of these decisions rapidly adds up, multiplying as decisions are repeated.

To understand the central role of operational decisions, consider two types of decisions a company might make about continuing or ending a business relationship:

- A ***strategic decision*** to renew the contract of a major channel partner.
- An ***operational decision*** to retain a specific customer account.

The channel renewal decision will be made once every year or two. It impacts sales, margins and market share so most companies will invest a lot of time and money trying to ensure the best result. Using analytics to understand the likely value, costs and tradeoffs of the contract will improve the strategic thinking that goes into the decision about whether or not to renew. It will also sharpen the company's ability to envision and negotiate for the most favorable terms.

A retention decision for a specific customer will also be made once every year or two. But it is one of **thousands,** maybe **hundreds of thousands**, of similar decisions made within that timeframe. Each decision determines whether, and how, the company will retain a specific customer. These operational decisions determine the actions the company takes in regard to one of its most valuable business assets—their portfolio of customers worth millions in customer lifetime value.

The value of retaining a single customer may not be significant and this decision may seem much less important than the channel renewal decision as a result. However, *the cumulative bottom-line impact of high-volume decisions such as this one can be substantial, easily exceeding that of a strategic decision* because the value of each customer renewal decision is multiplied by the number of customers in the portfolio.

Maximizing the value of Big Data means applying analytics to these operational decisions. These decisions are made in operational processes. A process-centric organization needs therefore to be able to consider operational decisions as part of its approach to modeling business processes.

MODEL DECISIONS AS WELL AS PROCESSES USING DMN

To model decisions, especially operational decisions, there is a well-defined set of iterative steps to develop an effective Decision Requirements Model using the industry standard Decision Model and Notation (DMN) approach.

A Note on Terminology

In the Decision Model and Notation Standard V1.0, Decision Requirements Diagrams and decision logic together create a decision model. This paper use Decision Requirements Model to refer to the models and diagrams and decision modeling when referring to the overall approach.

Decision Modeling

Decision modeling has four steps that are performed iteratively:

1. Identify Decisions.
   Identify the decisions that matter to the business process(es).
2. Describe Decisions.
   Describe the decisions and document how improving these decisions will impact the business objectives and metrics of the business.
3. Specify Decision Requirements.
   Move beyond simple descriptions of decisions to begin to specify detailed decision requirements. Specify the information and knowledge required to make the decisions and combine into a Decision Requirements Diagram.
4. Decompose and Refine the Model.
   Refine the requirements for these decisions using the precise yet easy to understand graphical notation of Decision Requirements Diagrams. Identify additional decisions that need to be described and specified.

This process repeats until the decisions are completely specified. As the DMN standard has moved through the approval process, the notation and overall approach have been described in various published materials [BABOK; Debevoise and Taylor; DMS 2015; Taylor et al].

Decision Requirements Diagrams

Decision Requirements diagrams are at the heart of this effort, using a core set of notational elements to clearly express how the decision should be made. These diagrams use the simple palette shown in Figure 2.

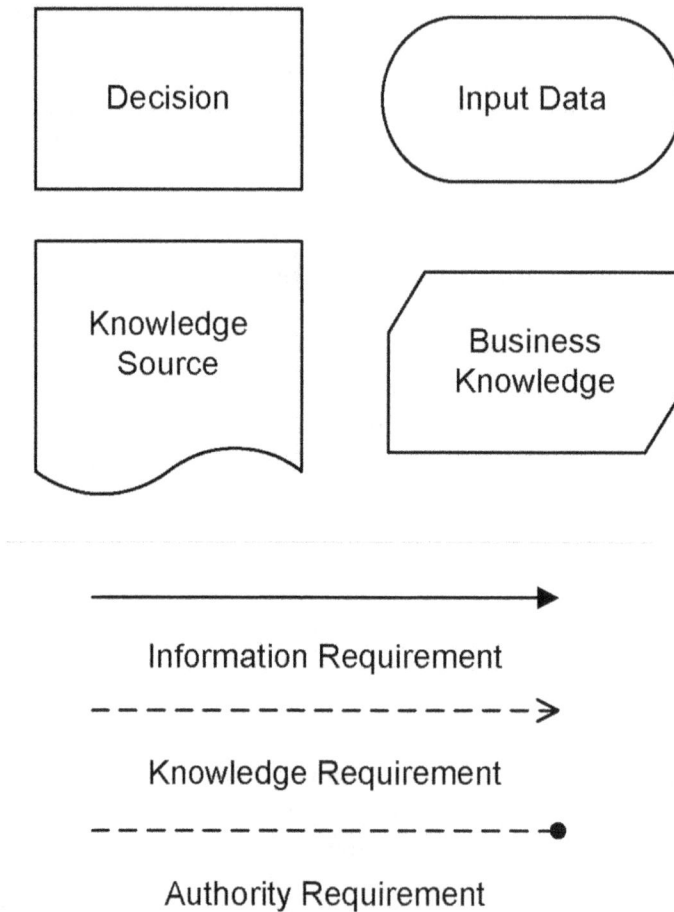

Figure 2: The DMN Palette [Debevoise and Taylor]

A Decision Requirements Diagram combines these elements to show how a decision is made:

- The decision and its component sub-decisions – the decisions that must be made precede it - are modeled.
- The business entities that describe outside data input to these decisions is modeled as Input Data.
- The policies, regulations, best practices, expertise and analytic insight required to make these decisions are modeled as Knowledge Sources
- If a decision cannot be made without a piece of Input Data then an Information Requirement is added to show that the specific piece of Input Data is required by that decision.

- If a decision cannot be made until another decision is made then an Information Requirement is added to show that one decision requires the result of the other.
- Finally Knowledge Sources are linked to the decisions they constrain, guide or influence – those they act as authorities for – using an Authority Requirement.

The result is a Decision Requirements Diagram shown in Figure 3 (the use of Business Knowledge models and Knowledge Requirements is not relevant at this point).

Figure 3: An example Decision Requirements Model
Source: DecisionsFirst Modeler

This Decision Requirements Model shows how the Select Marketing Offer decision is made, what the component sub-decisions are, as well as the data required to make the decision and the knowledge that must be applied to this decision to make it correctly and accurately.

FRAMING ANALYTIC REQUIREMENTS WITH DECISION REQUIREMENTS MODELS

Once a decision has been modeled in a decision requirements diagram the potential for applying analytics to make the decision a more data-driven one is generally much clearer.

Identifying analytic knowledge requirements

First specific analytic knowledge sources may have been identified as the decision was being modeled. It may be clear that the decision requires an assessment of risk, of fraud or of customer opportunity – all potential uses of Big Data Analytics.

Even if the initial model does not identify analytic knowledge requirements it can provide a framework for a conversation about analytics. Those working with the model can ask business owners to answer "if " statements about how the decision could be made more effectively:

- "If we knew which customers would renew, we could decide who to target with renewal offers more effectively."
- "If we knew which suppliers would deliver on time, we could pick suppliers that would help us deliver on time."

- "If we knew which refund requests were from people faking their identity, we could avoid paying out unnecessary tax refunds"

These questions are exactly the kinds of opportunities that Big Data Analytics address. A Decision Requirements Model provides a framework for identifying these opportunities and provides a robust framing of the analytic requirements identified.

Decision Requirements Models as Business Understanding

Established analytic approaches like CRISP-DM stress the importance of understanding the project objectives and requirements from a business perspective, but to date there are no formal approaches to capturing this understanding in a repeatable, understandable format. Decision Requirements Modeling closes this gap. Decision Requirements models develop a richer, more complete business understanding earlier for analytic teams. Decision Requirements models describe a clear business target, an understanding of how the results will be used and deployed, and by whom.

Scaling Analytics with Decision Requirements Models

Using Decision Requirements Models to guide and shape analytics projects also reduces the reliance on constrained specialist resources by improving requirements gathering and ensuring that business and process analysts can identify and describe analytic opportunities. They help teams ask the key questions and collaborate effectively because analytics, IT and business professionals can all build and understand the models.

Decision Requirements Models document analytic project requirements in a way that enables organizations to:

- Compare multiple projects for prioritization, including allowing new analytic development to be compared with updating or refining existing analytics.
- Act on a specific plan to guide analytic development that is accessible to business, IT and analytic teams alike.
- Reuse knowledge from project to project by creating an increasingly detailed and accurate view of decision-making and the role of analytics.
- Value information sources and analytics in terms of business impact.

OPERATIONAL DECISION DISCOVERY IN BUSINESS PROCESSES

This focus on using data, Big Data, and analytics to make decisions creates a challenge for most process-centric organizations. Process models, such as those built using the Object Management Group's Business Process Model and Notation (BPMN) standard, do a great job of modeling the flow of work through a process. They show assignments and integration points and the way data objects are created, modified and consumed in those processes. What they don't do is identify decision-making explicitly.

> There is a common misconception that the gateways shown in a business process are decisions. In fact gateways are better thought of as points in a process where the process branches based on the result of decision-making. In other words a gateway should generally be preceded by the decision that drives it.

Most, if not all, business processes require decisions to be made: claims must be approved or rejected before a claims process can complete, cross-sell offers must be selected and product discounts must be calculated before an order to cash process can complete and so on.

Explicitly modeling the decisions that happen in your business process ensures that the process model is closer to reality and identifies opportunities for analytics in the business process. For most organizations this is the critical approach, the one most likely to identify suitable decisions.

There are four approaches when looking for decisions in business processes:

Existing Decision Tasks

Some process models have already identified decision-making tasks, typically modeled as Rule Tasks in BPMN 2. The decision-making involved in these tasks may have been described using business rules or a description. Developing a Decision Requirements Model for each decision will clarify the decision-making, improve the management of the business rules involved and clearly show opportunities for analytics to improve the decision-making if they exist.

Manual Tasks

Many processes contain manual tasks, human tasks, focused on referral, escalation and approval. Unless these tasks involve manual input of data, and even sometimes when they do, the process is generally engaging a human at these points because a decision must be made. Identifying this as a decision and modeling it can improve the degree of automation of the process and identify the potential for Big Data Analytics in that task, whether it is automated or not.

Decisions modeled using process models

When a business process must handle multiple scenarios, modeling the decision-making in that process using only gateways and branches can become very complex. Nests of gateways with few intervening tasks often represent decision-making modeled in a business process. Only once the decision is clearly identified will the potential for Big Data Analytics to improve it be clear. Replacing such a nest of gateways with a single, explicit decision point—a Decision Task - and an associated Decision Requirements Model clarifies the behavior of the process, makes it easier to see if the process or the decision must change, and allows for changes in the decision-making approach to be independent from process change.

DECISION-LED PROCESS INNOVATION

While many opportunities for data-driven decision-making can be found by analyzing existing processes and process models, there is also an opportunity for organizations to engage in decision-led process innovation. Adding new decision tasks to a business process, decision tasks where Big Data Analytics will make for better decisions, can deliver dramatic process improvements.

Pre-empt processing

Many processes assemble data so that a decision can be made at the end of the process. These processes generally assemble all this data so that a person can make the decision once the data is all available. Because the decision is deferred to the end of the process, every decision requires every task in the process to be executed. Because this decision is generally poorly understood and left to the human decision-maker, little can be done to improve the process.

If, however, the decision is modeled and thereby understood a range of new options can be identified. First it may be possible to add a decision that attempts to decide first and execute the rest of the process later only if it is required. If the established decision-making approach is used, however, this will generally not work as the data required for the decision has not been assembled. The application of Big Data Analytics to the decision making approach can fundamentally change this reality.

First the use of analytics that can be automatically executed may allow parts of the decision to be made without human intervention. Second the use of analytics against new or external data sources, a key element of Big Data, may offer proxies for parts of the decision making – replacing an actual estimate for repair with a predicted cost of repair for instance. This increased analytic sophistication may effectively allow a correct decision to be made much earlier in the process, at least for some process instances.

Using Big Data Analytics to drive a pre-emptive decision in this way will shorten process execution. Additional decision points can also be added so that, as the process gathers more data, the process can keep trying to decide.

Route past manual reviews

In a similar vein many processes have manual reviews. Most organizations have already attempted to find out when they can avoid such a review and have automated straight through processing wherever they can. Big Data Analytics allow for new automated decisions before the manual review that route more process instances around the manual review, increasing straight through process rates. Two specific approaches offer real potential here.

The first approach is to use data mining techniques to assess completed processes that had a manual review step. These techniques will mathematically identify patterns in the data used by the process that match to transactions that will be approved by the manual review. Especially if the data in the process can be enriched with additional Big Data sources, surprising numbers of new rules can be identified and implemented to increase straight through processing.

Where the manual review involves a human user in an assessment of risk, where they must review data about customers and transactions to see how much risk there will be in handling the transaction, predictive analytic models can be used. This second approach takes data about historical transactions or cases as well as external data and uses it to build a predictive analytic model. Such a model calculates the probable risk involved in accepting a particular transaction. Often if this part of the human decision-making can be automated the rest of the decision model can similarly be automated and many more transactions handled without manual review.

In either case the organization can gradually flesh out a decision to automatically decide about additional transactions, gradually increasing the straight through processing rate.

Hidden Micro Decisions

"Micro decisions"[Taylor and Raden] refers to decisions made transaction by transaction, customer by customer. Companies often fail to recognize these as individual decisions, instead lumping them into bigger ones. For instance, instead of realizing that each price offered to each customer is a micro decision they think that "pricing" is a big, strategic decision. They therefore embed a single pricing task that looks up a standard price into a process. Such a task takes no account of the specific customer involved and hides the decision. Failing to consider these micro decisions as separate decision making opportunities means you cannot personalize or target them to individual customers. This in turn means you cannot leverage Big Data Analytics about customers to reward loyalty or otherwise differentiate your customers one from another.

Adding a micro decision task into a business process allows an explicit decision to be made for each customer. Data mining may be used to identify customer segments whose behavior is quite different from each other. Predictive analytic models may be built that predict customer churn, lifetime value or profitability. The way these different analytic elements are combined to make a decision about a specific customer can be modeled and this allows the process to have an explicit decision embedded in it that will treat each customer uniquely and appropriately.

Many processes have these opportunities and can replace default behavior with explicit decisions. A process with embedded micro decisions targets or personalizes itself such that each customer segment, even each customer, gets a "different" process.

CONCLUSION

Organizations are applying analytics, analyzing vast quantities of data, to drive improved risk assessment, reduce fraud and focus more clearly on their customers. Big Data Analytics deliver these powerful results by improving decision-making.

To deliver data-driven process innovation, organizations must discover, model and improve the decisions at the heart of their business processes. New standards and techniques are proving their worth putting Big Data Analytics to work in business processes.

Framing data mining and predictive analytics projects with a Decision Requirements Model links analytics to business results and helps ensure successful deployment.

By applying these techniques not only to the decisions already identified in an organization's business processes but also to pre-empt processing, route past manual reviews and deliver customer-centric micro decisions, organizations can deliver decision-centric process innovation.

REFERENCES

More information on DecisionsFirst Modeler is at http://decisionsfirst.com.

[BABOK] IIBA. Business Analyst Body of Knowledge v 3.0 (April 2015).

[Debevoise and Taylor] Debevoise, Tom and Taylor, James. The MicroGuide to Process and Decision Modeling in BPMN/DMN: Building More Effective Processes by Integrating Process Modeling with Decision Modeling (2014).

[DMS 2013] Decision Management Solutions, Predictive Analytics in the Cloud: Opportunities, Trends and the Impact of Big Data 2013 (2013).

[DMS 2015] Decision Management Solutions, An Introduction to Decision Modeling with DMN (2015).

[Taylor 2015] Decision Management Solutions, Analytics Capability Landscape: Identifying the right analytic capabilities for success (2015).

[Taylor et al] Taylor, Fish, Vanthienen and Vincent in iBPMS. Emerging Standards in Decision Modeling—an Introduction to Decision Model & Notation. Future Strategies, 2013. http://futstrat.com/books/iBPMS_Handbook.php

[DMN] Object Management Group. Decision Model and Notation (DMN) Specification 1.0. Current version at http://www.omg.org/spec/DMN/Current

[Taylor 2011] Taylor, James. Decision Management Systems – A Practical Guide to Using Business Rules and Predictive Analytics. IBM Press(2011).

[Taylor and Raden] Taylor, James and Raden, Neil. Smart (Enough) Systems: How to Deliver Competitive Advantage by Automating Hidden Decisions. Prentice Hall, (2007).

Value Streams Driving the Business Internet of Things

J. Bryan Lail and Gregory T. Taylor, Raytheon, USA

INTRODUCTION

The direction towards global markets and operations places stress on many business processes that originated in the days of primarily domestic business operations. The potential of a broader set of customers across more regions carries a set of complications where in-country policies, acquisition rules, workshare requirements, leadership expectations and differing infrastructure challenge morphing a domestic business model into the global scene. The Raytheon Company is stepping back to look at new value streams, or models across marketing, engineering, suppliers, manufacturing and information systems, which lead to improved business outcomes and improved affordability in the more complex global market.

We will demonstrate how the key shifts in business capabilities tied to these value streams will enable new business processes, as well as driving new technology and more efficient business operations. We will show a specific use case leading to the Internet of Things (IoT), but in a context relevant to our defense business with specific policies and mission needs, which we have labeled the "Business IoT". The Business IoT, combined with advanced analytics, brings powerful new agility and business efficiency by rigorous application to the new business process and direct relation to the future value stream.

VALUE STREAM RATIONALE

We propose that the greatest value to our industry from the Internet of Things is in enabling critical new value streams rather than incremental improvements to existing processes. Where the market and business environment are shifting, the company already has incentive to institute a fundamental new business approach. An advanced analytics capability designed for that new value stream makes information more actionable and useful for the business. The ability to use richer, actionable information in turn defines the targeted investment in the devices, connectivity and analytics.

The focus of this paper is on the strong tie between critical new value streams, advanced analytics and business-driven application of the Internet of Things. The methods discussed here can be found in the Business Architecture Guild's Business Architecture Body of Knowledge, or BIZBOK Guide.

THE RIGHT VALUE STREAM

A significant shift in the business model or product strategy provides the requirements for a new value stream. In the language of business modeling, the company has chosen to pursue a new customer segment, is opening up new channels to those customers and related revenue streams, or is offering a new value proposition to those customers. The business architect works with business leaders to map those market-driven changes into a new plan for internal business operations. Capability mapping provides a toolset to analyze the market strategy and provide the critical focus for the roles and processes that must change, how costs must be restructured, and how the team is formed.

For a large market shift, the capability map provides a key means to describe all the activities the business must perform, independent of current organization charts or specific processes as practiced currently. With an understanding of the heat map, or subjective evaluation on capability gaps by the team of experts in the business shift, a focus emerges for a future value stream that spans across the changes in roles, skills, processes, teaming, cost structures and other elements to provide new revenue channels. As one would expect in an existing company, the roadmap to develop this value stream will evolve in phases from existing capabilities, but it is a critical step to acknowledge that the future value stream is not restricted by current boundaries and processes in the company today.

A RAYTHEON VALUE STREAM

As an example, the Raytheon Company has been expanding internationally during the downturn in the U.S. domestic defense environment, but needs to expand the capabilities required to have a global presence. We assessed the business model for each of our key market strategies, and then used an industry standard framework to form heat maps for each market to identify the most critical shifts in business capabilities. A heat map for an individual market will look similar to the general example in Figure 1, where the framework is the same for each market but the heat, or capabilities identified as most critical for significant shift, is tied to that strategy and market environment.

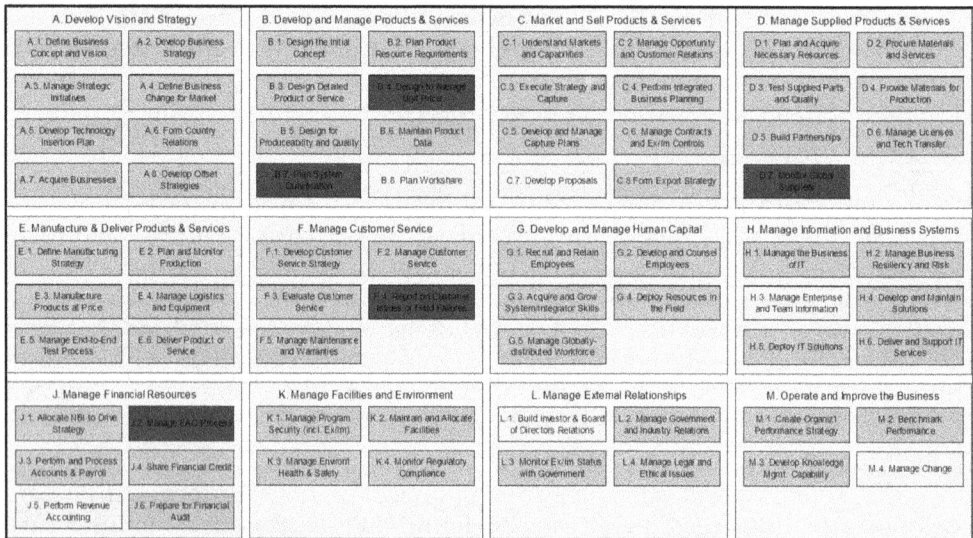

Figure 1: Generic Capability Heat Map

By weighting each heat map according to the size of the commitment to that market area, we were then able to normalize across all market strategies to find the biggest drivers for the whole business. Value streams then emerged from the related capability gaps in that final combined heat map, by finding opportunities for horizontal integration and similar elements of the lifecycle.

For example, a key value stream related to the challenges of growing globally ties to the growing customer expectation for co-development and co-production of products in their country, including some of their indigenous suppliers and workforce. We'll focus next on that value stream and business capabilities addressed within it.

There are many elements in a value stream resulting in a highly effective co-development and co-production approach, early on during negotiation and later in executing the program. In Figure 2 we focus in the middle, where the deal has been made with the customer, but the exact approach needs to be planned. Information from the international customer or representatives provides an understanding of possible skills in-country and the starting point for facilities and infrastructure. A coordinated team across engineering, supply chain management and manufacturing need to form the plan with new tasks and measurements in comparison to a standard domestic customer model or foreign sales negotiated through the U.S. government.

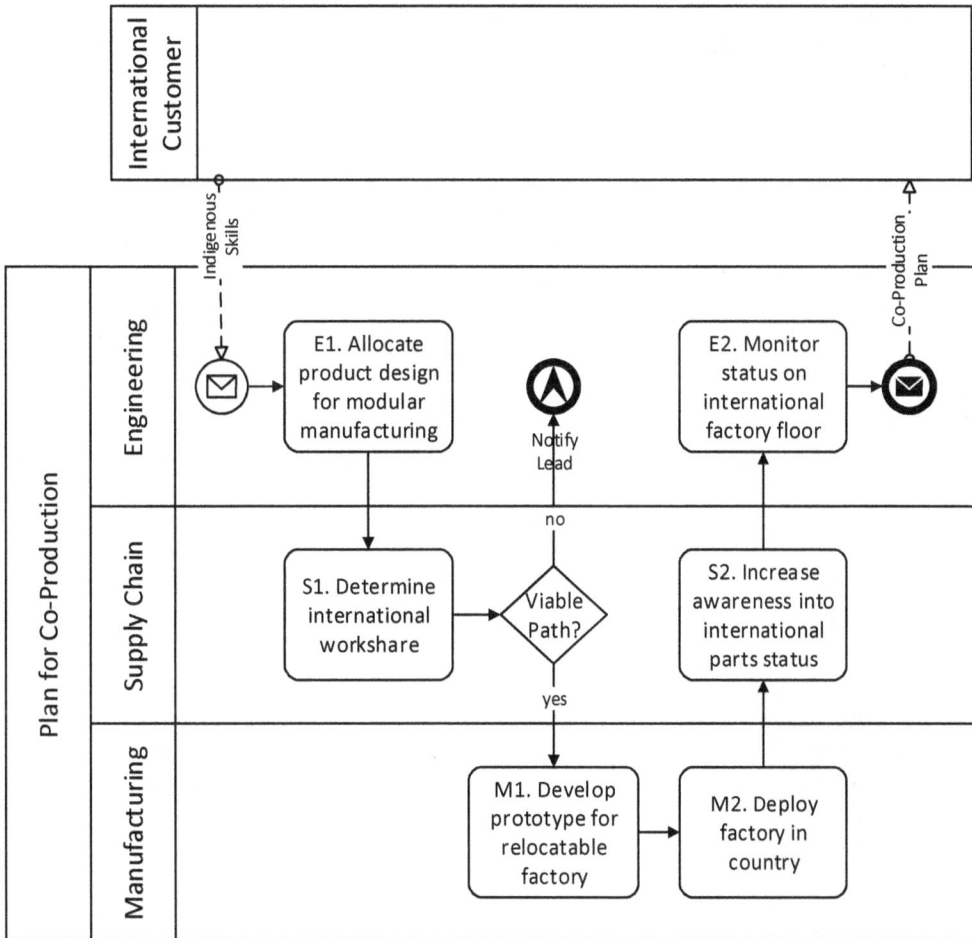

Figure 2: Co-production Process in International Value Stream

A new value stream for the business will likely include significant impact on skills, organization, information, and technologies, as well as new or tailored processes. Focusing on the process first, key stakeholders in engineering, supply chain management and manufacturing work together in a more collaborative fashion to determine the best approach for meeting in-country co-development or co-production requirements (as committed to by contract to win the program). The workflow in Figure 2 provides an example of a new process within the value stream, including how the business might implement the new approach (tasks M2, S2, and E2 will be used in a case study later in the paper).

Specifically, after a discussion below on the importance of advanced analytics to enable the new value stream and drive relevance into technology insertion, we'll come back to the global business implications for enhanced supply chain and factory floor information across countries.

ADVANCED ANALYTICS

Advanced analytics is broad term for a set of techniques and tools that focus on the future, to model and predict outcomes and behaviors, rather than examining historical data to understand the past, as in traditional business intelligence. It can be a powerful enabler to business, helping make sense of large volumes of fast moving unstructured and structured data, allowing business to maintain situational awareness of process and environment, and anticipate and adapt to change.

Advanced analytics applied to a critical business need, such as the international co-production process above, can accelerate the availability of the right information to the right business user at the right time. Finding the right approach for the international customer requires the engineer, supplier lead and manufacturing technician to collaborate in new ways and at a faster pace across a globally-distributed team. Analytics can provide the glue that delivers value from this collaboration and leverages a richer set of data coming out of the connected laboratory, engineering computing, supplier logistics and manufacturing facilities.

BUSINESS INTERNET OF THINGS

Our usage of the term Business IoT requires an implementation of the technology for a purpose solving a business need, rather than just more devices, sensors, data storage and analyst effort. The Business IoT is the foundation connecting all employees, devices and data throughout the entire business process lifecycle. It reduces the time and resource costs associated with traditional methods of information usage among less connected entities, providing better context and actionable intelligence.

Examples we'll build on here include applying IoT connectivity, sensing, data storage and analysis into a global supply chain, such as awareness of status on parts stored and delivered from many countries and companies. Those parts are then delivered to a factory floor that could be operating almost anywhere in the world with real-time monitoring to guide a factory worker on the other side of the globe.

ENABLING THE VALUE STREAM WITH ANALYTICS AND THE INTERNET OF THINGS

Now we tie these concepts together, where advanced analytics uses the Business IoT fabric to enable new value streams for the business. As shown visually in Figure 3, the new value stream could work as follows:

1. Sensor and processed data can be streamed and analyzed in near real-time at speed and scale
2. Deployed analytical models can notify users of interesting events
3. Users can conduct their own analyses using powerful statistical tools, making quick, collaborative decisions

4. Rich connected data sets enable additional analysis with emerging trends, promoting data-driven decisions back into the Business IoT

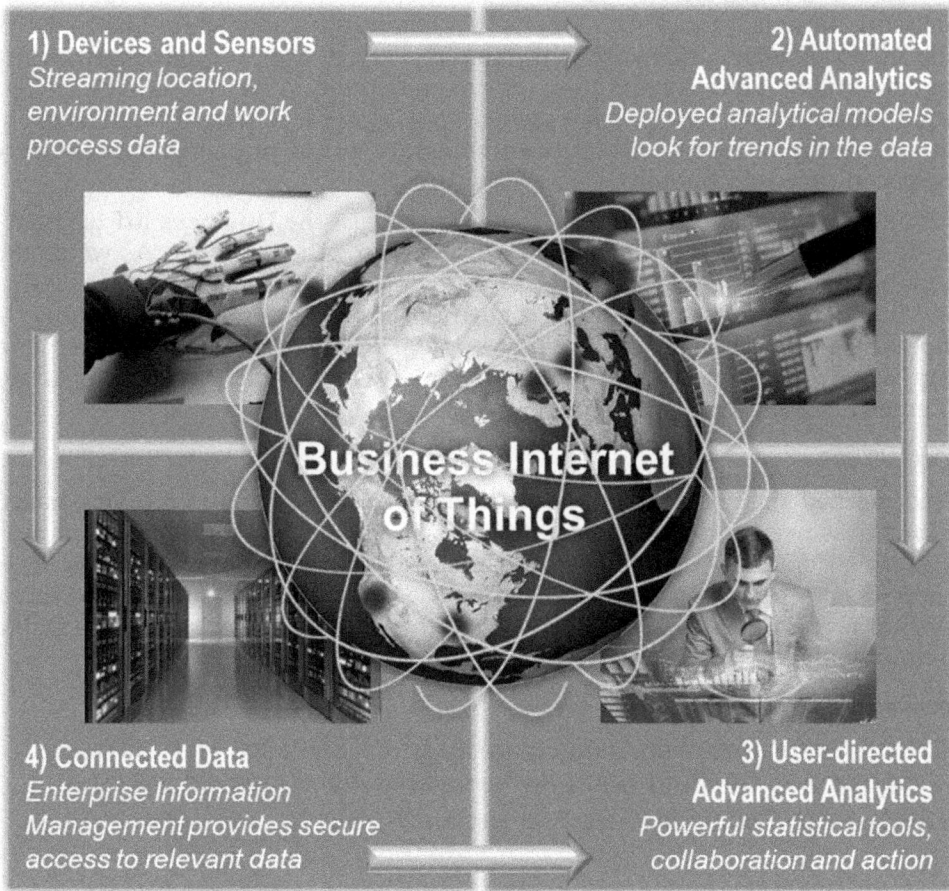

1) Devices and Sensors
Streaming location, environment and work process data

2) Automated Advanced Analytics
Deployed analytical models look for trends in the data

Business Internet of Things

4) Connected Data
Enterprise Information Management provides secure access to relevant data

3) User-directed Advanced Analytics
Powerful statistical tools, collaboration and action

Figure 3: Analytics and the Business IoT

CASE STUDIES AT RAYTHEON

A future case our company is assessing looks at a production facility focused on final integration needs for a globally-distributed supply chain, in order to operate effectively as a final assembly point. Sensors in a supplier storage area in another country report information about location of parts, status of testing and the state of the environment (e.g. temperature, humidity). A deployed analytical model monitors the data points and correlates with downstream enterprise system planning data, which determines that a part lot destined for use on the production line has been sitting in environmental conditions that may produce quality issues. An engineer is notified, who then validates the finding, using additional connected data sources and powerful statistical tools. The engineer then collaborates with local and international supply chain management to mitigate risk by engaging an alternate supplier and requesting requalification of the lot.

In another case, an international co-production facility is designed with sensors in gloves worn by assemblers used to collect movement data as work is performed (see a related article on the subject in WIRED magazine). A deployed analytical model, built with extensive historical movement data and subject matter expertise, monitors the stream of data and sees a trend that could result in a potential downstream quality issue. A quality engineer is notified and begins looking for causes using additional connected data sources and powerful statistical tools. The engineer validates the model's finding and collaborates via video conference with management at the co-production facility to do additional analysis and plan for risk mitigation. A part lot is set aside for requalification before it makes its way into a higher level assembly. The problem is discovered early enough that schedule is not impacted and delivery occurs on time and budget.

The use of Advanced Analytics in conjunction with the Business IoT is particularly compelling to Raytheon's international growth trajectory. As we create more business and governmental partnerships in-country, the need to enable new business processes, including partnering with in-country personnel, is imperative. The Business IoT removes latency between people, devices and data, while Advanced Analytics can help make sense of that data even at larger volumes and near real-time speed.

CONCLUSIONS

We described the connections between developing new value streams based on business need, with advanced analytics as the method for delivering value, extracting significant benefit from the business-driven Internet of Things. Raytheon has started down the road to bring these techniques together in a manner that prepares the company for the realities of doing business in the global environment.

REFERENCES

(BIZBOK Guide) Business Architecture Body of Knowledge v4.1, Business Architecture Guild, http://www.businessarchitectureguild.org 2014.

(WIRED Article) Ready to Wear, Mat Honan, WIRED Magazine Jan 2015.

Mining the Swarm

Keith D. Swenson, Sumeet Batra, Yasumasa Oshiro, Fujitsu America

1. ABSTRACT

Data mining and process mining are both tools used by the BPM professional in order find out how an organization is currently operating and to get an objective measure of how efficiently the organization is operating. Big data is a style of data analysis that reflects a return to large, centralized data repositories. Processing power and memory are getting cheaper, while the bandwidth among all the smart devices remains a barrier to getting all the data together in one place for analysis. Rather than centralize the data, this article considers the possibility that the data will remain close to the device, which is why analytics is moved to the data. Swarms of devices will be mined in order to retrieve intelligence about what those devices have been involved in. As with all technology advancements, we should move forward with our eyes open.

2. INTRODUCTION

The Internet of Things (IoT) will be composed of a tremendous number of intelligent devices connected and communicating with each other. These devices are smart themselves – that is they have processing power, memory – and they can communicate with the Internet. Historical technological trends predict that processing power will continue to grow at the device level. We can also predict that cost for storing and for transporting data will both decrease, but the course of the future depends upon how these costs are related to each other: is it ultimately cheaper to store or transport the data?

Being cheaper to store the data in the device means that we will see a paradigm shift in how we process that data. In a way similar to how Google distributed web search queries across a grid of computers, it is reasonable to see analytics functions distributed to the devices that form the Internet of Things.

Building on this, there are some very disturbing aspects to consider: Who owns this data when it is distributed over millions of devices? How can one protect privacy? Whether centralized or distributed, how can one assure the quality of the data? On the flip side, devices that mine information from other devices might be able to provide better service, and a better quality life than without.

3. HISTORICAL TRENDS IN COMPUTING

To justify the prediction that IoT devices will tend to store their own data, let's start by looking at some historical trends in centralization and decentralization in order to understand the general pattern.

Mainframe Origins

The first advances into the field of computing machinery were big, clumsy, error-prone electrical and mechanical devices that were not only large physically but extremely expensive, requiring specially-designed rooms and teams of attendants to keep them running. The huge up-front investment necessary meant that the machines were reserved exclusively for the most important most expensive and most valuable problems.

We all know the story of Moore's Law and how the cost of such machines dropped dramatically year after year. At first the cost savings meant only that such machines could be dramatically more powerful and could handle many programs running at the same time. Machine operating time was split into slices that could be used by different accounts at different times. Sharing across accounts presents an overhead and a barrier to use. The groups running the machines needed to charge by the CPU cycle to pay for the machine. While there were times that the machine was under-utilized, it was never possible to really say that there were "free" cycles available to give away. The cost-recovery motive can't allow that.

Emergence of Personal Computers

The PC revolution was not simply a logical step due to the decreased costs of computer machinery, but rather a different paradigm. By owning a small computer, the CPU cycles were there to be used or not used as pleased by the user. CPU cycles were literally free after the modest capital cost of the PC had been paid. This liberated people to use the machines more freely, and opened the way to many classes of applications that would have been hard to justify economically on a time-share system.

The electronic spreadsheet was born on the PC because spending expensive CPU power just to update the display for the user could not be justified. The mainframe approach would be print all the numbers onto paper, have the analyst mark up the paper, get it as right as possible, and then have someone input the changes once. The spreadsheet application allowed a user to *experiment* with numbers; play with the relationships between quantities; try out different potential plans; and to see which of many possible approaches looked better.

The pendulum had swung from centralized systems to decentralized systems; new applications allow CPU cycles to be used in new innovative ways, but PC users were still isolated.

Networking in the 1990s changed everything.

World Wide Web

The Internet transformed PCs from computation machines to communications devices. New applications arrived for delivering content to users. The browser was invented to bring resources from those remote computers and assemble them into a coherent display whenever the user demanded. Early browsers were primitive, and there were many disagreements on what capabilities a browser should have to make the presentation of information useful to the user. The focus at that time was on the web server which had access to information in a raw form, and would format the information for display in a browser. Simply viewing raw data is not that interesting, but actually processing that data in ways customized by the user was the powerful value-add that the web server could provide. Servers had plug-ins, and the Java and JavaScript languages were invented to make it easier to code these capabilities and put them on a server.

The pendulum had swung back to the mainframe model of centralized computing. Web servers, along with their big brother application servers, were the most important processing platforms at that time. The web browser allowed you to connect to the results of any one of thousands of such web servers, but each web server was the source of a single kind of data.

Apps, HTML5, and client computing

Web 2.0 was the name of a trend for the web to change from a one way flow of information, to a two-way, collaborative flow of information that allowed users to be more involved in the flow of information. At the same time, an interesting technological change brought about the advent of "apps" – small programs that could be downloaded, installed, and run more or less automatically. This trend was launched on smart phones and branched out from there. HTML5 promises to bring the same capability to every browser. Once again the pendulum has swung in the direction of decentralization; servers provide data in a more raw form and apps format the display on a device much closer to the user.

	Centralized	Decentralized
Computation	1970 Mainframe	1985 Personal Computer
Web Communications	1995 Web servers, App servers	2005 Web 2.0, Apps
Analytics	2010 Big Data	2020 *Analytics in the Swarm*

Cloud Computing & Big Data

Cloud computing and big data moved us beyond the basic provision of first-order data. Computing platforms can collect large amounts of data about how people are using the web platforms. The cost of memory has also dropped precipitously. There is no longer any need to throw anything away. The resulting huge piles of data can then be mined, and surprising new insights gained.

The results of analysis are often useful in ways that the designers of the devices never imagined possible. Cell phones automatically report their position and velocity to the phone company. Whether a cell phone is moving quickly – or not so quickly – on a freeway is important information about traffic conditions. Google collects this information, determines where the traffic is running slow and where it is running fast, and displays the result on maps using colors to indicate good or bad traffic conditions. *The cell phone was never designed as a traffic monitor!*

It took an insightful data scientist to realize that out of a large collection of information for one purpose, good information about other things could be concluded.

The Swarm

Big data means just that: data that is collected in such quantity that it is hard to move around. Even at the fastest transfer speeds, it would take days or months to move it to another location. Bringing the data to a special machine for analyzing is not possible. Instead the analysis must be done on the machine holding the data.

The theme of this chapter is to anticipate the next pendulum swing: big data style analytics will become available in a distributed fashion away from the centralized stockpiles of information.

While the challenges in Big Data are variety and velocity, what sensor technology or IoT brings is the variety of the data which had been previously leveraged is what we call "dark data." Dark data is attracting people as new data-source for mining.

Each hardware sensor collects specific data such as video, sounds (in stream), social media texts, stocks, weather, temperature, location, vital data etc. Traditional means of analysis of this data is a challenge since there is so much data, and it is useful for different purposes, that make it relatively difficult to aggregate in the traditional ways.

The key to analyzing those sensor data is how you extract useful data (metadata) or compress it, and how to interact with other devices or center server. Some say that a machine-to-machine (M2M) approach is called for. There are a number of reasons to anticipate these trends, as well as evidence that this is beginning to happen today.

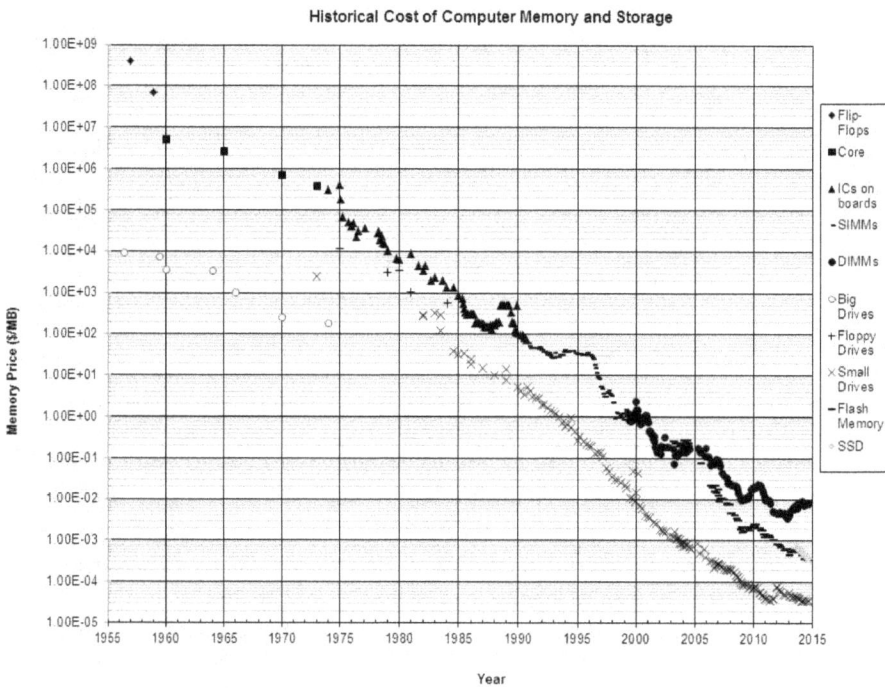

Figure 1: Historical Prices of Memory[1]

4. EVIDENCE FOR A NEW PARADIGM

We have seen that technologies tend to be introduced in a centralized mode, and later migrate to decentralized. There is another force that will drive the trend to keeping data on the device, and which is that data storage is becoming cheap far faster than data transmission.

---

1 Historical prices of memory and graphic compiled by John C. McCallum. See

http://www.jcmit.com/memoryprice.htm

Storage is getting cheaper

Figure 1 shows on a logarithmic scale how the price of storage of information has decreased exponentially over a long period of history. This figure shows a number of different devices. Along with cost decreases, size usually decreases, and speed increases. Hard disks have historically been the most cost-effective way to store information, but notice especially how solid state disks (SSD) have appeared in the last ten years. SSDs are rapidly approaching the price / performance range of hard disks. It is likely that IoT devices will use solid state memory for storing data because there are no moving parts, and therefor they are less likely to fail. SSD memory is remarkably small, with plans for a 1 terabyte SSD the size of a small fingernail to be available soon. Memory typically decreases in cost by more than 40% a year.

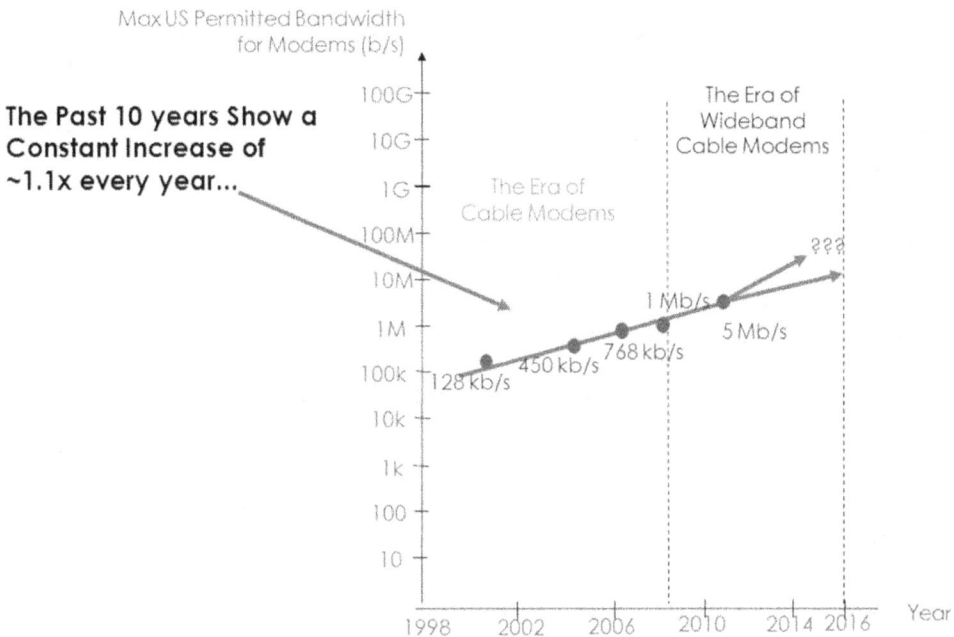

Figure 2. Upload Bandwidth Trend[2]

Bandwidth remains a Challenge

The ability to transmit information from point-to-point is also getting dramatically cheaper over time. The growth of the Internet has been both in capacity and speed. Most measure of Internet bandwidth focus on total bandwidth, which is the total ability to carry data throughout the world.

The IEEE 802.3 Ethernet Working Group reports[3] that the total global consumer Internet traffic was estimated to have a 34% compound annual growth rate (CAGR) from 2010 to 2015.

---

2 From IEEE 802.3 Industry Connections Ethernet Bandwidth Assessment

3 "IEEE 802.3 Industry Connections Ethernet Bandwidth Assessment," BWA Ad Hoc Report, 19th July 2012,

http://www.ieee802.org/3/ad_hoc/bwa/BWA_Report.pdf

In some way the measure of total bandwidth is misleading, because there is at the same time an increase in the total number of devices to connect. Each device receives a smaller fraction of the total bandwidth.

It is important to consider which of these trends is growing faster.

We can look instead at the growth of Internet traffic per person. Traffic per average user of the Internet grows from 7.3 gigabyte per month in 2010 to 24.8 gigabyte per month in 2015. That is a 28% growth rate *per person* in Internet traffic. However, the number of devices per person is increasing.

The number of devices on the Internet is growing dramatically as well.

Cisco reports[4] that the number of devices on the Internet will grow from 12.4 billion in 2013 to 20.6 billion networked devices by 2018. That is a 10% CAGR.

Gartner separates the count of "things" from the count of traditional consumer information devices like laptops, tablets and smart phones. By 2020, the number of smartphones tablets and PCs in use will reach about 7.3 billion units. In contrast, the growth of the number of networked things will grow from 0.9 billion in 2009, to about 26 billion by 2020[5].

Global stored data is growing faster than global IP traffic. According to the "Digital Universe" study[6], stored data is growing at 40% to 50% per year (i.e., doubling every two years) compared to IP traffic growth of 30% to 40% per year.

The Internet of things will appear in the home and office setting, and one restriction on the ability to transfer this capacity to centralized analytical sites is the upload speed of the broadband connection. Figure 2 shows the rate that upload bandwidth has been increasing in recent years at a mere 10% compounded rate. The number of devices will be growing faster than that, and the ability for those devices to collect data will far exceed the ability to move it out of the office or household.

What we can conclude from this that as data moves beyond simply being "big data" it will be not only increasingly hard to move, but it will also be hard to consolidate into centralized locations. Inexpensive, durable memory is getting smaller and more portable, and data will increasingly be collected and stored close to the location that it was collected.

Unnecessary duplication when attempting to centralize

The third consideration with regard to large data analytics lies in the nature of how uses for analytics seem to emerge from surprisingly unrelated data sets. We mentioned earlier that cell phone location and velocity data was able to yield information about traffic jams even though the telephone was never intended as a traffic monitor.

Cell phone location and velocity information are relatively small in size -- just a few bytes of information per phone, so the fact that this data might be duplicated into multiple data archives does not represent a particular problem. The phone company might collect this; a traffic data archive might collect this, etc. If your model is centralized, then you will collect data at your centralized archive for a particular

4 Cisco Visual Networking Index, http://share.cisco.com/vni14/

5 "Gartner Says the Internet of Things Installed Base Will Grow to 26 Billion Units By 2020," December 12, 2013, http://www.gartner.com/newsroom/id/2636073

6 Scott Kipp, Storage Growth and Ethernet,

http://www.ieee802.org/3/ad_hoc/bwa/public/sep11/kipp_01a_0911.pdf

purpose, but there may be many different purposed that the data is relevant for. This means that the data will tend to be duplicated for each possible use, and there may be many possible uses.

As we start to consider extremely large amounts of data, the idea of moving this multiple times in the network, and storing in multiple places becomes a real problem, particularly since the amount of data to start with is growing faster than the network is growing capability to move it. It stands to reason that data will tend to be stored close to the device that collected the data, and that search queries will be distributed out to the devices instead.

5.   POTENTIAL APPLICATIONS

We present a couple of possible applications of distributed analytics in order to describe how it might work in more detail. The applications are speculations at this time, and it is likely that far more compelling applications will be developed when the future actually arrives. Our focus here is mainly on the mechanism of distributing the analytics.

Finding Potholes in Roads - Cars

Traffic fatality statistics have been used for years to identify roads that need repair or redesign. It makes sense to focus investment on road and highways that have proven to be difficult for people in the past, and particularly have been shown to be unsafe. Fatalities, however, are a very blunt and very tragic measure of road quality.

One trend we see rising in parts of the world are dashboard cameras in vehicles that take continuous video of the road ahead, and sometimes include sound recordings. This opens an interesting opportunity for analysis. Potholes in a road might be detectable in two ways. Hitting a pothole might cause the car to rock momentarily which would be visible in the video picture by analyzing successive frames. The other would be to analyze the audio for a loud "thump" sound. By themselves, these indicators would be of little analytical value, but if across many vehicles, if the thump or the rocking motion is detected at the same place, it might be easy to determine that there is a pothole.

This example makes it clear that collecting all of the video of all of the dash-cams of all vehicles is such a large amount of data that collecting that together into one place for analysis is not even remotely possible. Imagine instead that each car keeps 30 days of video on board. The city might decide to look for potholes in a particular stretch of city street. The query would effectively ask each car: "Did you drive on Main Street between 5th and 45th Street this month, and if you did, did you encounter any loud thumps?"

Five thousand cars might respond with the location of such thumps and compared with each other. When the location of a particular sound matches the location on 20 other cars, then you have some significant evidence that there is a road problem requiring attention.

The primary analysis of the video or audio would be done on the dash-cam itself: frame-by-frame comparison to detect sudden shifts in view, or audio detection of the frequency spread usually caused by a tire against a surface obstacle. That analysis on the device saves having to transmit the video itself over long distances. The conclusion that there was a thump at a particular location can be communicated in a million times smaller amount of data than the entire video itself.

Fighting Crime with video

Another example of distributed analytics might be help in resolving crimes. Video surveillance is common in a store setting. One possible application of analytics might be that after a crime occurs, a query might go to the surveillance systems in a particular part of town, or in the branches of a set of stores, essentially asking the question: "Did you see anything unusual between 3:00 and 4:00pm on Jan 15th?"

If the video has nothing in that time, it might return nothing, but is might have pictures of people walking by, and investigators might select a couple of stills for further examination.

One form of distributed analytics is the incorporation of face recognition technology directly in the video monitoring system. Instead of saving hours and hours of video as direct video data, the conclusions of the face recognition are saved – for example, gender and estimated age – which saves a lot of space and we can therefore keep records for considerably longer.

Retail

While the practice of using data to make better decisions has been around for decades, most retailers still pride themselves in making critical business decisions based on their experience and gut feeling. Experience and gut feeling are definitely invaluable for any decision but the business decision outcomes based on combination of experience and real data, yield much better results.

Within retail, compared to brick and mortar stores, online retailers have distinct advantage as it is much easier for them to collect data on each and every click, purchase and login of the customers. It is also much easier for online retailers to test various web components and layouts based using A/B testing tools. The analytics tools market is quite mature to help the online retail world.

With the rise of technology trends like the dramatic rise of mobile phones usage, ubiquitous presence of WiFi networks, cheaper storage and new tools like Hadoop and Spark, Innovative online retailers are actually starting to use sensor based data (WiFi, Beacons, Lasers) to analyze customers "in-store" behavior and use that to make business decisions. The IOT, sensor-based analytics, when used properly can help provide retailers with deeper understanding of customer behavior, what they are looking at, how much time they are spending in each department; dwell times.

On the backend side of things, retailers can use this location data in real time to visualize customer and employee presence, optimize the floor plan layout and manage staff in the most optimal way. Having this kind of "in-store" data in real-time can really give a distinct advantage and level the playing field to compete against online retailers:

- Specifically, retailers can use IOT; WiFi, lasers and beacon based analytics to understand customer behavior inside the store, what they are looking at and how much time they are spending in each department.
- IOT-based analytics and apps enable Retailers to engage with customers at a very different level by providing highly relevant product suggestions, discount coupons, relevant promos, etc.
- WiFi and beacon-based apps enable retailers to leverage analytics and provide value added services like directions, specific details about product, product availability etc.

- There are numerous ways to leverage this technology, for e.g.: In hospitality industry, a museum can leverage these IOT based analytics to provide detailed information on museum artifacts making it a highly immersive experience for visitors

6. INTERNET OF THINGS

Some surprising opportunities where IoT products exist today:

Music Players

Millions of people today use a music discovery service known as "Last.FM." This allows users to find and listen to song in a way similar to the function that FM radio offered years ago, except for one thing: it knows what you are listening to. It can keep track of all the songs you have listened to. The action of recording that you have listened to a particular song is called *scrobbling*[7]. It can be configured to remember songs played on any number of devices, such as smart-phones, laptops, even dedicated MP3 players.

The cloud-based server tracks all the devices into a single account. You can easily go and find out how many times you have listened to a particular song in a multi-year time span.

It is easy to understand that the byproduct of this data collection is that they have accurate popularity information about what songs people are listening to, as well as associations between the kinds of songs that the same person might listen to. This information allows them to produce an "instantaneous top-forty" most popular songs listened to today, this week, and this month. The value of this information is such that it would be easy to imagine such a capability to *scrobble* the song might be built into all music players in the not-too-distant future.

Furniture and Household

Have you ever wanted your bed connected to the Internet? That is an option now on some of the high-end beds. A particular well-known brand offers "SleepIQ" which is a system that monitors heart rate, breathing rate, and movement to track how well someone is sleeping. It provides a graphical display of the data it has collected, and it suggests settings that you might use on the bed to get a better night of sleep. Like many things it is a mixture of attraction and repulsion. Who wants their bed to inform a cloud service of all their movements? At the same time, those with sleeping problems might greatly appreciate the additional insight into how well they are currently sleeping, and what to do about it.

An important use for IoT is keeping tabs on elderly. A company named "Lively" makes sensors that can be deployed around the home to monitor activity and communicate it. A concerned relative might be able to know when the refrigerator door is opened, or when the pill box is opened, and all this is tracked.[8]

It does not observe the inhabitants directly, but rather indirectly though the devices that they use regularly.

Such a system might save a life if it recognized that the pattern suddenly changed and alerted others to the problem. Lively voluntarily offers a privacy policy that promises to get users" consent before sharing their data with anyone and only after stripping out personally identifiable information. Lively is primarily in the business

---

[7] http://www.wired.com/2012/11/richard-jones-scrobbling/

[8] "Can legal system keep up with pace of innovation?" San Jose Mercury News, Feb 22, 2015

of collecting information, and so treating privacy as a primary concern is easy, however a company that delivers a refrigerator, for instance, may not have the same precautions in place for the data they collect.

Retail Opportunities

The state of the art in devices today keeps moving forward. Vending machines located in Japanese train stations now automatically detects gender or age of purchaser, and shows beverages accordingly. TESCO supermarkets can automatically detect when items are gone from the shelf and order replenishment. Also they monitor queue length in the cashier and manage appropriate number of active cashiers so as not to let customer wait.

The new Levi's stadium in Santa Clara has beacon technology which can guide visitor to the closest restroom, and helps food shops deliver ordered food to their seats.

Isetan, a large department store in Japan, differentiates themselves from others in service quality by analyzing store staff's behavior using beacon technology. They collected information showing which salespeople were in in location across many days. The correlated this with how well they contacted and served customers. They have found out that good performing store associates doesn't really walk around the store - which they were encouraged to do traditionally in the training. Instead, they stand in particular area of the store from which they can observe what the customer is doing and contact at the right timing. This insight was not known until they mined the data of the location of the sales personnel.

At the National Retail Federation show in January 2015, one food retailer said that they found that demand changes drastically according to the trend information such as stocks, news broadcasting, and online media. They hope to use analytics of data in order to predict the demand in real time. The essential point of analytics is to support decision-making. Retailers are relatively mature in employing diagnostic techniques, so predictive and prescriptive approaches are the next steps. If we can predict what happens and what should we do, we can even automate decision and take right action.

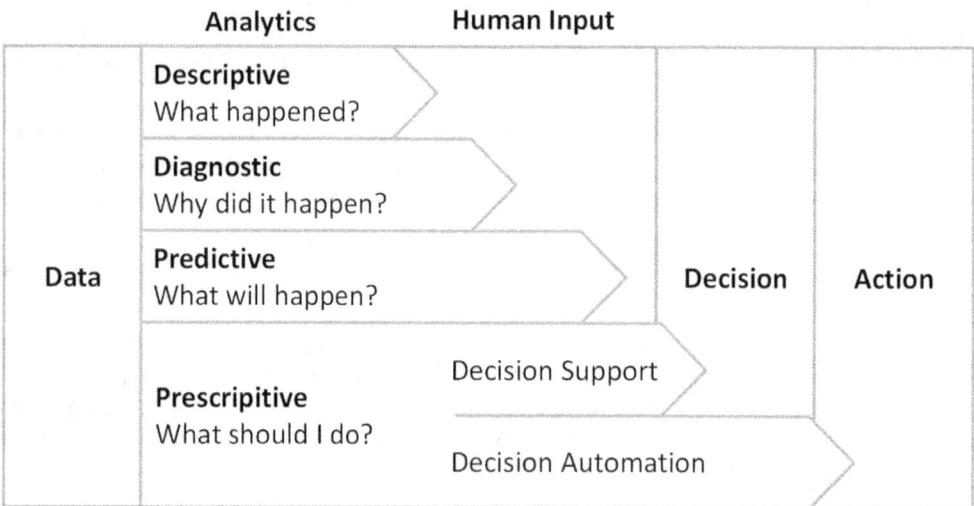

Figure 3. Varying Extents of Data Mining & Analytics (Gartner)

7. PERSONAL DATA WAREHOUSES

Earlier we gave evidence that the amount of data being collected is outstripping the ability to transmit that data to a central location for analysis. This was based on looking at the capacity of the Internet in relation to the growth of acquired data. A cloud-based analytics collector would be subject to this limitation because all the data would have to go through the Internet. Locally, devices on the IoT are likely to enjoy a much higher connectivity and bandwidth on the premises. Within a residential home you are likely to have a subnet with more bandwidth that is being used. The bottleneck is typically the connection to the Internet service provider (ISP).

At the same time, as the number of smart devices grows, it is unlikely that those devices will be uniformly endowed with analytics capabilities. It would seem logical that a new form of device will arise that will be configured to aggregate and mine data from other IoT devices: a Personal Data Warehouse (PDW). Imagine you wear an activity monitor for most of the day; but when running you use a GPS-enabled run tracker, with a heart monitor; and furthermore your shoes have activity monitors in them as well. A PDW might be programmed to consolidate the information from these different sources, and provide a single source for seeing progress toward exercise goals.

A PDW would be a general purpose device for collecting data and analyzing it. Such a device offloads processing from a centralized analytic capability, and provides effectively data compression to avoid the problem with data growing faster than telecom speed.

The deployment and distribution of PDWs will provide the same kinds of benefits that big data would provide, but it would not be centralized. Again, the pendulum swings to the decentralized capability by deploying the analytics capability into the field.

Privacy

Privacy considerations are essential. Applications like those above could only be proposed if there were at the same time sufficient privacy protection that the people owning the surveillance equipment felt that their own personal privacy would not be violated. Had we proposed ten years ago that your telephone would be used to determine where traffic jams were located; you might have considered that a large privacy violation, however, it is done today without alarm. It is more likely that applications will be proposed that have less of a privacy concern.

In the US there are very few laws that govern this data collection. If you set the collection up for yourself, it seems safe enough, but how can you know that the collected information will not find its way to others - particularly other businesses who value such information highly for their sales and marketing efforts. South Korea based LG Electronics was criticized for collecting information on the programs its television users watched – even if the users opted out of such collection. LG shifted its policy, but that triggered more complaints since consumers are denied access to some smart TV services unless they permit their viewing information to be shared with advertisers.

Tyranny of Complexity - Can it all be managed?

We must not ignore the one big challenge with distributed data mining: complexity. The advantage of a central data warehouse is that since there is only one, the programming of that one is consistent with itself. When distributing mining capability to the field, we run the risk that different data collectors will be analyzing the data slightly differently. This remains a large challenge, and one that we will have to wait and see how, or if, it is resolved.

8. SUMMARY

To summarize, we have covered how the growth of the IoT will bring about large stockpiles of data, but that data will not in general be be transported to a central, processing location. Mining that data has the potential to yield valuable byproducts. Instead of moving all the data to central repositories, it is more reasonable to envision a world where analysis of the data is distributed to the field, and only the result of the analysis need to be communicated back.

It is hard to imagine that all IoT devices will have sufficient capability to do this analytics on their own, particularly since the value is observed only when a collection of devices is monitored separately. We then speculated the emergence of a new, specialized device, a personal data warehouse that is able locally collect information from the devices around it, and at the same time offer regular analytic techniques to handle the distributed data mining in a coordinated way.

BPM to Go:
Supporting Business Processes in a Mobile and Sensing World

Rüdiger Pryss, Manfred Reichert,
Alexander Bachmeier, Johann Albach,
Ulm University, Germany

ABSTRACT

The growing maturity of smart mobile devices has fostered their prevalence in a multitude of business areas. As a consequence, business process management (BPM) technologies need to be enhanced with sophisticated and configurable mobile task support. Together with characteristic use cases from different application domains (e.g., healthcare and logistics), this chapter will give insights into the challenges, concepts and technologies relevant for integrating mobile task support with business processes. Amongst others, we will show how mobile task support can be enhanced with location-based data, sensor integration, and mobile task configuration support. The latter is based on a 3D model for configuring mobile tasks on smart mobile devices.

This chapter focuses on mobile task assistance in general and mobile task configuration in particular.

INTRODUCTION

In the computer industry, the emergence of smart mobile devices has opened up new and exciting perspectives. Nowadays, we carry computers in our pockets that wouldn't have been out of place on a supercomputer ranking of the 1990s. The ever-increasing ubiquity of these smart mobile devices and the dynamic nature of Business Process Management (BPM) technology demand new concepts and systems that may execute tasks on these smart mobile devices. For example, these would assist a physician during her daily work through sophisticated mobile task and process support may ease her work significantly (Pryss et al., 2015).

However, the smooth integration of smart mobile devices into the BPM landscape has revealed a multitude of specific challenges. One way to properly meet these challenges is through a sophisticated mobile task execution framework that can be smoothly integrated with existing BPM environments. A specific challenge in respect to such an integration concerns the proper configuration of mobile tasks. In this context, the chapter proposes an approach that enables the domain expert (i.e., the end user) to configure mobile tasks by a 3D process model, which is displayed in an augmented reality view on his smart mobile device.

Motivation

Although smart mobile devices have evolved rapidly (Geiger et al., 2014), they still show limitations that need to be considered when integrating them with BPM systems (Pryss et al., 2014). Current limitations include, amongst others, limited battery power, instantaneous shutdowns, data inconsistency, and unreliable network connectivity. As a consequence, one cannot simply migrate the execution of complete processes and their tasks onto mobile devices without coping with these issues.

The last years have shown a divergence towards smart mobile devices, with only a small number of tasks not ported to a smartphone or tablet in one way or another. Accordingly, users more and more expect from their smart mobile devices to assist them in fulfilling almost every task they have processed on their stationary PC. BPM technology should pick up this trend, not only due to emerging customer demands, but also because it opens up new and promising opportunities.

In general, BPM serves as an approach to analyze, model, automate, monitor, and optimize business processes in a variety of application domains (Weske, 2012). Particularly, BPM improves business IT alignment and serves as a glue between information technology on one hand and the various business stakeholders (e.g., staff, customers, and business partners) on the other (Knuplesch et al., 2012). In this context, *BPM to Go* represents our vision of coupling smart mobile devices with BPM technology in order to enable flexible process and task assistance of mobile (knowledge) workers. Amongst others, the following areas need to be touched to make this vision a reality:

1. Mobile task execution & configuration
    a. Smooth integration of mobile tasks in existing BPM environments (Pryss et al., 2015)
    b. Tackling challenges of a mobile execution context (e.g., instantaneous shutdowns) (Pryss et al., 2014).
2. Distributed mobile processes (e.g. cross-departmental as well as cross- organizational scenarios) (Zaplata et al., 2010).
3. Collaborative mobile processes (e.g., mobile checklists for collaborating knowledge workers) (Mundbrod & Reichert, 2014).
4. Mobile office in combination with BPM (e.g., using personalized smart mobile processes) (Ko et al., 2009).
5. Cyberphysical systems & Internet of Things in combination with BPM (Atzori et al., 2010).

Contribution

This chapter focuses on mobile task assistance in general and mobile task configuration in particular.

The primary goal of mobile task assistance is to enable end users to work on their business tasks using smart mobile devices instead of stationary PCs. Smart mobile devices not only allow performing these tasks almost everywhere, but also enable measurements on the spot. Furthermore, the interaction of mobile workers with smart mobile devices fosters process and task flexibility as well as a faster completion of business processes. Figure 1: Mobile task approaches depicts three approaches for integrating smart mobile devices with BPM. The support of these mobile scenarios reveals challenging issues that need to be properly addressed, e.g., in respect to process exception handling (Pryss et al., 2013) and task failure management (Pryss et al., 2014).

Beyond the collaborative and mobile aspect, the connectedness of smart mobile devices and their sensors allows for the integration of additional context information and parameters with business process execution. For example, a location parameter may be used to store information about the location a particular task has been performed (Pryss et al., 2013).

The usage of smart mobile devices need not be limited to the execution of single tasks. As demonstrated later in this chapter, the ability to perform task configurations on the *Go* opens up new opportunities. Our idea for mobile task configuration revolves around the concept of a 3-dimensional, augmented reality view of processes, which is generated using a common Android smart mobile device. Based on this view, domain experts and users shall be enabled to configure and optimize mobile tasks on the *Go*.

To the best of our knowledge, there are no comparable approaches dealing with mobile task execution and configuration. In particular, the configuration of mobile tasks directly on a smart mobile device has not been properly addressed so far. However, there exist approaches that characterize a *mobile context* through a set of parameters (Kocurova et al., 2012). Usually, only few contextual parameters are considered and these mainly focus on process characteristics (Yang et al., 2012); e.g., to be able to decide what shall happen with a task if a device is unavailable. In turn, no parameters are maintained to characterize the different kinds of failures (e.g., low battery power).

The remainder of this chapter is structured as follows: First, we discuss lessons learned in the context of real-world scenarios and relate them to the *"BPM to Go"* vision. Second, we describe relevant aspects of mobile task execution along an example from the healthcare domain. Finally, we present an augmented reality engine being able to display a 3D representation of processes on a smart mobile device to assist users in configuring mobile tasks.

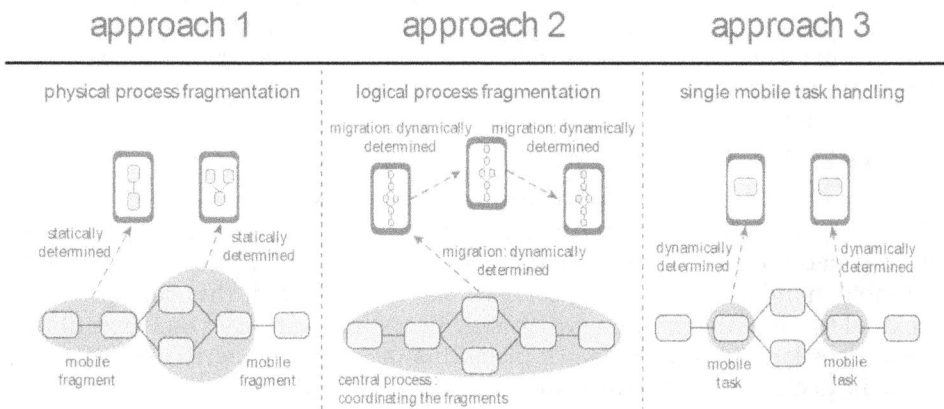

Figure 1: Mobile task approaches

BACKGROUND INFORMATION AND CONSIDERED SCENARIOS

In the context of our research on mobile processes (Pryss et al., 2014, Pryss et al., 2010), a number of approaches have been designed that provide robust ways to deal with the challenges of mobile task support. To further evolve these approaches (cf. **Error! Reference source not found.**), both their feasibility and their limitations were investigated in a number of real-world scenarios. The three considered approaches differ in respect to the part of the process known to a device, the information exchanged, and the way the tasks are synchronized between the devices.

To confirm the importance of mobile task support, different application scenarios from the healthcare, automotive and psychology domains were investigated. As will be shown in the course of this chapter, the benefits of enhancing scenarios with smart mobile devices are manifold. For example, through the use of smart mobile devices, the efficiency of how tasks are performed can be improved. As another benefit, data can be collected and recorded at the right time and place (Schobel et al., 2014). The occurrence of erroneous data can be decreased since data can be processed and checked on the device actually running the data collection procedure.

While some of the discussed challenges are known to mobile app developers in general, the execution of mobile tasks in the context of business processes particularly raises demands in respect to robustness and usability. We present four categories of challenges to be addressed in this context.

Challenge 1: Process-related

Regarding process-related challenges, the focus should be on data consistency. In general, network connectivity will be unstable, compared to a physically immobile system like a workstation or server. During any point in the execution or configuration of a process, network connection problems or power issues might arise. Consequently, the challenge is to keep the data of executed process consistent even when unexpected exceptions occur.

Challenge 2: User Behavior

An issue not specific to mobile environments, but of higher relevance compared to stationary devices, concerns the user as a source of irregularities. For example, a user might inadvertently shut down his device or put an application currently executing a task into a sleeping state. Since the multi-tasking capabilities of smart mobile devices are not yet up to the standards known from other systems, the application will have to respond in a safe way to, for example, an unexpected shutdown of the device. Note that this is particularly important in the context of Challenge 1 (i.e., data consistency) as well.

Challenge 3: Mobile Context

The mobile space opens up new opportunities regarding process execution. Specifically, the location and time context may be utilized to foster process and task support. In general, the location of smart mobile devices can be determined within a reasonable margin of error using sensors like GPS. In turn, this data provides a contextual factor of the process, which may be utilized to restrict task execution to those devices located near the work place this task shall be performed. Note that this might decrease the distance to be covered by an actor in the process when performing individual tasks.

Challenge 4: Sensors

Nowadays, most smart mobile devices are equipped with a plethora of sensors. This includes sensors to locate a device using a satellite positioning system (GPS), cameras and microphone. Other sensors available are heartbeat sensors, thermometers, or blood sugar sensors. Smart mobile devices equipped with them may be used to provide physical data during process and task execution, mitigating the need to capture this data by using specialized devices or – even worse – requiring manual user input.

The particularities of smart mobile devices should be considered as specific challenges when targeting a mobile task execution. However, the sensors of these mobile devices are also able to provide valuable parameters in the context of process execution. When dealing with real-world scenarios, several of these parameters could be used as an integral part of the processes, proofing their validity and importance in a business process context. When investigating the real-world scenarios, we identified a large number of parameters that can be related to the four categories mentioned above. To give an impression, for each considered real-world scenario,

Table 1: parameter validity in real-world scenarios shows parameters of the four categories that turned out to be relevant.

SCENARIO	DATA CONSISTENCY	SHUTDOWNS	LOCATION	CAMERA
HEALTHCARE (WARD ROUNDS)	✓	✓	✓	✓
AVIATION (AIRLINE CATERING)	✓	✓	✓	✓
LOGISTICS (WAREHOUSING)	✓	✓	✓	✓
AUTOMOTIVE (PRODUCTION)	✓	X	✓	✓
PSYCHOLOGY (QUESTIONNAIRES)	✓	X	✓	X

Table 1: parameter validity in real-world scenarios

MOBILE TASK EXECUTION & CONFIGURATION SUPPORT

BPM not only deals with the modeling, configuration and execution of business processes, but also with their monitoring and evolution. The presented work deals with task configuration support, specifically the implementation of this support on smart mobile devices. We have designed an example of a process demonstrating how smart mobile devices and features enabling mobile configuration support may serve to enhance scenarios.

We consider a scenario involving a nursing home and a patient with dementia. A nurse performs her scheduled rounds to check the status of all patients she is responsible for. To assist her in accomplishing this procedure, she is equipped with a smart mobile device that is linked with a BPM system. Thereby, the procedure around a single ward round shall be implemented as a process in the BPM system and its corresponding tasks be executed as mobile tasks on her smart mobile device. The simplified scenario referring to a particular patient is depicted in Figure 2 (in terms of the BPMN notation). The latter also shows how data is exchanged between the smart mobile devices of the actors involved in the process.

After finishing the care of a patient, the nurse shall visit the patient scheduled next, as displayed on her smart mobile device. As part of the process, the device can display the tasks that need to be performed for a particular patient. In particular, we consider patients suffering from dementia and – most of them – from diabetes as well. To reflect the latter, one of the tasks involves a routine check of the patient's blood sugar level. When the nurse enters the room of a specific patient, an automated check is performed as to the whereabouts of the patient. To facilitate this check, every patient has been equipped with a small tracking device that permits indoor and outdoor localization, thus decreasing the possibility of a disoriented patient that might wander off and get lost outside the area of the nursing home.

Assume that the smart mobile device of the nurse queries the patient's tracking device and determines that the patient is currently not available in her room. The task execution engine on the mobile phone is further able to indicate to the nurse that the respective patient is currently in the cafeteria. The nurse may now choose to send a notification to the patient's device, informing her that she is needed in her room. The nurse declines the request and decides to walk to the cafeteria and take the patient with her back to the room in order to be able to administer the required tests.

The nurse administers a blood sugar test on the patient using a computerized measurement strip. The blood sugar level is then automatically stored in the electronic patient record. At the same time, the blood sugar value is compared with thresholds set by a doctor. Assume that the system discovers that the levels are elevated, but not high enough to warrant immediate action. As defined by the parameters of the process, the doctor will be notified about the blood sugar levels and an appointment be automatically added to calendar of the doctor.

The nurse finishes the test and proceeds with the next patient (i.e., the next process will be started and executed). Without any interaction of the nurse, an event was created by the device after the test strip had been used as the number of test strips has reached a level below the threshold set. As part of this event, an automatic request is sent to the person managing the devices that the supply of test strips for this device needs to be replenished.

A logistics expert is notified about the situation and proceeds with the nursing home's storage facility to gather the required test strips (i.e., the device may be restocked at the next opportunity). He is also equipped with a smart mobile device that includes augmented reality features. Once notified about the task, the device determines the location of its owner and can, if requested, show the location of these test strips in the warehouse and navigate him to the aisle in question.

Once the logistics expert reaches the location of the test strips, the camera of his smart mobile device is able to scan the barcode in the field of view of the camera. Once the camera recognizes the barcode of the needed package of test strips, the package is marked on the augmented reality view.

This feature serves to minimize the possibility that a wrong set of test strips is taken from the warehouse. The expert takes the visually marked package of test strips and delivers them to the desk, where the blood sugar testing device can be restocked in the near future.

In summary, the scenario makes use of the following parameters:

- *Mobile Context*: Location of patient, nurse, logistics expert
- *Mobile Context*: Date and Time
- *Mobile Context & Process Related*: Device crashes
- *Sensors*: Blood sugar level
- *Sensors*: Camera (product barcodes)
- *User Behavior*: Instantaneous shutdowns

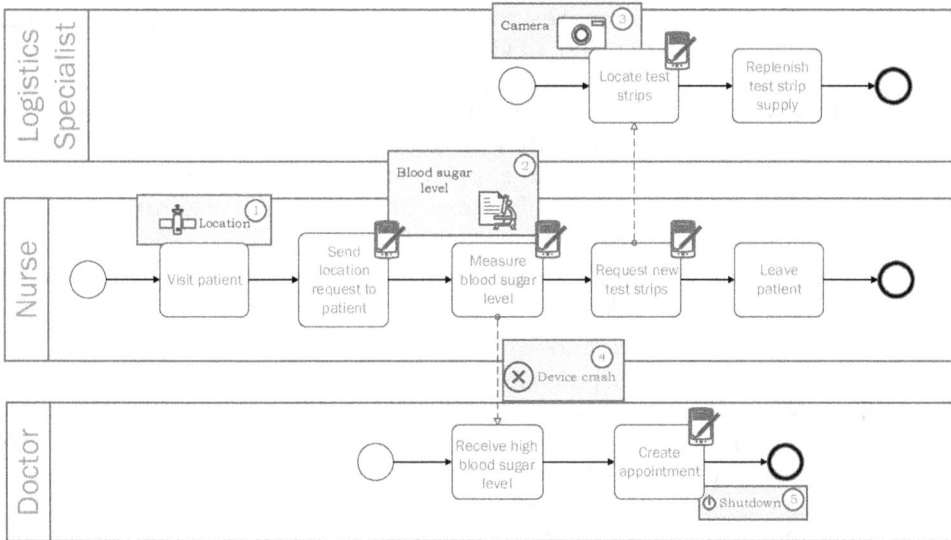

Figure 2: Nursing home Scenario

Regarding the parameters and challenges advocated in the previous section,

Figure 2: Nursing home Scenario shows specific parameters (numbered rectangles) that may be applied to this scenario. We briefly summarize their significance as follows:

(1) *(Mobile Context)* The location of the nurse and the patient needs to be determined as required by the possible situations described for the scenario (e.g., patient is not in her room).

(2) *(Sensors)* Blood sugar levels are determined using a smart mobile device.

(3) *(Mobile Context & Process Related)* During the transfer of the blood sugar levels, the smart mobile device of the nurse might crash. Regarding this scenario, data consistency is crucial as incomplete or erroneous data might have severe consequences on the patient's health. Once the device is safely restarted, therefore, the data must be completely transmitted to the BPM backend.

(4) *(Sensors)* The logistics actor uses the camera of a smart mobile device to correctly identify the correct test strips.

(5) *(User Behavior)* Assume that when using the smart mobile device, the doctor receives the required data to make an appointment, the doctor shuts down his device. In such a case, exception handling techniques must be applied to determine whether the appointment has been created correctly once the device becomes available again, or another doctor must be notified about the situation.

As the scenario illustrates, the use of smart mobile devices provides new possibilities in terms of available process parameters. This scenario only illuminates the task of executing processes on smart mobile devices.

In general, in many business processes scenarios various difficulties and exceptions must be tackled at the time a process leaves the planning stage and is implemented for real-world execution. In this particular context, the sheer number of parameters and execution anomalies are often not foreseeable during design time. By equipping users with the ability to view and modify their specific tasks directly on the smart mobile devices, the overall process execution can be significantly improved. In this context, the ability to modify, remove or add parameters becomes an issue. In particular, we propose that the parameterization may improve overall process execution in case the parameter operations (i.e., add, remove, and modify) may be applied at the place a task will be executed. Such a configuration scenario constitutes mobile task configuration on the *Go*.

As we envision mobile task configuration on the *Go*, a scenario comprising the following three steps can be realized:

(1) A user works on a task and wants to modify one of the parameters. Therefore, she uses her smart mobile device to identify the task corresponding to the process she is working on. Based on this information, a model is created which provides information about the process and the mobile task for which she wants to change the current parametrization.

(2) Using the model, she can modify, remove or add parameters.

(3) Once the parameters are changed, the user may view the modified task and process. Following this, the parameters can be discarded or saved. In the letter case, new process instances will be executed based on the modifications.

3D MOBILE TASK CONFIGURATION SUPPORT

Our implementation of this vision is based on a 3D augmented reality engine that is able to display processes and parameters. Additionally, it enables users to modify processes, mobile tasks and parameters directly on the smart mobile device.

Currently, we base our mobile task configuration support on two different procedures. These procedures identify the mobile tasks that shall be modified. First, for tasks which are currently executed, we use the parameters and the current location of a user to identify them. Second, for tasks which are not executed, the smart mobile device uses a marker approach (1) to identify a task. After the procedure to identify a task that shall be modified, the smart mobile device uses its internal or server side storage to fetch the data for this task and display all relevant information on the mobile screen (2). Using gestures, the user is now able to view the task and its process based on the 3D augmented reality engine (3).

This section focuses on our implementation of a 3D augmented reality engine that can be used to display a process using a marker or running process information to determine the process that needs to be displayed. We provide an in depth explanation of the architecture and the underlying computational model. We show how our engine can display processes and tasks using a system of markers as task identifiers (we restrict our explanations to this procedure of task detection due to the lack of space.). Additionally, we present the way users can modify the representation of the model, including the possibilities of zooming into specific sections of the model. Furthermore, the task configuration view is shown. Finally, we discuss aspects we revealed when using our approach in practice.

Architecture

The architecture of the prototype is shown in Figure 3. It can be divided into three parts: (1) an augmented reality framework, (2) a graphics engine and a (3) process parser. The AR-component allows us to recognize different markers (e.g., QR-Codes) using the smart mobile device's camera system. As the next step, after the marker is recognized, a process is loaded, parsed and computed. After this procedure, it can be visualized by the graphical component. Each instance of the involved components operates in its own thread (one for the AR-component, one for every parsed process, and one for the renderer). This approach became necessary to deal with user demands (e.g., response time). Usually, after the process is loaded and parsed, only up to two threads are running. Consequently, there are still enough capabilities for fluid interactions, considering that many modern smart mobile devices make use of a quad core CPU architecture.

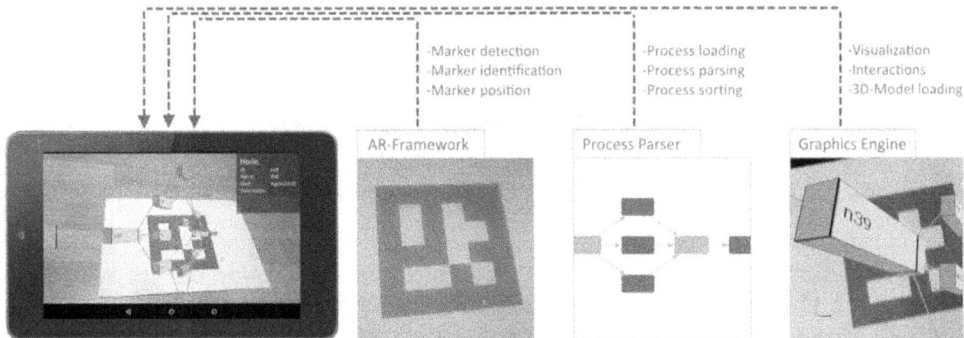

Figure 3: Architectural model

Computational Model

Before a user may interact with a graphical representation of a process, it is necessary to create separate objects, which - once linked together - will form a 3D representation of a process graph. To simplify this task, objects can be produced using a variety of 3D modeling tools. The current prototype is able to load the exported *.OBJ model format (cf. Figure 4), which stores a model's geometries and its materials in two plaintext files along with required textures. Those files are loaded in the prototype's own parser and represent single nodes of a process graph. The second input information are XML files that contain process data.

For example, they contain nodes with several attributes as well as edges controlling the flow. Note that we currently use process models based on ADEPT (Dadam & Reichert, 2009). Then, the parser creates single objects out of parsed information, fills them with their attributes, and optimizes them to minimize crossovers in edges. Finally, the parser notifies the renderer that new graph data is available. Once the renderer gets informed, the loading of 3D models that correspond to the process graph's nodes is initialized and edges between them are established using lines.

When a previously linked marker is visible to the camera, the process graph can be drawn onto the screen. Thereby, a mapping between graph data and its visual representation exists. This mapping is used to get additional information about rendered objects (e.g., to provide touch events for these objects).

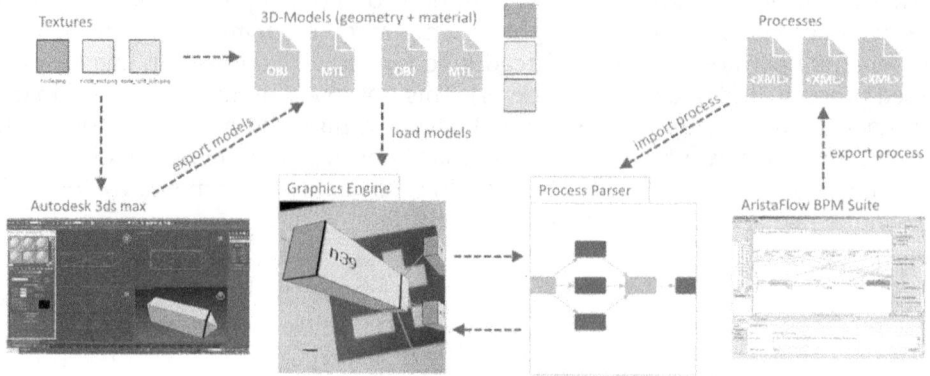

Figure 4: computational model

Process Representation

The visual representation of the graph consists of the previously loaded 3D models, which represent the nodes of the graph (cf. Figure 5). Each node has its own visual counterpart, thus every node type has a different visual representation. At the moment, four types are supported: start/end, conditional join/split, parallel join/split and plain tasks. Additionally, a second model in front of nodes contains the name of the node using a bitmap texture. All nodes are connected by edges according to the edge type.

All nodes and edges are placed on the plane, spanned by the x- and y-axis. Only backward directed edge types are placed behind a node's plane. This allows us to provide the user with the entire graph without overlapping edges on the first plane, and limiting the possible overlaps on the second one.

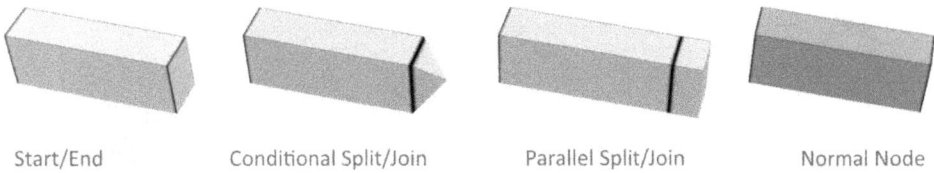

| Start/End | Conditional Split/Join | Parallel Split/Join | Normal Node |

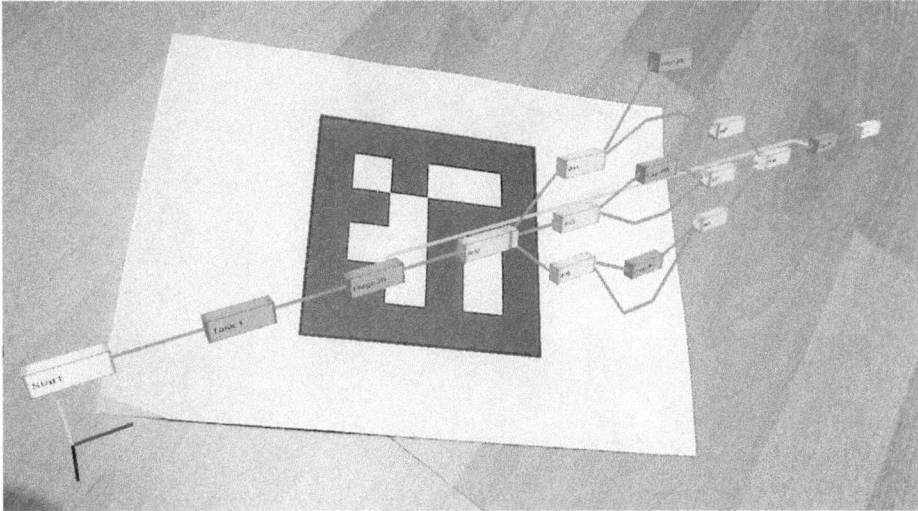

Figure 5: Example process with corresponding marker

Interaction Dimensions

As we lifted the two dimensional graphical process representation to the third dimension, we gained additional interaction possibilities (cf. Figure 6). The third dimension allows us to move a process, like its two-dimensional counterpart on two axes and zoom into it, which corresponds with a translation on the third axis.

Additionally, it is possible to rotate the complete process visualization along the three axes, which provides a useful feature (frequently reported by users) to interact with process graphs. In particular, this feature provides a better overview on the backward directed edge types on the second plane (and behind the actual graph). Furthermore, with a single touch, it is possible to extract information about nodes and visualize the details for mobile task configuration on the mobile screen.

To provide a better experience during the interaction with such processes, an option to pause the marker detection was introduced. Note that the user is not required to keep pointing the device's camera towards the marker.

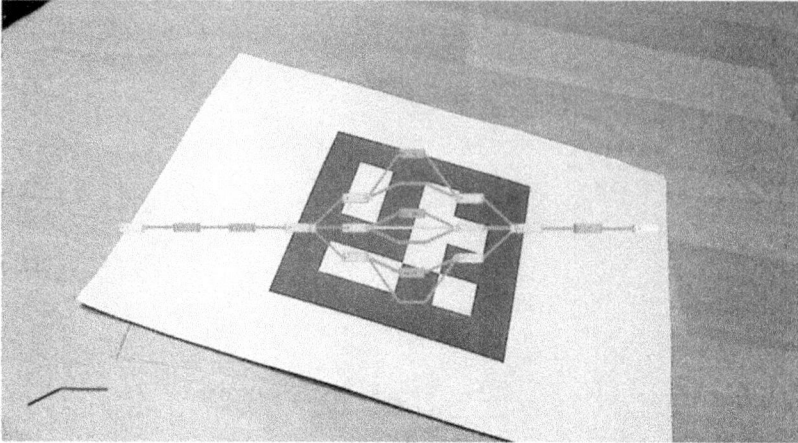

Translation

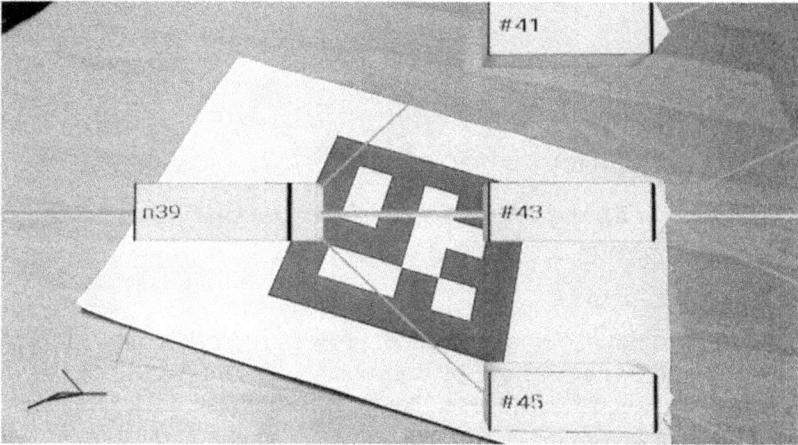

Zoom

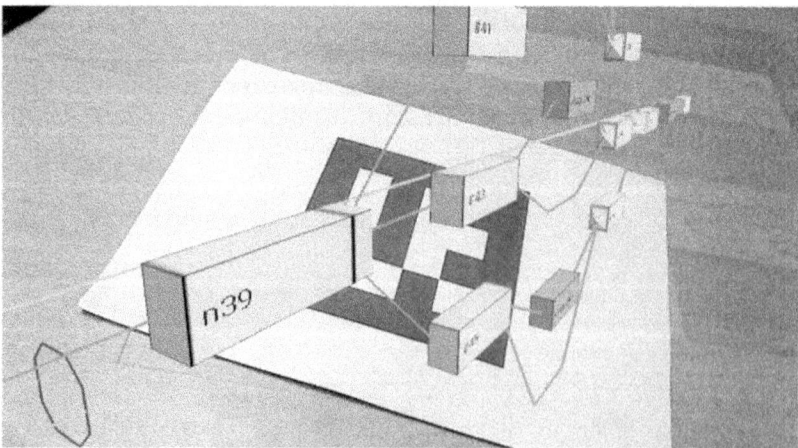

Rotation

Figure 6: user interface to modify Process representation

Task and Process Operations

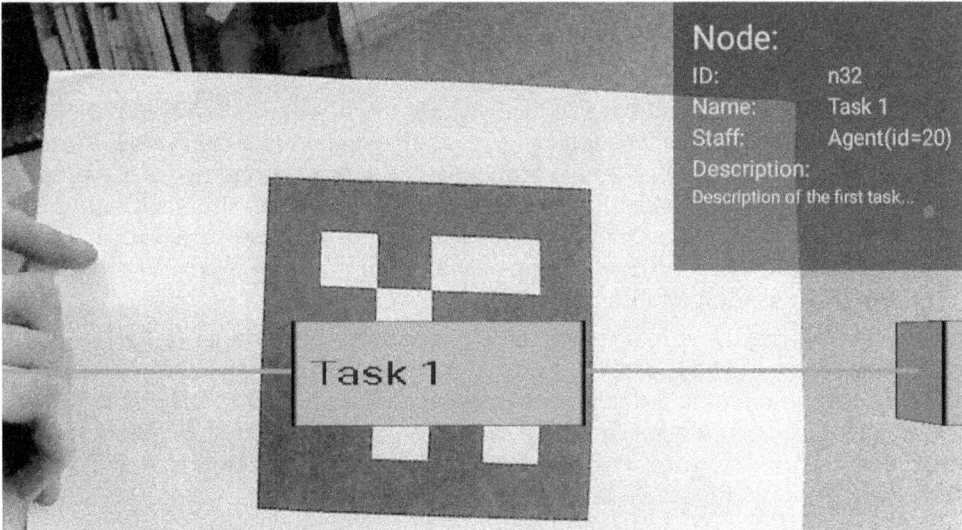

Figure 7: Task view with corresponding marker

Finally, the framework includes algorithms to process all relevant attributes (e.g., actor, parameters, etc.) of mobile tasks. Following this, users may modify or analyze attributes like shown in Figure 7.

Lessons Learned

The currently implemented 3D model has a few limits. Models, seen as single objects, should have a suitable size. If models are exported with wrong scales, the renderer will use them without rescaling, resulting in a misleading or miscalled representation. Additionally, the parser for the *.OBJ file format does not support the full feature set offered by the exported models. This means that single geometries of those models should have one material with at least a diffuse map as texture. Furthermore, single texture maps should be stored in a format supported by Android. Only the PNG format was used during testing, but JPEG and many other formats should work as well, depending on the Android version and its support for the format in question.

Looking at a complete graphical screen consisting of multiple models, the GPU usage has to stay within limits. The texture sizes and triangle counts of geometries should stay within a reasonable limit to maintain a fluid experience during usage.

Mobile Task configuration using 3D Models

The architecture (cf. Figure 3) and computational model (cf. Figure 4) we presented have shown their feasibility in practice. In particular, we were able to meet the requirements of a fluid and useful experience to configure mobile tasks directly on a smart mobile device. Altogether, 3D models are a proper technique to show process graphs on smart mobile devices. In particular, domain experts have reported that using such models - combined with the interaction possibilities - meet their requirements to configure mobile process tasks. In addition, our approach has shown its flexibility in practice. At the beginning of the project, we only used process models based on ADEPT (Dadam et al., 2009). In turn, for integrating process models based on BPMN (Weske, 2012) with our framework, only minor changes became necessary. In general, to be flexible has been a major challenge (Reichert & Dadam, 1998; Reichert & Weber, 2012) in the context of BPM frameworks that must be properly addressed. Finally, the integration of a marker component to identify mobile tasks has been reported as very useful.

Assume that within a warehouse, a clerk wants to check whether one of the used shelves is related to a business task (e.g., to manage goods for this shelf). Furthermore, the clerk wants to check the parameters of the corresponding mobile process task that manages the goods of this shelf. For this purpose, the shelf has a QR-code that may be utilized by the smart mobile device of the clerk to identify it. Based on the QR-code information, the clerk is able to modify and analyze the corresponding mobile process task and its parameters.

However, we learned that many more challenges must be addressed. For example, at the moment we only support the Android mobile operating system. In turn, other mobile operating systems must be addressed as well. In addition, the different ways of implementing mobile applications (Schobel et al., 2013) must be also carefully considered to properly meet the requirements of integrating sophisticated mobile task configuration support with existing BPM environments.

CONCLUSION

This chapter introduced a novel approach for configuring mobile tasks of business processes. The presented approach using 3D models allows for a new support of users to configure mobile tasks. In general, the goal to provide a sophisticated mobile task configuration support is challenging. We have shown that in various BPM scenarios such configuration support is promising. We have further shown that in mobile scenarios, a sheer number of parameters and execution anomalies may result to capture the process context properly. Finally, we have shown that in a mobile context these parameters are often not foreseeable during planning stages. Consequently, new techniques must be provided to configure these parameters on the *Go*. We have additionally learned that user acceptance is crucial in the context of mobile task configuration support.

Our approach has shown its feasibility, but many more challenges have to be addressed in this context. Altogether, we consider mobile task execution and configuration support as shown in this chapter as one challenging and promising category of *BPM to Go*. Our future work will consider distributed and collaborative processes in the context of *BPM to Go* as well.

REFERENCES

(Reichert & Dadam, 1998) Reichert, M. and Dadam, P.: ADEPTflex-Supporting Dynamic Changes of Workflows Without Losing Control. Journal of Intelligent Information Systems, Special Issue on Workflow Management Systems, 10(2): 93-129, Kluwer, 1998.

(Dadam & Reichert, 2009) Dadam, Peter and Reichert, Manfred: The ADEPT Project: A Decade of Research and Development for Robust and Flexible Process Support - Challenges and Achievements. Computer Science - Research and Development, 23(2): 81-97, Springer, 2009.

(Dadam et al., 2009) Dadam, P. and Reichert, M. and Rinderle-Ma, S. and Lanz, A. and Pryss, R. and Predeschly, M. and Kolb, J. and Ly, T. and Jurisch, M. and Kreher, U. and Goeser, K.: From ADEPT to AristaFlow BPM Suite: A Research Vision has become Reality. In: Proceedings Business Process Management (BPM'09) Workshops, 1st Int'l. Workshop on Empirical Research in Business

Process Management (ER-BPM '09), Ulm, Germany, September 2009, LNBIP 43, Springer, pp. 529-531, 2009.

(Ko et al., 2009) Ko, R. and Lee, S. and Lee, W.: Business process management (BPM) standards: a survey. Business Process Management Journal, 15(5), 744-791, 2009.

(Atzori et al., 2010) Atzori, L. and Iera, A. and Morabito, G.: The internet of things: A survey. Computer networks, 54(15), 2787-2805, 2010.

(Pryss et al., 2010) Pryss, R. and Tiedeken, J. and Kreher, U. and Reichert, M.: Towards Flexible Process Support on Mobile Devices. In: Proc. CAiSE'10 Forum - Information Systems Evolution, Hammamet, Tunisia, June 2010, LNBIP 72, Springer, pp. 150-165, 2010.

(Zaplata et al., 2010) Zaplata, S. and Hamann, K. and Kottke, K. and Lamersdorf, W.: Flexible execution of distributed business processes based on process instance migration. Journal of Systems Integration, 1(3):3-16, 2010.

(Knuplesch et al., 2012) Knuplesch, D. and Pryss, R. and Reichert, M.: Data-Aware Interaction in Distributed and Collaborative Workflows: Modeling, Semantics, Correctness. In: 8th IEEE Int'l Conf on Collaborative Computing: Networking, Applications and Worksharing (CollaborateCom'12), Pittsburgh, Pennsylvania, United States, October 14–17, 2012, IEEE Computer Society Press, pp. 223-232, 2012.

(Kocurova et al., 2012) Kocurova, A. and Oussena, S. and Komisarczuk, P. and Clark, T.: Context-aware content-centric collaborative workflow management for mobile devices. In COLLA 2012, The Second International Conference on Advanced Collaborative Networks, Systems and Applications, pages 54-57, 2012.

(Reichert & Weber, 2012) Reichert, M. and Weber, B.: Enabling Flexibility in Process-Aware Information Systems: Challenges, Methods, Technologies. Springer, 2012.

(Weske, 2012) Weske, M.: Business process management: concepts, languages, architectures. Springer Science & Business Media, 2012.

(Yang et al., 2012) Yang, Y. and Lu, W. and Domack, J. and Li, T. and Chen, S. and Luis, S. and Navlakha, J.: Madis: A multimedia-aided disaster information integration system for emergency management. In Proc 8th Int'l Conf on Collaborative Computing: Networking, Applications and Worksharing (Collaboratecom), 2012.

(Pryss et al., 2013) Pryss, R. and Musiol, S. and Reichert, M.: Collaboration support through mobile processes and entailment constraints. In Proc 9th Int'l Conf on Collaborative Computing: Networking, Applications and Worksharing (Collaboratecom), 2013.

(Schobel et al., 2013) Schobel, J. and Schickler, M. and Pryss, R. and Nienhaus, H. and Reichert, M.: Using Vital Sensors in Mobile Healthcare Business Applications: Challenges, Examples, Lessons Learned. In: 9th Int'l Conf on Web Information Systems and Technologies (WEBIST 2013), Special Session on Business Apps, Aachen, Germany , 8 - 10 May 2013, pp. 509-518, 2013.

(Geiger et al., 2014) Geiger, P. and Schickler, M. and Pryss, R. and Schobel, J. and Reichert, M.: Location-based Mobile Augmented Reality Applications: Challenges, Examples, Lessons Learned. In: 10th Int'l Conf on Web Information Systems and Technologies (WEBIST 2014), Special Session on Business Apps, Barcelona, Spain, April 3-5, 2014, pp. 383-394, 2014.

(Mundbrod & Reichert, 2014) Mundbrod, N. and Reichert, M.: Process-Aware Task Management Support for Knowledge-Intensive Business Processes: Findings, Challenges, Requirements. In: IEEE 18th Int'l Distributed Object Computing Conference - Workshops and Demonstrations (EDOCW 2014), Ulm, Germany, IEEE Computer Society Press, pp. 116-125, 2014.

(Pryss et al., 2014) Pryss, R. and Musiol, S. and Reichert, M.: Integrating Mobile Tasks with Business Processes: A Self-Healing Approach. In: Handbook of Research on Architectural Trends in Service-Driven Computing. pp. 103-135, 2014.

(Schobel et al., 2014) Schobel, J. and Schickler, M. and Pryss, R. and Maier, F. and Reichert, M.: Towards Process-Driven Mobile Data Collection Applications: Requirements, Challenges, Lessons Learned. In: 10th Int'l Conf on Web Information Systems and Technologies (WEBIST 2014), Special Session on Business Apps, Barcelona, Spain, April 3-5, 2014, pp. 371-382, 2014.

(Pryss et al., 2015) Pryss, R. and Mundbrod, N. and Langer, D. and Reichert, M.: Supporting medical ward rounds through mobile task and process management. Information Systems and e-Business Management, 13(1): 107-146, Springer Berlin Heidelberg, 10.1007/s10257-014-0244-5, 2015.

Unlocking the Power of the Internet of Things Through BPM

Stuart Chandler, Virtusa, USA

Two major technology developments require organizations to pay close attention to the Internet of Things (IoT)—in order to be effective and run their businesses more efficiently and capitalize on revenue-generation opportunities. These include the explosion and the continued rapid growth of touch points through which businesses can connect to their customers. Whether it's through websites, mobile devices, POS systems, kiosks or social media, all of these touch points invite disruption and generate massive amounts of data.

The second development is the emergence of advanced analytic tools, such as Big Data, which allow organizations to make use of data they previously could not access at all. It's now possible to process all the data that IoT networks produce and convert those into meaningful information. Armed with this new information, businesses can alter their business processes to perform more efficiently and more intelligently, and ultimately achieve better business results.

Consider the hypothetical case of John Simpson as he and his wife and their three girls travel from New York to California for his best friend's wedding. Because John taps into a travel service that has integrated the IoT networks of an extensive travel industry supply chain, he can book his entire trip—airline, rental car, hotel and restaurants—all through one Web portal. The same portal even lets him buy tickets to Disney Land to take advantage of the extra time his family has before the wedding. John is enjoying a seamless and customer 'delight' experience.

Not only is the supply chain integrated across all the major travel service providers, but also connected to the National Weather Service. So when major thunderstorms break out on the day of the trip in Kansas City (where John and his family need to catch a connecting flight) the IoT network connected to the entire supply chain immediately identifies John's trip as one that requires changes.

The intelligence built into this IoT network not only allows the system to automatically present John with a new flight plan, it also alerts the rental car company and the hotel that his arrival will be delayed. The system even knows to cancel his dinner reservation for the first night and to push the visit to Disney Land to one day later. John just needs to review the new itinerary on his smartphone and press <Accept>.

But in today's world, this level of "magic" just simply does not happen. In reality, when the weather in Kansas City occurs, John may not know until it's too late unless he has subscribed to a weather message alert on his weather app. Even then it is just an alert, and he will still have to contact the airline to determine the options and make his own decisions for new flights. Furthermore, he will have to contact the car rental company, the hotel, the restaurants and Disney Land. John's got a busy day ahead of him, thanks to the weather!

John faces this challenge because systems across industry supply chains don't talk to each other. They use different technologies and different data models, and each business within the supply chain is protective of their territory. There's just no way to bring them all together seamlessly to deliver the kind of story he wants to hear.

But customers don't want to hear this. And if businesses take a good look at the challenge from the standpoint of the technologies that are available today, it's actually not impossible to deliver experiences such as the one that John dreams of.

In this article, we discuss the challenges the IoT presents as well as the opportunities, but more importantly, we also cover the capabilities of the key tool that makes it possible to leverage the IoT within individual companies and across supply chains—Business Process Management. We also demonstrate how BPM can enable your organization to wrap its arms around all the opportunities the IoT offers and how BPM demystifies what it takes to manage all the data generated by the IoT.

So Just What Is the Internet of Things?

As defined by Webopedia, the Internet of Things (IoT) refers to a network of physical objects connected to the Internet that have the ability to communicate with other Internet-enabled objects, devices and systems. The IoT extends Internet connectivity beyond traditional devices—such as desktops, laptops, and smart devices to everyday things that can also utilize embedded technology to interact with each other—all via the Internet.

The basic concept of the IoT has existed almost as long as the Internet, but its practical application to drive and enhance business processes has just started to take off in recent years in terms of enhancing customer experiences, facilitating innovation for companies, and disrupting traditional models for delivering products and services. Businesses can create their own IoT through an interconnected network of physical objects and applications that they embed with electronics and software sensors.

Connectivity and communications across an IoT network can then be managed by a software system that enables the objects to exchange data with each other and automatically make intelligent decisions on how to change their behavior. An IoT network can also exchange data with internal company databases so that the performance of corporate assets, employees, customers and business partners can all be monitored and managed.

Each object in an IoT network is uniquely identifiable through its embedded computing system and is able to interoperate across the existing Internet infrastructure. The objects can refer to a wide variety of devices such as healthcare monitoring devices, utility system sensors, devices that assist field technicians, and home-based systems such as entertainment and appliances.

Given the number of objects that a business can add to its IoT network, the IoT can generate large amounts of data aggregated at a very high-velocity—thereby increasing the need for smarter processes and more intelligent data indexing, storing and processing.

Massive Data Sets Present Complex Challenges

The IoT can and does produce massive amounts of data. This creates several complex challenges when it comes to harnessing the IoT in a way that allows businesses to transform the data into actionable information and generate business value:

- **Varying Forms of Data**: The IoT produces structured data, such as databases, and complex unstructured data, such as social media and proprietary data constructs. The data comes in a wide variety of formats from all the different objects that co-exist on an IoT network. Take for example, the challenge of integrating video data with temperature readings so that a software system can identify a suspicious object. Enterprises need to find a way to extract, transform and load the data, and then tie all the data together to generate actionable information. In addition, enterprises need to determine which data should be actionable rather than ignored.

- **Varying Objects**: An IoT network can include a wide variety of physical objects and mobile devices that transmit data while also defining the context and the situation in which the data was produced. Each object and device requires an interface, and the data produced must be converted so information from multiple devices can be fed into a system that then makes decisions on how to manage all the devices across the IoT network. The variety of devices could include assets on a manufacturing line and various customer touch points as well as devices communicating information from field personnel.

- **Lack of Standards**: When enterprises try to orchestrate the multitude of applications collecting data from the IoT, they need to create standards. But not everyone has agreed on what the IoT standards should be. This creates a problem because businesses with a common supply chain need standards in order to exchange data and effectively service their shared customers.

- **Privacy**: The need for privacy can limit the use of an IoT network. Just how much information are customers willing to let a business access? They may not want to provide all their data to their product and service providers—particularly when it comes to medical and financial information. Businesses will thus need to gain customer trust if they want to tap into all the data they produce when using a product or service.

- **Trust**: This challenge involves the willingness to accept the concept of software systems making decisions on behalf of humans. Fully leveraging an IoT requires trust from within the company and trust from customers that any decision an IoT management system makes will turn out to be the right decision. Consider the case of cars that can drive themselves. Is the general public ready to sit in the back seat and assume the on-board IoT network will get them where they are going—safely?

- **Compliance**: As is the case with internal corporate systems, businesses will also need to ensure that their IoT networks comply with any relevant industry regulations. Given the variety of IoT devices, the varying data structures and the amount of data that an IoT network can produce, achieving compliance can become very complex and expensive.

With greater connectivity to many more devices than ever before, the IoT also creates a whole new set of customer activities and demands to which businesses must react. When calling an airline to reschedule a flight, customers will expect the airline to automatically notify all the other businesses that are providing services on that trip. Businesses thus need to create new processes in order to orchestrate the process effectively—within their own business workflows and in conjunction with the workflows of their supply chain partners.

IoT Opportunities Well Worth the Investment

Along with the challenges of the IoT come many new opportunities that could cause disruptions in the way consumers interact with their product and service providers. These opportunities and potential disruptions make overcoming the challenges of the IoT well worth the investment.

The use of smartphones as payment instruments is a prime example. Instead of consumers carrying multiple credit and debit cards with them, they can now store all these cards on their smartphones, and many businesses now accept smartphone payment transactions. This disruption is inserting a new brand, such as Apple Pay, in between consumers and the credit card companies. The new process gives smartphone providers another opportunity to interface directly with consumers while taking away opportunities from the credit card companies.

The IoT can produce tons of new information on customer and supply chain activity as well as employee and asset performance that businesses simply could not tap into previously. Acquiring and processing this data intelligently can expose many new opportunities that businesses can capitalize on to increase the revenue generated by their existing sales channels. They can also create new revenue streams while reducing operating costs, enhancing customer interactions, and improving business-process efficiencies. Businesses also gain new opportunities to disrupt, innovate and jump in front of customers—by handling all activities and needs with one interaction involving many inter-connected events across a supply chain.

For example, healthcare organizations can now create better quality of life for their patients—with immediate access to data outputs produced by home-based and mobile health monitoring systems. Before, patients had to communicate symptoms over the phone, or their care provider needed to be present. There were thus islands of measurement and medical insights that patients and care providers had to manually bring together.

But now, thanks to the IoT, medical devices can take readings on a patient's vitals and reach out to medical organizations through a smart process that alerts personnel when readings indicate a problem—such as a person with dementia who wanders away from their home in cold weather. Also consider the case where a medical device connected to an IoT prompts a doctor or nurse to proactively call a patient at home with vital signs that indicate a health incident may be imminent.

Envision the value of a utility company providing a home monitoring system that detects a natural gas leak. By connecting with the house's IoT, the system can automatically shut down the electric system while also notifying emergency personnel and warning the homeowner to leave the house immediately.

In the travel industry, customers want to know about and have the ability to change more than just one part of their trip logistics. They want one place where they can see all their logistics on their mobile device and then click just once to update the entire itinerary. If a sudden weather event impacts the trip, a smart IoT network will know who the customer is, and if the travel logistics need to be adjusted. It then provides an automated process to update the entire supply chain.

The many ways in which IoT networks can inter-connect across supply chains and across different industries are almost endless. If a homeowner's boiler on an IoT network fails and then links with a weather reporting service to verify cold weather is ahead, the IoT network could trigger a connection to the homeowner's service provider to initiate action. Taking it further, replacement options could trigger financing, including government funding options if qualified. The opportunities are endless.

UNLOCKING THE FULL POWER OF THE IoT

Orchestrating the complexities of the IoT is the prime opportunity for businesses today—with a particular focus on enabling connectivity, extracting and loading the multitude of data, and then transforming that data into information that can be acted upon intelligently. Business Process Management (BPM) methodology holds the key to achieving successful orchestration across all the complexities that the IoT presents.

BPM, which is commonly applied to many business functions, focuses on improving business performance by managing and optimizing a company's business processes. BPM enables businesses to improve efficiency, increase effectiveness and react more nimbly to changes. BPM also provides a framework to visualize, enable and execute complexities in business. Successfully applying BPM methodology thus directly impacts the cost-savings and the revenue-generation capabilities of a business.

When it comes to the IoT, BPM provides the core tenet for successfully orchestrating all the major components:

- Physical objects operated as assets by the company—such as machines on a manufacturing production line.
- Physical objects operated as products by customers—such as home-based utilities, HVAC systems and medical monitoring devices.
- Customer mobile devices—that can record physical movements as well as social media activities.
- Employee mobile devices—that can record customer sales and service interaction results.
- Devices and software systems that monitor and measure all the customer, employee, asset and product devices.

Applications that generate data and business-process actions run on each IoT device as well as on corporate core systems. BPM applications apply intelligence to each device and core or back-office system that influences and impacts overall business process decision-making and execution.

As BPM orchestrates all of the activities among the IoT components, company personnel know when to act and how to act intelligently—based on a customer, asset, product or employee that needs assistance, or that acts in a manner indicating an opportunity for selling a new product or service. With activities determined by BPM, IoT devices can be connected to each other, and personnel can consume the information easily through instantaneous access to then make service and sales decisions.

Rather than waiting for a customer or employee to call for help, or waiting for an asset or product to break—BPM essentially makes it possible for personnel to proactively address situations in real time—by collecting all the data an IoT device generates and orchestrating better and timely outcomes. BPM also streamlines synchronization and the decisioning of other IoT devices while orchestrating the necessary actions—based on pre-determined rules—to make decisions on how to best service customers, employees, assets and products.

BPM APPROACHES TO OVERCOMING THE IOT CHALLENGES

Part of the BPM development process to overcome the IoT challenges involves determining the true value of data generated by all the various devices that a business can interact with, both from the perspective of the business and the perspective of the customers. Not every device that a business has access to should be connected to an IoT. BPM provides a structured way to think about the data each device produces and what customers need.

If the two are not aligned, BPM helps the business adjust. BPM can also provide a structure to create proper decision-making processes for customers so that they too can interact with devices in the most efficient way possible.

One of the key paradigms to realize while applying BPM is that businesses can't simply build applications that become hardened to the point where they act in isolation. Before building applications to manage an IoT network, businesses need to leverage BPM so applications can talk to each other and act smartly as to how to react to the output of other IoT applications.

The output of one application thus triggers processes in other applications. Rather than an island of execution that has no value beyond the decision an application initially triggers, integrating the application with other applications enables other processes to occur automatically. Taking this approach allows BPM to define the applications that are necessary to truly harness an IoT network.

To be truly effective, BPM should also be considered from the customer perspective rather than the business perspective. Otherwise, businesses will create barriers for customers who want to buy and use products and services. Considering the IoT from the lens of the customer viewpoint gives customers more options. If the business first determines what the IoT should do for customers, it can then harness those things that are effective while ignoring those that are not.

Mobile technologies, for example, can give patients the ability to communicate their vitals to their healthcare provider no matter where they are. This is much more desirable and creates a much higher quality of life compared to being tied down to their home or hospital bed unnecessarily. The IoT thus gives healthcare providers the ability to enable patients to function according to their terms by moving the devices that track their vitals—through mobility.

Ultimately, BPM helps businesses leverage process-centric software to create greater efficiencies and handle more complexity in how they interact with customers. This is critical, because no human can deal with all the complexities of the IoT.

Even Better Outcomes in the Near Future

When it comes to the IoT, BPM characterizes a business in terms of its execution to create more efficient and more adaptable processes. Instead of just asking customers to give you their information and selling them a product or service, applying BPM to the IoT creates processes that define exactly how to proceed from customer product requests to receiving payments, and from customer service requests to resolutions—along with all the process elements that create efficiencies and generate the best outcomes along the way.

Businesses that share customers across a supply chain will need to develop standards to share information and allow customers to dictate which of their business relationships will own the window into the other parts of their ecosystem—the travel industry and utilities are prime examples. Processes will need to be encapsulated and embedded across the travel supply chain so the airline industry, for example, could act as the primary decision entity over a traveler's entire trip. If the flight changes, the airline can then shift the logistics for the hotel, the car rental, leisure activities and restaurants.

In the utility sector—heating, electricity, water and telephone companies can benefit from integrated IoT networks that tell each other when the performance of one of their systems will impact the others. This will eliminate the need for customers to interact separately with each utility. By leveraging BPM, utilities can ultimately share embedded processes with each other to alter the usage of their respective services in order to balance the overall outcome for home owners. Imagine if all the utilities of a home could act in concert when an emergency strikes.

When it comes to creating an integrated IoT network backed by BPM across supply chains, many industry giants are likely to balk. Some may think that asking a company to grant access to another company that can then go into an application and alter the actions of a product or service on behalf of a shared customer is asking too much.

But undoubtedly, some companies will push the envelope, just like Apple is doing with Apple Pay and its relationship to the credit card companies. In other industries, Goliaths may fight against integrated supply chains, but they will likely find themselves getting toppled before they realize it. The demands of consumers—and those companies willing to provide services in the way consumer want them—will continue to nip at the heels of the giants. The time has arrived for the Goliaths to get nimble and start breaking some eggs.

In the coming years, as more devices connect to IoT networks, and as management systems grow more intelligent, BPM can help your company set the stage for even better outcomes—within your business and across all your supply chains that share customer interactions. And with the additional information the IoT generates, more consumer activities can be encapsulated and acted upon. This will vastly improve customer service and generate many more new opportunities to sell additional products and services.

Who knows, within the next couple years, maybe *your* company will cause the next major disruption that rocks your industry!

Creating the Information Foundation for iBPM

David RR Webber, Horizon Industries, USA

PREFACE

The old adage is, "You don't know what you don't know." How can we create intelligent software to augment BPM processes with decision-making by leveraging predictable information assets?

ABSTRACT

When creating predictable information assets solution, architects face a bewildering array of competing approaches and theoretical philosophies. What choices make the most sense in the context of iBPM (intelligent BPM), and what are their pros and cons? How can we handle multilingual needs in a pluralistic distributed workforce?

Big strides are being made in the ability to semantically package knowledge and information that can be processed logically and predictably. Tools that integrate into BPM solutions can provide a smooth and rapidly deployable information infrastructure. Existing open source and open standard software assets are considered along with complementary industry products.

INTRODUCTION

Leveraging Information

So often we see software applications struggle to be successful. One of the core reasons is likely a poor original or later extended information model with linkages and definitions lacking precision and purpose. The duplication of content and reuse of tables out of context are then further issues. These same challenges apply to BPM solutions also.

Today's information technology departments are struggling to meet the ever accelerating demands of managing information and sharing information across internal and external systems.

What we present here are concepts and tools along with practical examples in the context of BPM that can provide the essential foundation for a successful information architecture approach.

We also show ideas and the potential for transcending traditional software applications development to extract the most benefit from investing in an information architecture approach. Accelerating how BPM software applications themselves are built and delivered by automating common programming tasks. There really is no choice for successful agile businesses given the accelerating demands for services and solutions that analyze the enterprise data assets and extract competitive business value.

Information and iBPM

The Gartner Group has identified the 10 core components of iBPM solutions[1]. Every single one of those components has a dependency and need for clear and distinct information that is semantically robust that can be leveraged to drive the iBPM capabilities beyond where they are today. Here we examine how and discuss actual implementation details. First we look at what is needed to make up that information foundation.

The Semantics of Information

There is a lot of religious fervor involved in semantics. There are no right or wrong methods and approaches nor mathematical proofs that apply for modeling information and semantics. Consequently people have taken approaches that suit their purposes and are most familiar and comfortable for them. They also gravitate toward communities that embrace those modeling techniques and advocate for them.

What we have learned however is that there are best practices and techniques that yield more optimal results whatever particular brand of approach is being used and especially for iBPM purposes. Particularly for creating the information architecture underpinning that provides consistent, predictable and robust iBPM solution delivery.

We have also learned overall that abstraction techniques work along with neutral representations; rather than sole reliance on a specific technology such as historically with W3C XSD schema. Being able to handle a pluralistic ecosystem of formats and syntaxes and products is a major need for iBPM solutions.

The overall complete semantic view for information is shown in the Figure 1 here and the various components that constitute a complete view. An iBPM will need to manage and leverage all the components shown. For reference, with W3C XSD schema, the aspects captured are Structure, Annotations and Content model.

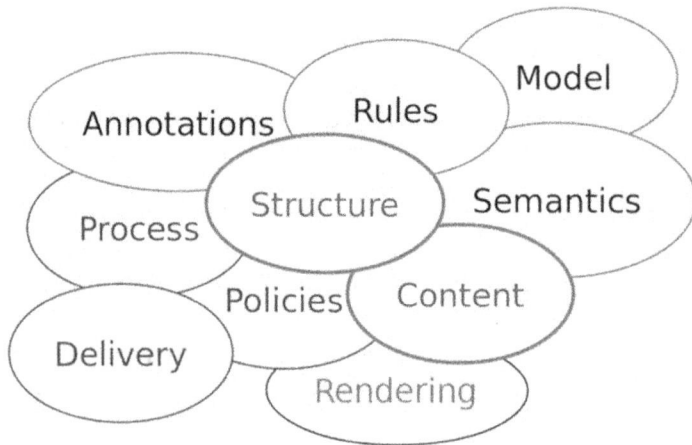

Figure 1: Information Semantic Components

Next the associated chart below here shows the swim-lanes and ecosystems that exist today from the perspective of deploying iBPM applications.

UML Technologies	W3C Schema	XML Technologies	Web
UML	XSD	XML	HTML
XMI	Namespace	XQuery	JavaScript
Patterns	Enumerations	XSLT XPath	JSON
Associations	Cardinality	Elements	REST
Stereotypes	Facets	Attributes	SQL
Inheritance	Complex Types	Content	
	Objects	SOAP	
Audience:	**Audience:**	**Audience:**	**Audience:**
Data Modellers / Designers	Software Developers and Middleware Engineers	General content delivery and applications; content engineers; rules representation systems; multimedia delivery; geospatial systems	Web application developers
		Open-XDX	

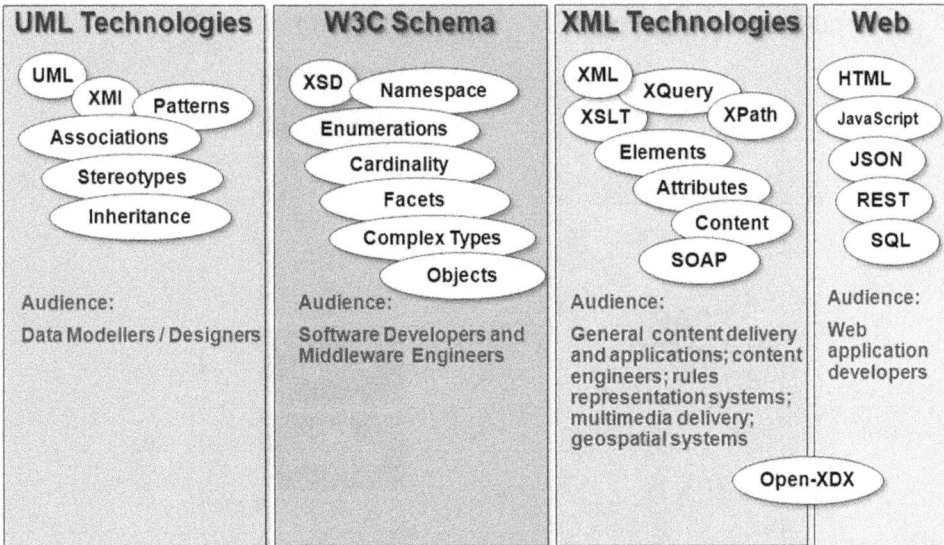

Figure 2: Technology Delivery Swim-lanes

The swim-lanes and communities help understand the overall challenges and preferred technology tools with approaches. However what we need to understand are the techniques and methods that span across the whole ecosystem and provide consistent value.

BUILDING THE FOUNDATION

Leveraging Semantic Abstraction

When we drill into the overall semantics of information we realize that there are three key facets of knowledge.

- Information Structure and relationships,
- Content Rules with dependencies and then
- Definition formally of a component and the business concepts associated with it.

These are also enshrined programmatically in W3C RDF, however you do not need to exclusively use RDF in order to gain the benefits of this understanding. Any representation that enshrines those concepts is equivalent and a simple transformation can render RDF/OWL representations.

The schematic here shows the approach used by the OASIS Content Assembly Mechanism (CAM) standard[2], and the abstraction approach that is using a plain XML representation to create templates of information content around the Structure, Rules and Documentation (annotations).

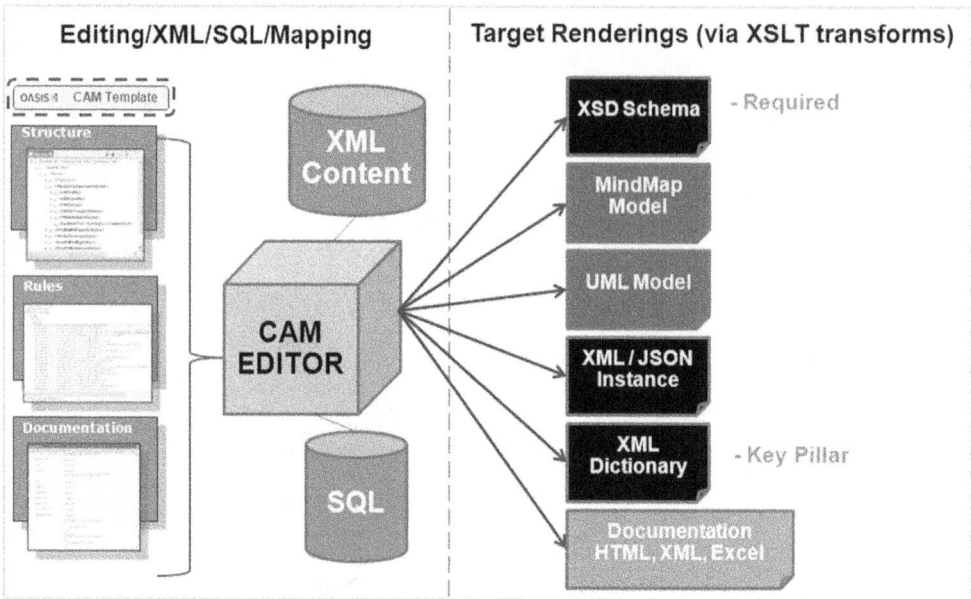

Figure 3: CAM Template Delivery

The importance of using plain XML and what this enables cannot be overstated. It allows rapid solution delivery using familiar XML tools such as XSLT programming in tandem with Java and SQL as needed. By way of example; the CAM Editor open source toolset is able to render CAM templates as UML/XMI, Core component dictionaries, XSD schema, Mind Maps, Hibernate bindings, BPM forms and HTML reports. Next we consider further lessons learned with information best practice.

Reliable Techniques

With neutral abstraction definitions, the first order of business is to ensure predictable information labeling by applying consistent Naming and Design Rules (NDR). The ISO11179 specifications, UN/CEFACT Core Components Technical Specifications (CCTS) and then US government National Information Exchange Model (NIEM)[3] initiatives have all worked on NDR specifications and leveraging and enhancing each other's work.

The core basis for a NDR is consistent naming using three components, the item name, the context and the representation term. To illustrate this consider this example: "Person"; this triggers the classic responses of person what, person where and person how? So "Person" by itself does not give enough context for machine representation and processing in an iBPM. More accurate therefore would be an example from CCTS – PersonName and the full definition of the components. Additionally each component identified should pass the NDR checks shown in Figure 5.

Example – Person Name

- Person Name (ABIE)
    - *Verified Details?* (ASBIE)
  - First Name (BBIE)
  - Middle Name (BBIE)
  - Last Name (BBIE)
    - *Previous Name?* (ASBIE)
  - Language Code (BBIE)

Language Code may exist independently of Person Name

Verified Details and Previous Name are flags that denote additional information about the entity they are associated with

There are three component items aspects:

structure relationships; content rules; definitions (RDF triple)

Figure 4: CCTS Example - PersonName

Notes: ABIE, BBIE and ASBIE are terms used in CCTS. They equate directly in XML to ABIE=Parent Element, BBIE=Child Element and ASBIE=Attribute.

The list of representation terms is shown in Figure 5 below and is again an area of best practices and community preference rather than exact science (especially when applied to non-English based domains).

Naming and Design Rule (NDR)

- The NDR checks are based on the Core Components Technical Specification (CCTS) as interpreted by the NIEM NDR guidelines.

- Consistency in use of upper and lowercase naming convention is checked

- The naming representation terms are inspected for leaf element items and attributes

- The naming convention is evaluated to look for use of these terms in the name itself (representation terms): 'Amount', 'Count', 'BinaryObject', 'Graphic', 'Picture', 'Sound', 'Video', 'Image', 'Code', 'Category', 'Currency', 'EMail', 'DateTime', 'Date', 'Time', 'Indicator', 'Format', 'Length', 'Width', 'Height', 'Weight', 'Level', 'Measure', 'Mode', 'Method', 'Numeric', 'Number', 'Price', 'State', 'Status', 'Rank', 'Flag', 'Frequency', 'Format', 'Size', 'Unit', 'Value', 'Version', 'Rate', 'Required', 'Percent', 'Quantity', 'Qty', 'Description', 'Comment', 'Reason', 'Location', 'Instructions', 'Text', 'Title', 'Type', 'Year', 'Month', 'Day', 'Name', 'URI', 'URL', or 'URN'; or that ends with 'Days', 'Hours', 'Minutes', 'ID', 'Id', 'Identification' or 'Identifier'

- A domain may use specialized terms that are not shown here and this can be configured accordingly.

Figure 5: Naming and Design Rules Representation Terms

Overall the need is to be able to evaluate a given information template and produce metrics that can guide developers toward semantically robust solutions.

Notice the use of the representation terms 'Name', 'Details' and 'Code' in Figure 4 above to indicate the type of information component. This qualifies the component and allows further determinations. For example the term 'Date' delimits the content and then further checks can be made to ensure a content rule is defined setting out the date formatting, (such as YYYY-MM-DD), allowed for that component. If the content rule is missing, an error can be noted in the evaluation report for the template.

In the CAM toolset, there is such an evaluation report that combines NIEM best practices with practical lessons learned building interoperability and information exchanges combined with enabling components reuse and reliability. More details of that can be found in the presentation deck available from the Slideshare web site – on the NIEM Evaluation Report [4]. The end objective for this is to build a consistent information foundation.

This information foundation consists of the tables and components that underpin the iBPM processing. The CAM toolset is used to capture as template representations the database records and information assets that power the overall application solution. These templates then can be used to generate software components, and allow analytics tools to function consistently [5]. The next step is cataloging all the components being used, evaluating them also and then ensuring they are consistently defined across the whole enterprise.

Dictionaries and Components Registry

For an iBPM solution you need to ability to collect the information components definitions into a formal dictionary and registry. The diagram here shows the key concepts.

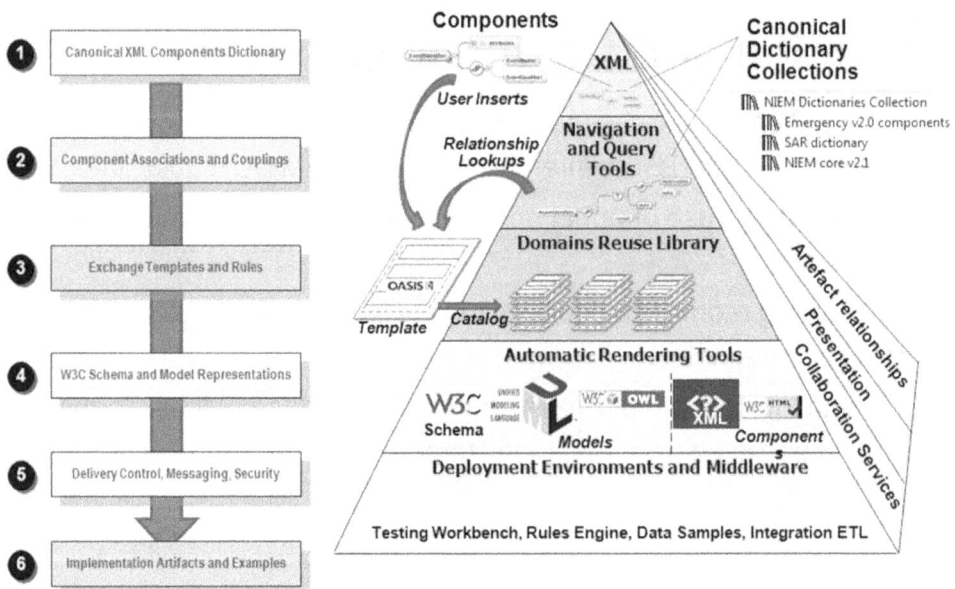

Figure 6: Dictionary and Registry Orchestration

As the diagram shows the dictionary representations along with the templates of the actual usage within the iBPM application then drives the generation of the physical software that is needed including BPM forms, records and tables, software bindings and information exchange patterns (as with examples shown previously in Figure 3 above).

Dictionaries are also critical in enabling multilingual representations. Each component in the dictionary can contain language translations. Additionally each component can be linked to the business concept and term definition (again with multilingual definitions) stored in a SKOS [6] repository such as the open source iQvoc project [7] is providing. The work that ISO/TC 154 is doing to create a Business Terminology Repository (BTR) is following this approach [13].

Next we consider practical use cases of iBPM solutions and how they have been delivered leveraging the techniques discussed.

ORCHESTRATING THE IBPM SOLUTION

Example Use Case

The State of California needed a solution for managing children in its care and looked to BPM to provide the necessary business process management. The diagram here shows the overall high level business process involved.

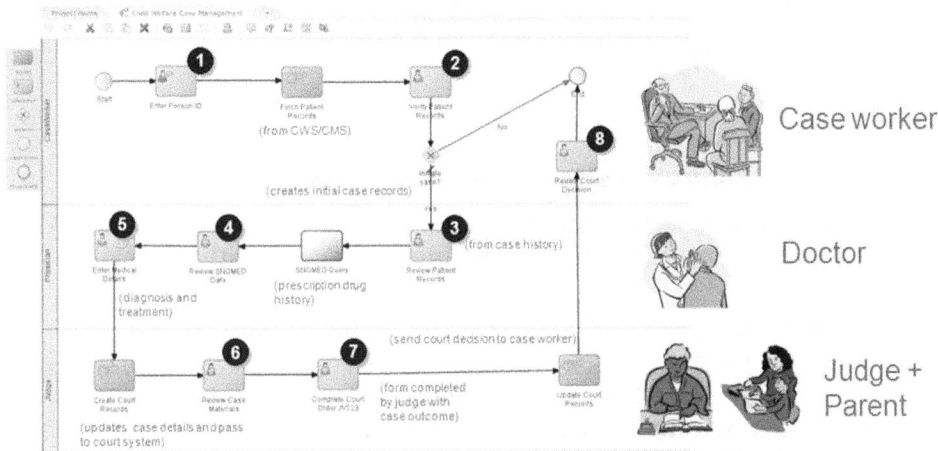

Figure 7: California Child Welfare Business Process

One such prototype solution can be found described at our reference resource [8] including the California business problem definition and then the technical approach. What we are interested in is how the information foundation allowed extremely rapid prototyping and model-driven composition to occur. The whole software set was built in three weeks and included marquee components illustrative of an iBPM. Namely, mobile device and interface delivery; intelligent prescription drug information analysis using the SNOMED drug repository [9] and SPARQL semantic queries; and connectivity with NIEM based court systems along with PDF document rendering. These capabilities were delivered predominately using open source software tools and components for software enablement along with the Oracle BPM SOA suite solution set.

For the mobile device integration we were able to generate simple inline XSD schema definitions of the information components and then load those into JDeveloper and generate the interface forms directly. This saved many hours of coding by hand in a form editor. Similarly for each of the task forms throughout the BPM process. Next the PDF forms content integration was delivered using the Open-XDX smart exchange tool. This takes a CAM template definition and builds a WSDL or RESTful exchange directly without coding. More information and online interactive examples can be found at this demonstration website [10]. The following diagram illustrates how the CAM templates and the embedded information in them drive the Open-XDX integration component.

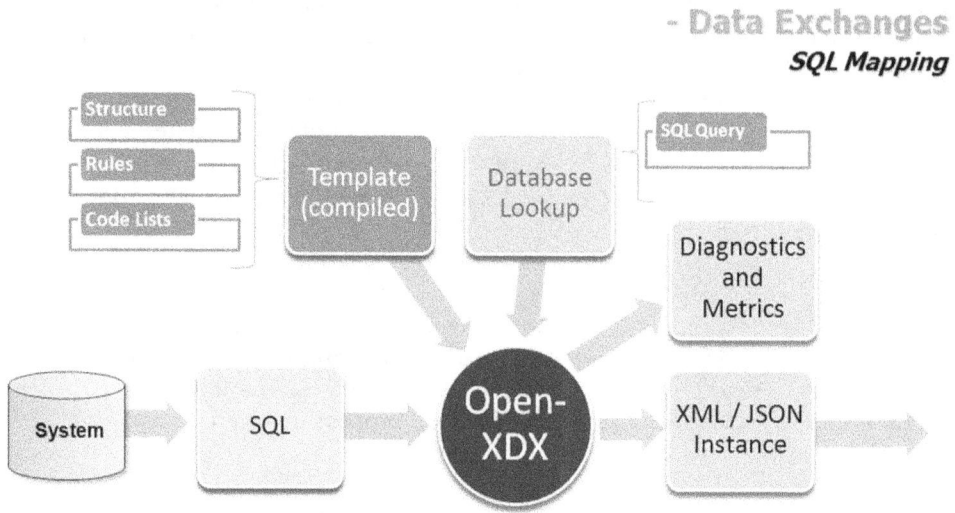

http://www.youtube.com/watch?v=oVXtJIZVvRA

Figure 8: Open-XDX functional overview

This is a classic example of how robust information semantics can drive iBPM solution smart components directly by using intelligent tools with minimal coding needed.

Building Data Bindings

A further key need for BPM tools is the data bindings to database repositories for record storage. These can be SQL or NoSQL based. A use case is creating Hibernate ORM Java persistence framework (JPA) bindings directly from the CAM templates of the component tables and information components. The Hibernate ORM [11] is used underneath several prominent BPM solutions and many other application solution products. Having consistent data binding definitions that provide reliable semantics of the content is then critical to enable iBPM solution analytic tools.

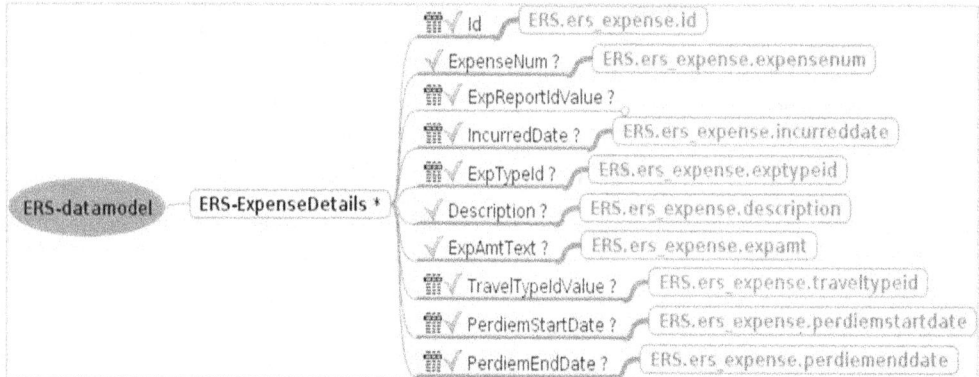

Figure 9: Example Hibernate ORM Binding

Key: optional items are denoted by the ? after; items with content restraints are noted with a preceding symbol; mapped items are denoted with the check mark symbol; then the right most item bubbles are the physical database mapping to the physical database schema.table.column item.

The key aspects shown in Figure 9 are the correlation between existing SQL database table and columns with the NIEM conformant NDR components and naming conventions in the Hibernate Java binding (note: just one table (Expense Details) and a selection of the columns are shown). The ability to create these templates and mappings provides the semantic foundation desired to then drive artifact generation and programming across the solution.

In this case the CAM Editor is able to reverse engineer these directly from the existing database tables. Alternatively for new systems, the editor can create the tables models and SQL mappings and then generate the actual database tables themselves automatically via the Hibernate bindings.

CONCLUSIONS

We have presented some aspects of automation of iBPM through the use of semantic information assets. There are many more opportunities with extended tools such as analytics engines and event management tools where a clear knowledge of the semantics of the information throughout the business processes is critical for accurate reasoning.

On the level of software delivery the consistent information representation also helps drive production of the iBPM solution itself through the generation of software artifacts directly. The examples presented include database configuration scripts, user forms and information extraction and formatting utilities.

In the California example [8], the information flows from the external case management systems into the BPM application provide another illustration of the need to have consistent information representations. From these the prescription drug information is extracted and passed to the SNOMED [9] smart query to provide diagnostic information to guide the doctors assessment of the patient. Then information is passed to the court systems using NIEM [3] based messaging. The court systems themselves can then react to these requests, such as case prioritization, based on knowledge of the structure components and content. Analytic tools could be deployed in the future to determine patterns across the State in terms of patient outcomes and treatments.

Always the need is for consistent information. In the case of California there are thousands of points of presence providing medical services to children throughout the state and those systems need to be aligned through the use of consistent naming and design rules based on NIEM and the resulting information exchanges integrated. That foundation then allows iBPM solutions to leverage those information assets into the future.

The role of open source tools is also important, being able to provide solutions independently of particular software products, licensing and providers. The SNOMED resources from NIH are one example and then the other is the CAM tools [12] that support use of BPM systems by facilitating the provision of the consistent information foundations.

REFERENCES AND RESOURCES

[1] [Gartner Group 2014) iBPM 10 Core Components – see
http://www.futstrat.com/books/iBPMS_Handbook.php

[2] (OASIS 2003) OASIS Content Assembly Mechanism (CAM) standard specification - https://www.oasis-open.org/committees/cam

[3] (NIEM 2005) National Information Exchange Model – http://www.niem.gov

[4] Naming and Design Rules Evaluation Reporting presentation -
http://www.slideshare.net/drrwebber/cam-editor-niem-evaluation-report

[5] CEUR Proceedings (2010) – details of Content Validation Framework automation (CAM/CAMV): http://ceur-ws.org/Vol-649/paper2.pdf

[6] (W3C 2009) "SKOS Primer" http://www.w3.org/TR/skos-primer/ and
ISO/TC154 – International Organization for Standardization – Technical
Committee for Processes, data elements and documents in commerce, industry and administration

[7] The iQvoc SKOS project site: http://iqvoc.net/

[8] Video describing the California Child Welfare Project
http://goo.gl/1PuEBn

[9] The NIH SNOMED resources site - http://www.nlm.nih.gov/research/umls/Snomed/snomed_main.html

[10] Open-XDX demonstration website
http://verifyxml.org/OpenXDX-page.html

[11] The Hibernate ORM site - http://hibernate.org/

[12] The CAM Editor tools site – http://www.cameditor.org

[13] ISO/TC 154 committee website - http://www.isotc154.org

Advanced Complex Adaptive Organizational Systems BPM/Workflow Design

Mark Casey, Miyian.com, USA

INTRODUCTION

Current BPM/Workflow systems, communication architectures, and other software designs encompass only a small fraction of the thousands of processes, actors, and cases active at any one time in a large organization (such as a hospital). Trying to model and manage this huge, complex adaptive interwoven mesh of systems, processes, and goals requires new designs and architectures that more accurately reflect the way humans naturally understand and model our surroundings, communicate with each other, and make good decisions. We must make our systems reflect this optimized way, then aggregate their capabilities so the organization acts like a million smart, wise, aware people at once.

There is a new approach and infrastructure called Complex Adaptive Systems – Organization (CASO) to understand and run organizations. It is possible to create designs and architectures to monitor, manage, and optimize ALL the processes, actors, and cases, and successfully adapt the recent huge advances in **Models**, **Communication**, and **Decision-making**.

We have, over thousands of years, evolved a fairly optimized way of finding success in our world. We make mental models of different kinds, keeping track of all the near and far threats and opportunities, understanding the relationships between them, and focusing dynamically on only the important ones at hand. Yet we have problems making accurate models of what a group of people are doing together and cannot hold in our collective heads more than a small fraction of the information or processes that are generated by an organization.

We have evolved better and better communications abilities, from gestures to speech to drawings to writing. We are now quite adapt at communicating locally, with our highly developed eyes, ears, mouths, and brains. Note that we most frequently used gestures and speech and pictures to communicate, until writing came along. Since then, we have stubbornly stuck with only the old ways of communicating that technology provided, talking on a few phones on a desk and writing voluminous amounts of paper that few people read or remember or can even find.

Decisions are a little different: inside our own heads, we are experts at understand how to make things better, with less effort, more consistently. We efficiently gain information, turn it into insight and knowledge, and convert it to wisdom. To a point. When we move out of our heads into the world with other people, we many times cannot correctly spread the decision-making power to those not at the top, or let them even understand what is happening enough to make good decisions. Leaders cannot keep track of the thousands of decision points or options, much less know what technology is becoming cost-effective and thus should be implemented. As an organization we forget the lessons we has learned in the past and many times never know what others in our industry is doing well. This severely hurts organizations at all levels.

Current BPM systems only encompass part of an organization's business activities. The biggest business drivers are (AIIM - IBM, 2012)

- Improved process productivity
- More effective internal collaboration
- Faster case resolution
- Higher quality customer experience
- Stronger compliance/reduced risk
- Better management visibility and control
- Faster customer response

MODELS

Then

As we go through a day's work, we keep mental models of important processes or goals, modifying them in real time to match what is going on around us. We focus on a few that are important at that minute, keeping others in our consciousness in a kind of descending order of importance or impact. We can quickly construct new ones, combine several into one (to "see a bigger picture"). Conversely we can drill down into a smaller subset of a process to focus on what is happening there, often revealing that subset is actually an intersecting piece of a different, larger process. But outside of our head, it is very hard to share this understanding and modeling of the organization we have. We try to write voluminous descriptions, but they get lost and no one reads them. We try to draw pictures, but they are static and don't reflect the day to day movement of the processes and workflows. We try to explain verbally to each other, but most of us can only keep a small model in our heads at one time while sharing it with another. And we forget a lot of things. Or never even know about them.

Now

It is important to remember that modeling systems should operate the way humans do naturally. They should focus on the main or most important processes first, then expand to include sub processes and other more distant issues in an organization. For instance, in the surgical department of a hospital, the first process that should get decision-making services is the patient flow. The next one should be the physician flow. The next one should be the nurse flow. These flow processes are supported and constrained by sub processes, such as availability, cost/profitability, timing, etc.. Those subsystems should come next. Farther down the line, processes supporting systems such as education, physical facilities, sterility, product and service mix, and scheduling come next.

Advances in sensors, graphics and video displays along with logarithmic jumps in computing and communications power will allow us to replicate an actual organization's many activities and states in a near-real-time world computer model. This provides a central view of the organization to all within it, greatly simplifying everyone's understanding of what is going on, and what needs to be focused on at any one time. As the organization's processes change or cases mature, we can quickly reflect this in the computer models. For the first time we can model the idealized processes (workflows), the movements of the intelligent agents within (cases, groups), and the thousands of little and big changes, both physical and non-physical, that occur all over the organization, and reflect them in the model. Archival modeling using big data analytics are starting to reveal patterns and opportunities, and the plunging costs of doing this will allow federated modeling of each person, level, and section of an organization.

COMMUNICATION

Then

When working with others, we almost exclusively use words to paint a "picture" of the process we are focusing on. Trying to include all the side and intersecting processes while we "paint", as well as the variations the current case presents compared to a commonly agreed upon template, causes most people at some point to lose the mental "picture", especially how one process impacts another. Writing this down or even using rectangles and arrows in a diagram can only capture a small fraction of the entire living, intersecting, and moving process milieu we are trying to commonly understand. Making a video is very useful, but takes too much time. Visualizing the state of a patient or process is very difficult at best, and electronic communications within the organization are usually confined to faxes and phone calls, with "advanced" organizations merely sharing static webpages when conferencing. We still use mostly our fingers to interact with technology and software, and it only interacts with us via words, and rarely, pictures.

Now

Smart, aware mobile phones and tablets which will soon have 2D and 3D projection capabilities are now cost effective, potentially allowing all members of an organization – including its customers – to participate quickly and efficiently in advancing and optimizing the work and business. Large, high definition wall displays are now cheap enough to cover almost every wall, vastly increasing the amount of information and knowledge available to all.

Audio/video recognition and understanding is now at the level where we can interact with technology by merely speaking, listening, watching, and moving our bodies. All these technologies are now cost-effective and must become ubiquitous within the organization.

DECISION-MAKING

Then

As we get more experienced and skilled at our level in an organization, we gather information, intelligence, insight, knowledge, and wisdom of how to make our area – and sometimes the whole organization - run better or smoother. Some of this we can impart to others or put down in print or pictures, but the amount soon increases way beyond our – or even the whole organization's – ability to use it effectively, or even just keep track of it all.

This usually results in three things: we forget about many of the important processes or cases when they fall out of our focus; we constantly miss some things that are very important (or even critical); and we repetitively and manually adjust, change, tweak, and intervene in processes to make them come out right. There is no way for an average employee to easily automate or integrate the "easier" or "lower level" interventions we do every day, which would let us concentrate on more important or bigger issues.

There is also no way to easily orchestrate or coordinate multiple, remote, or higher processes via technology, so we still do most of that in our heads or in static documents that are hard to locate and understand when needed. This manual approach means we also have to wait for a higher authority to make crucial decisions rather than fixing or optimizing a situation on the spot. We also let insight, knowledge, and wisdom walk out the door each time a person quits. This lack of institutional memory and wisdom keeps us from evolving to a more optimized organization.

Education and learning is part of decision-making, and the complex organization of today contains many points where an employee needs to learn something right away, something that is not learned in a university degree program. Learning how to deal with a complex case, how to operate a piece of technology, or how to understand a new concept or practice demands just-in-time learning and education. Tracking and monitoring talent levels, skill development, and education achievements is necessary to ensure employees can do what is required of them, and are justly rewarded.

Now

CASO decision-making includes the concept of a virtual agent (VA). There will be one VA for each process step, actor (including humans), model part, and decision-making component. The VA will act in the best interest of the real process step/actor/model part/decision-making component, making its life and work easier thru AI and automation.

Decision-making systems should initially focus on the primary or most important processes first, making or aiding decisions that affect the overall progress of the process or goal. In surgical services in a hospital, that would be the overall movement of the patient (aka surgical case). Certain states (criteria, milestones and artifacts) are critical to the case moving forward. These should be initially focused on by the decision-making system. As each state is successful, the case can move one more step forward in the process, moving through surgical candidate evaluation, pre-op (registration, imaging, anesthesia evaluation, trauma management, timing, financing, etc.), intra-op, post-op, and rehab.

The next process that should get decision-making services is the physician flow. The next one should be the nurse flow. These flow processes are supported and constrained by sub processes, such as availability, resources management, cost/profitability, timing, etc. Those subsystems should come next. Farther down the line, processes supporting systems such as education, physical facilities, sterility, product and service mix, and scheduling come next. It can then expand to include sub processes and other more distant issues in the organization.

As the number of subsystems (processes) increases, layers of decision-making must be added, to handle coordination, choreography, orchestration, and multi-level process intelligence. Larger tactical and strategic goals such as organizational intelligence and business intelligence will be added at a higher level, as they exist as both a basic process for the top of the organizational hierarchy and a more distant process for line level processes.

CASO decision-making (as well as models and communication) includes the concept of federation. This means that each position in an organization's org chart (CEO, CFO, Directors, Managers, etc.) will contain its own separate decision-making system/service with all the components – rule engines, evaluation engines, big data at their level, analytics, intelligence, automation, orchestration, etc. It will be fed not only by data and processes at its own level, but from levels below and beside it. It will feed up into higher organization chart positions.

This is analogous to the way organizations are run today. A worker has a certain number of primary processes, and mentally models and manages them (with the help of some written policies, etc.). The worker's manager aggregates responsibility for and accepts data from the workers, and models and manages their own primary processes, feeding data and other things up to their director. To understand what decision-making systems or processes should be developed first, just look at the way the humans are doing it now. Of course reengineering can always make it better, but the decision to either forklift a new process model, or just tweak the existing one is part of the optimization process.

As an organization is transformed using the CASO concept, more and more complex decision-making will become useful. More and more process, both large and small, will be optimized, adding to the complexity of the whole system. This includes interlinking more and more subsystems so they can share data and collaborate; and increased use and complexity of human-facing systems to facilitate communications and collaboration and innovation. It also includes larger process sets, such as public health, medical population management, and skill set authorization.

Decision-making systems are starting to take hold in organizations, usually in helping people move from one step in a customer-facing process to another. Some systems are helping employees move through very simple processes. Tools and technologies are becoming available recently that allow organizations to use systems that act the way we think. Decision-making today is moving more and more from people to computer systems, starting with tasks and situations such as self-provisioning logic, automatic data distribution, automatic cross linking in sales, process step management, data, image, and sound understanding and semantical correlation.

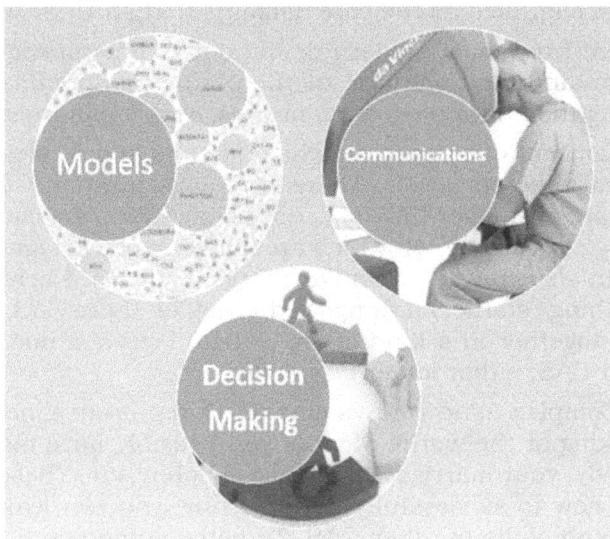

Figure 1 – CASO Models, Communication, Decision-making

LEARNING AND EDUCATION

As smart as we make our hardware and software, if the people in an organization are not able to understand or use them properly, the system will fail or be dis-optimized. Every day, all people come upon a situation where they need to learn about something right away. They also have some things they need to learn about in the short term, and some things they need to learn in the long run.

The current system of college degrees and industry certifications have their place, but must be supplanted by just-in-time learning systems that pervade the organization. A robust learning and education system is critical for an organization to become truly optimized. This system has several parts, federated like all CASO components. There should be a role/skills/certification tracking system that keeps records on every employee, a correlation system that matches needed skills/roles to that tracking system, and a learning/education planning systems that produces roadmaps to meeting the organization's needs. At a lower level, every corner of an organization should have an on-the-spot, just-in-time learning system for use by employees and customers. It would provide short learning modules on the use of machines, processes, scientific activities (e.g., assessing a postpartum mother, inserting an IV), upcoming meeting agenda items, CASO principles, etc.

The learning and education system will of course use audio, video, images, text, simulations, and other media types. A media management system that manages *all* the media in an organization is a must, so both prepared media (learning videos, etc.) and meeting media (audio/video recording and transcriptions of *all* meetings) will be managed and available when needed. Both the learning/education and media systems will have their own modeling and decision-making subsystems, federated, of course.

COMPLEX ADAPTIVE SYSTEMS – ORGANIZATIONS (CASO)

CASO is a subset of the general science of Complex Adaptive Systems (CAS), In addition to organizations, Miyian also conducts CAS R&D in the domains of Complex Adaptive *engineering, technology, learning, media*, and *humans*. These have been identified as the core domains that all CAS contain.

CASO is different from most modern definitions of organizations, as it seeks to define, understand, and optimize *all* the parts of an organization, big and small, organizing them into processes, models, and communications.

CASO has the concept of *scoping*, in which (just as in real life), allows one to view the world at different levels. There is the organization CAS as a whole, which is composed of smaller CAS (e.g., divisions), which are composed of even smaller CAS (e.g., departments), which are made up of even smaller CAS (e.g., rooms). CAS can also consist of similar things distributed across the organization (e.g., all things sterile, all things pediatric). All these CAS, big and small, are interlocked together in a kind of fog or ball. Pieces of one CAS make up parts of another CAS, either larger or smaller.

CASO and all Complex Adaptive Systems (CAS) represent a new paradigm, a new way of looking at the world. Most of you possibly have mastered a CAS, such as your body, your marriage, a science, a hobby, etc. These are CAS also, so if you know how to successfully optimize one, you can learn to map over the knowledge and skills to other CAS. To better understand CASO, look at parts of an organization that have already been optimized – in a hospital, the operating room is an example. Attention to minute details within the OR in processes, models, materials, and communications have been worked out to produce the best possible outcome.

Scoping examples

Each level will have its own federated *Processes/Workflows/Cases*, and its own *Intelligence/Knowledge/Decision-making* services, and its own *Communications/Input/Display* services

- Business Capabilities (using Healthcare as an example)
- Belong to Business Domain (Hospital)
  - Governed by *Business Principles* (Provide Quality, Efficient, Effective Healthcare, Profitable, etc.)
    - realized by *Business Processes* (methods) (Patient passing through system)
      - Performed by *Business Role* (people, teams) (Surgeon, Nurse, Manager, Director, etc.)
        - *Business Functions* are roles individuals and units play to meet business objectives (PreOp, IntraOP, PostOp, etc.)
          - *Business Services* is the realization of the Business Capability (Diagnostic Capabilities, Critical Care level Phase I and II services, Medical / Surgical level services, Rehab services, etc.), also IPSO - Input, Storage, Processing Output, etc.

- Vision
  - Goal
    - Objective
      - Strategy
        - Tactic
          - Policy
            - Case (defined as agent/environment within a process)
              - Event separation
              - Rule / Decision

- The Information Chain
  - Data
    - Information
      - Reasoning
        - Evaluation (cost/benefit, risk/reward)
          - Insight
            - Knowledge
              - Wisdom

OPTIMIZATION OF BPM MODELING, DECISION-MAKING, COMMUNICATIONS

Optimizing BPM/CM modeling

CASO Approach to Process/Workflow/Case Management
- On The Fly Process/Workflow/Case modeling
- *Deterministic* evolving to *Dynamic/Relative/Probabilistic*
- Start with Static ("most probable") Workflow, move towards Dynamic Template/Roadmap/Tree
- Move Unpredictable Input towards Predictable Output
- Probabilistic Evaluation & Decision making
- Reuse of previously constructed P/W/C components that did not change, or as a starting point for reconstruction
- Processes/Workflows cross each other and interlock, can be incomplete, mature, etc.

Optimizing Decision-making
- Goal oriented, adaptive case management based on state / approach / outcome probabilities (Pucher, 2014)
- The AI subsystem will maintain an internal content and state management system to manage decisions and artifacts
- manage decisions and artifacts
- Federated & Orchestrated BI / BPM / AI / Data / Analytics
- Use of HPC cloud distributed components and supercomputers to manage the thousands of an organization's processes, agents, and evaluation / decision engines / predictive modeling / real-time state modeling / big data analytics (IBM Watson Analytics)
- Repositories of data marts / cubes, of goal seeking knowledge / experience cubes are dynamically created / updated / modified according to current states / goals of system at each level of scoping

Optimizing Communications
- Automated semantic understanding of data / documents / audio / video into AI analytic systems (Web 2.0) (O'Reilly, 2005)
- Model communication goals on natural human interfaces ("The Mirror")
- Voice input / output – natural language recognition, automatic advanced audio dictation
- 2D and 3D displays that display current states / outcomes in near real time (MIT MediaLab doppelab)
- Visualizing just the group of CAS and goals/processes you are interested in at any one time
- Ubiquitous videoconferencing / collaborations / meetings, automatic advanced video recognition
- Use of augmented reality systems (Google Glasses) (Augmedix.com)

CASO optimization

To be optimized, a CASO must have several conditions. It must be set up the right way; it must be allowed to quickly modify its organizational structure and activities; it must be able to self-organize at certain levels, within a firmly determined structure. It must actively seek to identify and recognize the abilities and talents of its members, allowing them to move within the organization to their most useful and productive role. Decision-making must be moved as close to the decision spot as possible, pushing authority down to match responsibility.

The three critical CASO optimization areas discussed above are also identified as "The Mirror (communications), the Org Chart (decision-making), and the Factory Hotel (models)" (Casey, 2014MUSE, 2014)

All current technologies and BPM concepts will be integrated into a CASO design and architecture. (Casey, ConceptsInCASO, 2014)

CASO design and architecture combines and integrates newly successful advanced technologies and capabilities from different industries into an organization, such as:

- Automated multi-level process management and supply chain / fulfillment systems (Amazon.com)
- Automated AI Deep Learning (IBM Watson Analytics) (Google Voice) (Cognitive Science & Design)
- Advanced semantic voice recognition (Google Voice) (Apple Siri) (Google Knowledge Graph)
- Advanced 2D and 3D (virtual reality) dashboards and simulations (Breakaway Games, Healthcare) (Rockwell Automation) (SSIH.ORG) (PharmaTimes)
- Machine learning and risk prediction (Etiometry 2013)
- Constraint optimization and risk allocation in scheduling planning (MIT CSAIL laboratory)
- Mobile tablets, smartphones, and targeted Apps
- Augmented Reality systems (Atheer Medical) (AR Healthcare - YouTube)

There are four pillars of CASO optimization: (FourPillars, 2009)

- *Process* (BPM/WM/CM)
- *Technology* (computing, communications, I/O)
- *Learning* (knowledge bases, education)
- *People* (openness, collaboration, support, interfaces, interactions, talent)

CASO User Modification

Because CASO change so quickly and have so many variations in processes and cases, it is critical that users and super-users (as opposed to IT people) be able to modify models, communications, and decisions, on the fly and in a structured way. Primary functions will be produced by programmers, but users must be able to modify the system both to modify the model or decision-making logic and design the communications the way that works best for them.

CONCLUSION

CASO is a new way of looking at organizations, one that more closely matches the way humans look at the world. It uses the natural human experience, thought processes, and interfaces as a guide to designing organizational systems and processes.

CASO seeks to identify and manage all the parts of an organization, from the largest primary value process to the smallest detail of the smallest process. BPM/WM/ACM are a critical part of CASO, taking a much bigger role in the organization by eventually expanding beyond business to managing all processes. CASO focuses on modeling, communication, and decision-making within the organization, providing a dynamic and configurable framework that can integrate all existing systems within an organization, both physical and conceptual. A primary concept of CASO is using advanced technologies that have already been successful in other domains and industries.

CASO is also future-proof in being able to absorb any new technologies or connections with other external systems. Common characteristics of all complex adaptive systems, which CASO inherits, are only touched upon briefly in this paper, which focuses primarily on BPM.

REFERENCES

AIIM - IBM. (2012). *Broadening the Scope for Advanced Case Management.* IBM. Retrieved from http://public.dhe.ibm.com/software/data/sw-library/ecm-programs/IBM-AdvancedCaseManagement-2013-Final.pdf

(*Amazon.com.* Retrieved from http://www.amazon.com

Apple Siri. Retrieved from http://www.apple.com/ios/siri/

AR Healthcare - YouTube. Retrieved from https://www.youtube.com/results?search_query=augmented+reality+for+healthcare

Atheer Medical. Retrieved from https://www.youtube.com/watch?v=Vwshf8jXMh4

Augmedix.com. Retrieved from http://www.augmedix.com/index

Breakaway Games, Healthcare. Retrieved from http://www.breakawaygames.com/serious-games/solutions/healthcare/

Casey, M. (2014). *2014MUSE.* miyian.com. Retrieved from http://www.markboulder.com/origin/originportal/MARKATMIYIANDOTCOM2014MUSE.pptx

Casey, M. (2014). *ConceptsInCASO.* Retrieved from http://www.markboulder.com/origin/originportal/TechnologiesAndBPMConceptsInCASO.doc

Cognitive Science & Design. Retrieved from https://developers.google.com/events/io/sessions/326460111

Etiometry 2013. Retrieved from http://www.technologyreview.com/news/515461/machine-learning-and-risk-prediction-in-the-icu/

(2009). *FourPillars.* research paper by Mark Casey.

Google Glasses. Retrieved from
    https://developers.google.com/glass/distribute/glass-at-work

Google Knowledge Graph. Retrieved from
    https://developers.google.com/events/io/sessions/351343657

Google Voice. Retrieved from
    http://www.google.com/insidesearch/features/search/knowledge.ht
    ml

IBM Watson Analytics. IBM.COM. Retrieved from
    http://www.ibm.com/analytics/watson-analytics/

Internet of Things. (n.d.). Retrieved from
    http://en.wikipedia.org/wiki/Internet_of_Things

(n.d.). *mark@miyian.com.*

MIT CSAIL laboratory. Retrieved from http://www.gizmag.com/mit-better-
    siri/35725/

MIT MediaLab doppelab. Retrieved from http://doppellab.media.mit.edu/

O'Reilly, T. (2005). *CEO.* www.oreilly.com. Retrieved from
    http://www.oreilly.com/pub/a/web2/archive/what-is-web-20.html

PharmaTimes. Retrieved from http://www.pharmatimes.com/Article/15-02-
    20/Healthcare_is_about_to_go_virtual.aspx

Pucher, M. J. (2014). *Adaptive Case Management Blog.* http://www.isis-
    papyrus.com/. ACMISIS. Retrieved from
    https://acmisis.wordpress.com/

Rockwell Automation. Retrieved from
    https://www.arenasimulation.com/industry-solutions/healthcare-
    simulation-software?gclid=COyN3u2x-sMCFZGIaQodUVIAMw

SSIH.ORG. Retrieved from http://www.ssih.org/

Viewing the Internet of Events through a Process Lens

Wil van der Aalst, Eindhoven University of Technology, The Netherlands

ABSTRACT

The spectacular growth of event data is rapidly changing the Business Process Management (BPM) discipline. It makes no sense to focus on process modeling (including model-based analysis and model-based process automation) without considering the torrents of factual data in and between today's organizations. Hence, there is a need to connect BPM technology to the "internet of events" and make it more evidence-based BPM. However, the volume (size of data), velocity (speed of change), variety (multiple heterogeneous data sources), and veracity (uncertainty) of event data complicate matters.

Mainstream analytics approaches are unable to turn data into insights, once things get more involved. Therefore, they tend to focus on isolated decision problems rather than providing a more holistic view on the behavior of actors within and outside the organization. Fortunately, recent developments in process mining make it possible to use process models as the "lens" to look at (low) level event data. Viewing the internet of events through a "process lens" helps to understand and solve compliance and performance related problems. In fact, we envision a new profession—the process scientist—connecting traditional model-driven BPM with data-centric approaches (data mining, statistics, and business intelligence). Process mining provides the process scientist with a powerful set of tools and prepares BPM for a highly connected world where processes are surrounded by devices emitting events.

INTRODUCTION

Organizations are competing on analytics and only organizations that intelligently use the vast amounts of data available will survive. Process-mining techniques enable the analysis of a wide variety of processes using event data. For example, event logs can be used to automatically learn a process model (e.g., a Petri net or BPMN model). Next to the automated discovery of the real underlying process, there are process-mining techniques to analyze bottlenecks, to uncover hidden inefficiencies, to check compliance, to explain deviations, to predict performance, and to guide users towards "better" processes. Dozens (if not hundreds) of process-mining techniques are available and their value has been proven in many case studies.

See, for example, the twenty *case studies* on the webpage of the IEEE Task Force on Process Mining (IEEE 2013). The growing number of commercial *process mining tools* (Disco, Perceptive Process Mining, Celonis Process Mining, QPR ProcessAnalyzer, Software AG/ARIS PPM, Fujitsu Interstage Automated Process Discovery, etc.) further illustrates the uptake of process mining. The recent Massive Open Online Course (MOOC) on process mining attracted over 41.500 participants (Coursera 2014).

Process mining provides the interface between process models and event data. On the one hand, conventional Business Process Management (BPM) and

Workflow Management (WfM) approaches and tools are mostly model-driven with little consideration for event data. On the other hand, Data Mining (DM), Business Intelligence (BI), and Machine Learning (ML) focus on data without considering end-to-end process models. Process mining aims to bridge the gap between BPM and WfM on the one hand and DM, BI, and ML on the other hand. Here, the challenge is to turn torrents of event data ("Big Data") into valuable insights related to process performance and compliance.

Figure 1: Process models can be seen as the glasses through which one can see structure in otherwise puzzling event data

This paper does not focus on specific process mining algorithms. Instead, it focuses on the interplay between event data and process models. As illustrated in Figure 1, process models can be used to view event data in such a way that actionable knowledge can be extracted. Process models can be used to extract real value from event data. However, this is only possible if model and data are aligned. This is where process mining plays a crucial role.

This paper coins the term "process lens" and demonstrates that processes can indeed be used to interpret confounding event data.

INTERNET OF EVENTS

In (Aalst 2014) the term *Internet of Events* (IoE) was coined to refer to all event data available. As described in (Hilbert and Lopez 2011; Manyika et al. 2011), society shifted from being predominantly "analog" to "digital" in just a few years. Society, organizations, and people are "Always On". Data is collected *about anything, at any time,* and *at any place. Event data* are the most important source of information. Events may take place inside a machine (e.g., an X-ray machine or baggage handling system), inside an enterprise information system (e.g., a order placed by a customer), inside a hospital (e.g., the analysis of a blood sample), inside a social network (e.g., exchanging e-mails or Twitter messages), inside a transportation system (e.g., checking in, buying a ticket, or passing through a toll booth), etc. Events may be "life events", "machine events", or both.

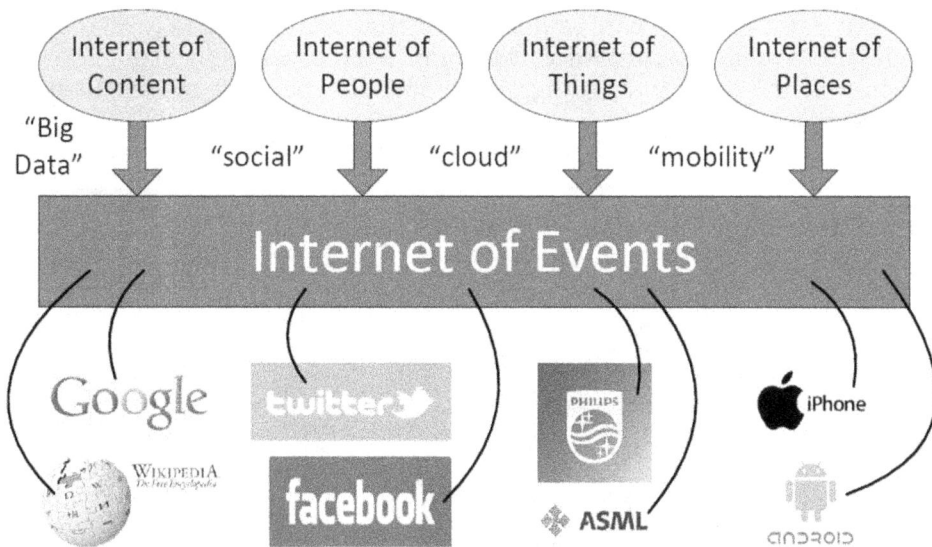

Figure 2: The Internet of Events (IoE) is based on the Internet of Content (IoC), the Internet of People (IoP), the Internet of Things (IoT), and the Internet of Locations (IoL).

Figure 2 aims to characterize the types of events available for analysis. As shown the Internet of Events (IoE) is composed of:

- The *Internet of Content* (IoC): all information created by humans to increase knowledge on particular subjects. The IoC includes traditional web pages, articles, encyclopedia like Wikipedia, YouTube, e-books, newsfeeds, etc.
- The *Internet of People* (IoP): all data related to social interaction. The IoP includes e-mail, Facebook, Twitter, forums, LinkedIn, etc.
- The *Internet of Things* (IoT): all physical objects connected to the network. The IoT includes all things that have a unique id and a presence in an internet-like structure. Things may have an internet connection or tagged using Radio-Frequency Identification (RFID), Near Field Communication (NFC), etc.
- The *Internet of Locations* (IoL): refers to all data that have a spatial dimension. With the uptake of mobile devices (e.g., smartphones) more and more events have geospatial attributes.

Obviously, the IoC, the IoP, the IoT, and the IoL are partially overlapping. The spectacular growth of IoE impacts BPM, e.g., process improvements will increasingly be driven by analytics. At the same time, organizations have difficulties exploiting the data they have. Therefore, we propose *process models to be used as lenses to view data* that are otherwise confusing.

PROCESS LENS

To use a process model as a "lens" to observe the data from a particular viewpoint, it is not sufficient to have a model and data. Both (i.e. model and data) need to be aligned. This can be achieved through process mining. Based on the event data, a model can be discovered that is automatically aligned with the data. Through conformance checking, it is possible to align normative models with the data and highlight discrepancies between modeled behavior and observed behavior.

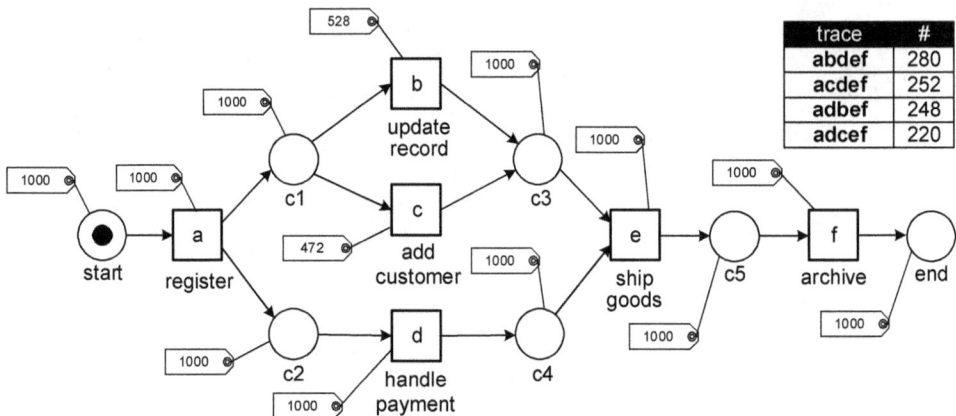

Figure 3: A process model discovered for an event log with 1000 cases. The model is expressed in terms of a Petri net.

To introduce the notion of process discovery, we consider Figure 3, which shows an event log and a discovered process model. The event log holds information on 1000 cases: 280 cases followed the trace **abdef**, 252 followed the trace **acdef**, etc. The activity names have been shortened to a single letter, e.g., **a = register**. In fact, the event log in Figure 3 is significantly simplified by abstracting away many aspects. Normally, each *event* refers to a *case* and an *activity*. An event also has a *timestamp* and may refer to the *resources* used; there may be *transactional information*, and any number of attributes. In the example log, such information is missing. Cases and events cannot be distinguished, but the compact representation allows us to illustrate the basics of process mining. There are 280 cases that followed the same sequence of activities: **abdef**. The event log in Figure 3 has 5000 events, e.g., 1000 **a** events that always happen first.

The discovered process model in Figure 3 is expressed in terms of a Petri net. In the initial state shown, only the transition having activity label **a** can occur. A transition (represented as a square) can occur if all input places (represented as circles) have a token (represented by a black dot). If a transition occurs, tokens are consumed from all input places and produced for all output places. After the occurrence of **a** in Figure 3, there are tokens in **c1** and **c2**. Hence after **a** either (1) **b** and **d** occur or (2) **c** and **d** occur (in any order). Then **e** occurs, followed by **f**. The end state is the state with a token in **end**. Note that the process model is able to replay all 1000 cases: they all start in the initial state and finish in the desired end state. Figure 3 also shows the number of times each place and transition is visited, e.g., **b** occurs 528 times.

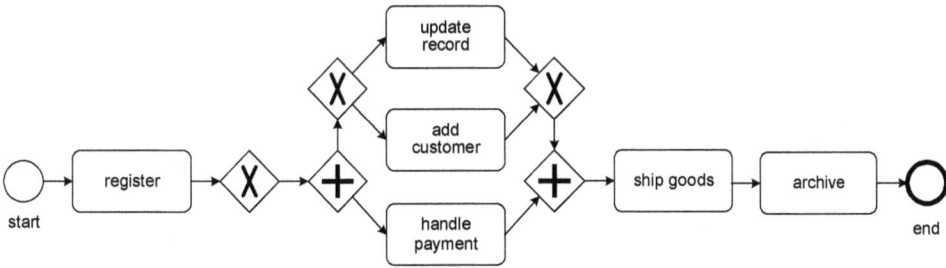

Figure 4: A BPMN model corresponding to the discovered Petri net in Figure 3.

The BPMN model in Figure 4 has the same behavior as the Petri net model in Figure 3. We would like to stress that the notation is less relevant here: Automatic translations are possible and "observed behavior does not have a preference for a particular syntax" (although people like to believe differently). Only things that can be related to event data matter!

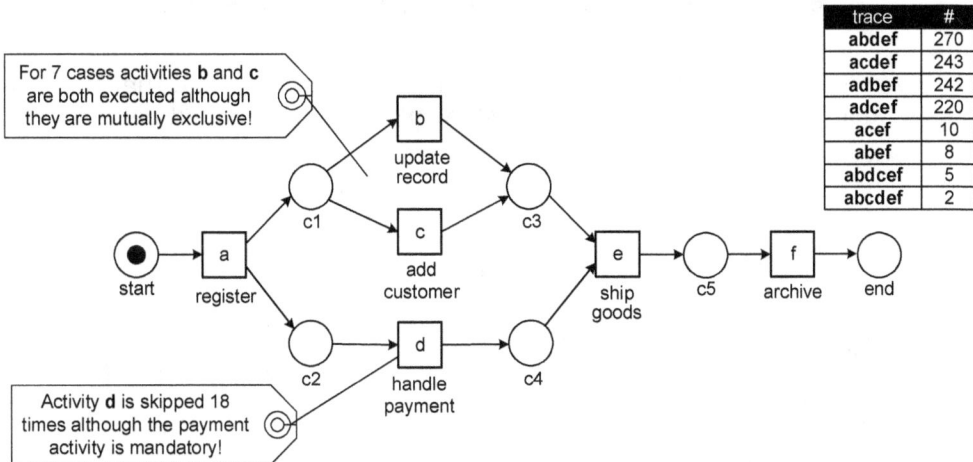

trace	#
abdef	270
acdef	243
adbef	242
adcef	220
acef	10
abef	8
abdcef	5
abcdef	2

Figure 5: The event log now has 25 cases that do not fit into the normative process model. By replaying the event log one can see that activity d is sometimes skipped and activities b and c are both executed although the model does not allow for this.

Process models can be discovered automatically or made by hand. In both scenarios, it is possible to *check conformance*. This is illustrated in Figure 5. Assume that sometimes **d** is skipped or both **b** and **c** occur. Hence, reality as described in the event log deviates from the model. Figure 5 shows some diagnostics. Conformance checking techniques will immediately reveal such deviations. Note that the process model is used as the "lens" to show non-conforming behavior.

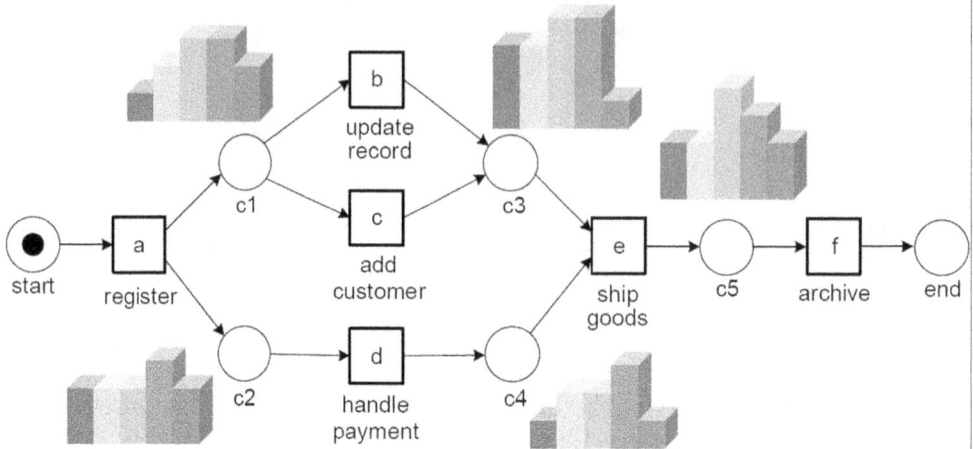

Figure 6: By replaying the event log on a discovered process model, one can see where the bottlenecks are in the process.

Replay can also be used to show bottlenecks, see Figure 6. Note that the process model is now used as the lens to show performance-related behavior.

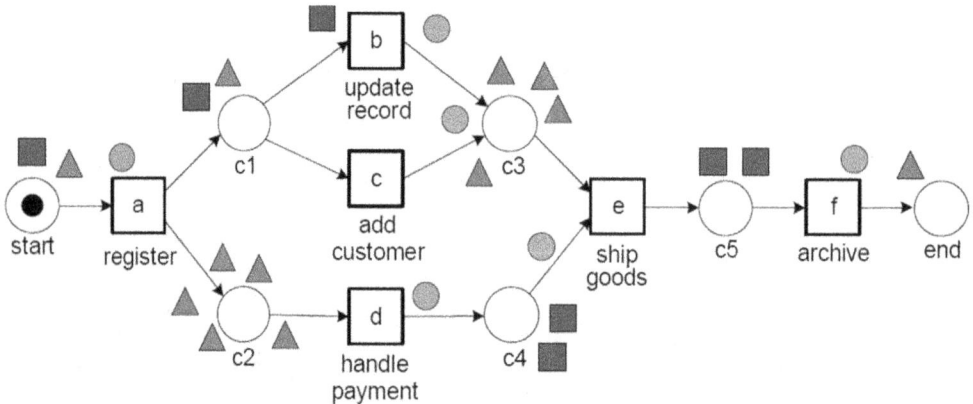

Figure 7: By mapping running cases onto the model, one can see the "traffic jams" in an organization.

It is also possible to replay streaming event data, i.e., align cases to the model while they are still running. This can be used to show the "traffic" in the process, as illustrated by Figure 7. There are three types of cases (represented using triangles, squares, and circles). In Figure 7 one can see the congestion of particular case types at any point in time.

trace	#
abdef	205
acdef	180
adbef	170
adcef	160
abedf	150
acedf	135

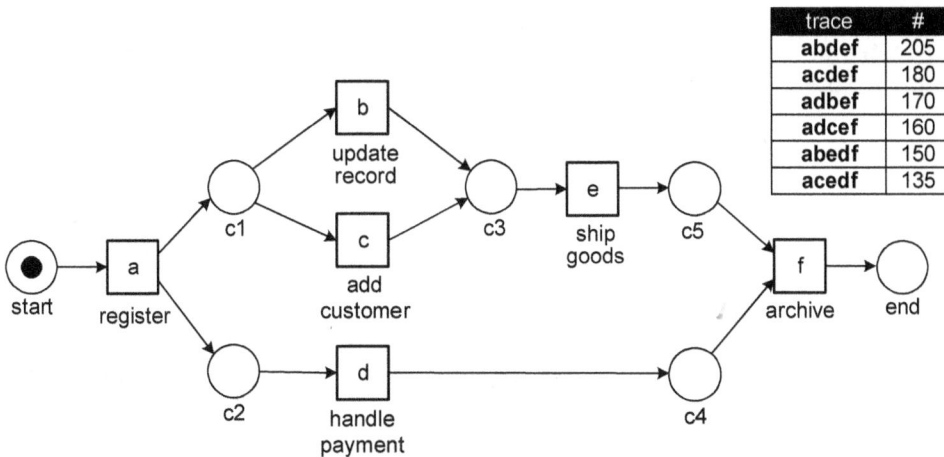

Figure 8: Due to concept drift, the model is changing. Hence, the model needs to be adapted continuously to avoid misleading diagnostics.

The event log in Figure 8 describes the same process, but in a later period. Again 1000 cases are recorded, but now the shipment (**e**) often occurs before the payment (**d**). This was not possible according to the original model. The Petri net shown in Figure 8 shows the updated process model also allowing for this new behavior.

The change from the process in Figure 3 to the process in Figure 8, illustrates that the simple dashboards and reports provided by contemporary Business Intelligence (BI) tools are inadequate. One needs to look *into* the process and cannot reduce reality to a few Key Performance Indicators (KPIs). Suppose one is interested in the delay between payments (activity **d**) and shipments (activity **e**). This corresponds to the sojourn time of tokens in place **c4** in Figure 3. The process could have been instrumented to measure these delays. However, after the drift these times can be negative. Shipments (activity **e**) happen before payments (activity **d**), and statistics can become very misleading. If activities are skipped, similar problems occur. Hence, it is vital to align event data with an up-to-date process model. Existing BI tools not supporting process mining, cannot cope with such issues. To use a BI tool, an idealized process is assumed and only high-level measurements are performed.

Process mining provides a way to look into the process and view event data in a process-centric manner. Process models provide the lenses to make sense of event data. The volume (size of data), velocity (speed of change), variety (multiple heterogeneous data sources), and veracity (uncertainty) of event data necessitates state-of-the-art techniques that are able to reliably and efficiently interpret recorded events.

PROCESS MINING IN THE LARGE

The reader is referred to (Aalst 2011) for an introduction to process mining. Process mining extends far beyond process discovery. The alignment of process models and event data enables all kinds of analytics, e.g., decision point analysis, bottleneck analysis, time prediction, resource recommendation, and compliance checking.

The spectacular growth of event data provides numerous opportunities for process mining in any business. However, there are also challenges related to "process mining in the large". Fortunately, recent developments show that process mining is quite scalable compared to classical data mining techniques. Some examples:

- Many process-mining techniques (but obviously not all) are linear in the size of the event log. If the number of activities is limited, then the time needed to discover a process model corresponds to the time to traverse the data.
- There are some discovery approaches that are more time consuming and computing alignments (e.g., for conformance checking or performance analysis) is known to be time consuming. Fortunately, there are generic techniques (Aalst 2013) to decompose large process mining into many smaller ones that can be solved much faster.
- There are many ways to distribute process-mining problems. Next to the process-mining specific approach in (Aalst 2013), many subproblems can be trivially distributed using MapReduce approaches exploiting, for example, Hadoop for distributed storage and distributed processing.
- Events logs can be decomposed for performance and scalability reasons. However, it is often also useful to partition the log and then compare the results. Techniques and tools for comparative process mining are emerging and essential for conducting process mining at a larger scale, e.g., for comparing different departments, regions, customer groups, or periods.
- The notion of "process cubes" can be used for comparative process mining. Events are stored in the cells of a multidimensional database. This is closely related to Online Analytical Processing (OLAP) technologies that aim to answer multi-dimensional analytical queries using operators such as slice, dice, roll-up, and drill-down.

The above developments illustrate that process mining fits well with other developments in the context of Big Data.

TOWARDS A PROCESS SCIENTIST

Hal Varian, the chief economist at Google, said in 2009: "The sexy job in the next 10 years will be statisticians. People think I'm joking, but who would've guessed that computer engineers would've been the sexy job of the 1990s?". The later article with the provocative title "Data Scientist: The Sexiest Job of the 21st Century" (Davenport and Patil 2012) generated lots of attention for this new profession. Indeed, just like computer science emerged from mathematics in the seventies and eighties, data science is now emerging from computer science, statistics, and management science. However, let's not forget about processes. As argued in this paper, processes provide the lenses to look at event data from different angles. The focus on data analysis is good, but should not frustrate process-orientation. In the end, good processes are more important than information systems and data analysis. The old phrase "It's the process stupid" is still valid. Hence, we advocate the need for *process scientists* that will drive process innovations while exploiting the Internet of Events (IoE).

REFERENCES

(Aalst 2011) W.M.P. van der Aalst. Process Mining: Discovery, Conformance and Enhancement of Business Processes. Springer-Verlag, Berlin, 2011.

(Aalst 2013) W.M.P. van der Aalst. Decomposing Petri Nets for Process Mining: A Generic Approach. Distributed and Parallel Databases, 31(4):471–507, 2013.

(Aalst 2014) W.M.P. van der Aalst. Data Scientist: The Engineer of the Future. In K. Mertins, F. Benaben, R. Poler, and J. Bourrieres, editors, Proceedings of the I-ESA Conference, volume 7 of Enterprise Interoperability, pages 13–28. Springer-Verlag, Berlin, 2014.

(Coursera 2014) Process Mining: Data science in Action. Coursera Course, November 2014. https://www.coursera.org/course/procmin.

(Davenport and Patil 2012) T.H. Davenport and D.J. Patil. Data Scientist: The Sexiest Job of the 21st Century. Harvard Business Review, pages 70–76, October 2012.

(Hilbert and Lopez 2011) M. Hilbert and P. Lopez. The World's Technological Capacity to Store, Communicate, and Compute Information. Science, 332(6025):60–65, 2011.

(IEEE 2013) IEEE Task Force on Process Mining. Process Mining Case Studies. http://www.win.tue.nl/ieeetfpm/doku.php?id=shared:process_mining_case_studies, 2013.

(Manyika et al. 2011) J. Manyika, M. Chui, B. Brown, J. Bughin, R. Dobbs, C. Roxburgh, and A. Byers. Big Data: The Next Frontier for Innovation, Competition, and Productivity. McKinsey Global Institute, 2011.

Section 2

WfMC Structure and Membership Information

WHAT IS THE WORKFLOW MANAGEMENT COALITION?

The Workflow Management Coalition (WfMC), founded in August 1993, is a non-profit, international organization of BPM and workflow vendors, users, analysts and university/research groups.

The Coalition's mission is to promote and develop the use of collaborative technologies such as workflow, BPM and case management through the establishment of standards for software terminology, interoperability and connectivity among products and to publicize successful use cases.

WORKFLOW STANDARDS FRAMEWORK

The Coalition has developed a framework for the establishment of workflow standards. This framework includes five categories of interoperability and communication standards that will allow multiple collaboration products to coexist and interoperate within a user's environment. Technical details are included in the white paper entitled, "The Work of the Coalition," available at www.wfmc.org.

ACHIEVEMENTS

The initial work of the Coalition focused on publishing the Reference Model and Glossary, defining a common architecture and terminology for the industry. A major milestone was achieved with the publication of the first versions of the Workflow API (WAPI) specification, covering the Workflow Client Application Interface, and the Workflow Interoperability specification.

In addition to a series of successful tutorials industry wide, the WfMC invested many person-years over the past 20 years helping to drive awareness, understanding and adoption of XPDL, now the standard means for business process definition in over 80 BPM products. As a result, it has been cited as the most deployed BPM standard by a number of industry analysts, and continues to receive a growing amount of media attention.

Workflow Reference Model

The Workflow Reference Model was published first in 1995 and still forms the basis of most BPM and workflow software systems in use today. It was developed from the generic workflow application structure by identifying the interfaces which enable products to interoperate at a variety of levels.

All workflow systems contain a number of generic components which interact in a defined set of ways; different products will typically exhibit different levels of capability within each of these generic components. To achieve interoperability between workflow products a standardized set of interfaces and data interchange formats between such components is necessary.

A number of distinct interoperability scenarios can then be constructed by reference to such interfaces, identifying different levels of functional conformance as appropriate to the range of products in the market.

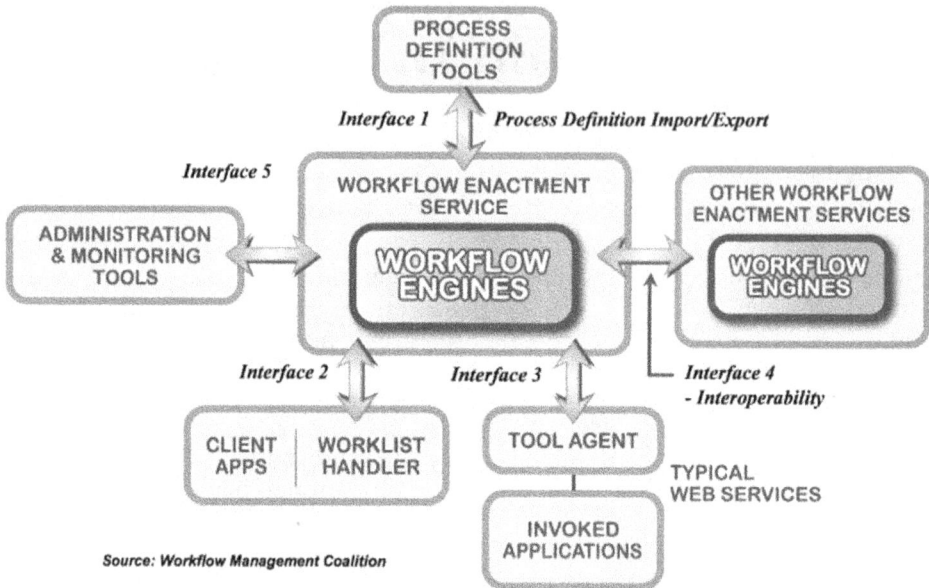

Source: Workflow Management Coalition

WORKFLOW REFERENCE MODEL DIAGRAM

XPDL (XML Process Definition Language)

An XML based language for describing a process definition, developed by the WfMC. Version 1.0 was released in 2002. Version 2.0 was released in Oct 2005. The goal of XPDL is to store and exchange the process diagram, to allow one tool to model a process diagram, and another to read the diagram and edit, another to "run" the process model on an XPDL-compliant BPM engine, and so on.

For this reason, XPDL is not an executable programming language like BPEL, but specifically a process design format that literally represents the "drawing" of the process definition. Thus it has 'XY' or vector coordinates, including lines and points that define process flows. This allows an XPDL to store a one-to-one representation of a BPMN process diagram.

For this reason, XPDL is effectively the file format or "serialization" of BPMN, as well as any non-BPMN design method or process model which use in their underlying definition the XPDL meta-model (there are presently about 60 tools which use XPDL for storing process models.)

In spring 2012, the WfMC completed XPDL 2.2 as the *fifth* revision of this specification. XPDL 2.2 builds on version 2.1 by introducing support for the process modeling extensions added to BPMN 2.0.

BPSim

The Business Process Simulation (BPSim) framework is a standardized specification that allows business process models captured in either BPMN or XPDL to be augmented with information in support of rigorous methods of analysis. It defines the parameterization and interchange of process analysis data allowing structural and capacity analysis of process models.

BPSim is meant to support both pre-execution and post-execution optimization of said process models. The BPSim specification consists of an underlying computer-interpretable representation (meta-model) and an accompanying electronic file format to ease the safeguard and transfer of this data between different tools (interchange format).

Wf-XML

Wf-XML is designed and implemented as an extension to the OASIS Asynchronous Service Access Protocol (ASAP). ASAP provides a standardized way that a program can start and monitor a program that might take a long time to complete. It provides the capability to monitor the running service, and be informed of changes in its status.

Wf-XML extends this by providing additional standard web service operations that allow sending and retrieving the "program" or definition of the service which is provided. A process engine has this behavior of providing a service that lasts a long time, and also being programmable by being able to install process definitions.

Awards

The Workflow Management Coalition sponsors three annual award programs.

1. The **Global Awards for Excellence in BPM & Workflow**[1] recognizes organizations that have implemented particularly innovative workflow solutions. Every year between 10 and 15 BPM and workflow solutions are recognized in this manner.
   WfMC publishes the case studies in the annual Excellence in Practice [2] series.

2. WfMC inaugurated a Global Awards program in 2011 for **Excellence in Case Management**[3] case studies to recognize and focus upon successful use cases for coordinating unpredictable work patterns. Awards are given in the category of Production Case Management and in Adaptive Case Management which are both new technological approaches to supporting knowledge work in today's leading edge organizations. These awards are designed to highlight the best examples of technology to support knowledge workers.
   Several books[4] have been published recognizing the winning teams. In 2013, WfMC updated the program to "WfMC Awards for Excellence in Case Management" to recognize the growing deployment of Production Case Management.

3. The **Marvin L. Manheim Award For Significant Contributions** in the Field of Workflow is given to one person every year in recognition of individual contributions to workflow and BPM standards. This award commemorates Marvin Manheim who played a key motivational role in the founding of the WfMC.

---

[1] BPM Awards: www.BPMF.org

[2] *Delivering BPM Excellence:* Published 2013 by Future Strategies Inc. http://futstrat.com/books/Delivering_BPM.php

[3] Case Management Awards: www.adaptivecasemanagement.org

[4] *Empowering Knowledge Workers:* Published 2013 by Future Strategies Inc. http://futstrat.com/books/EmpoweringKnowledgeWorkers.php

How Knowledge Workers Get Things Done. Published 2012 by Future Strategies Inc. http://www.futstrat.com/books/HowKnowledgeWorkers.php

Taming the Unpredictable: Published 2011 by Future Strategies Inc .http://futstrat.com/books/eip11.php

The Workflow Management Coalition gives you the unique opportunity to participate in the creation of standards for the workflow industry as they are developing.

Your contributions to our community ensure that progress continues in the adoption of royalty-free workflow and process standards.

THE SECRETARIAT

Workflow Management Coalition (WfMC)

www.WfMC.org

Author Appendix

JOHANN ALBACH

Research Associate, Database and Information Systems Institute, Ulm University, Germany

Johann Albach is a student at Ulm University targeting at a Bachelor degree in Computer Science. His research interests include web technologies, real-time computer graphics on desktop and mobile environments, and business process management. In his Bachelor thesis he has been developing a mobile framework that allows visualizing interactive 3D process models induced by markers.

ROY ALTMAN

Manager of Analytics & Architecture, Memorial Sloan Kettering Cancer Center, USA

Roy Altman is responsible for HR Analytics and Application Architecture at Memorial Sloan-Kettering Cancer Center. Previously, Roy was founder/CEO of Peopleserv, a software/services company. Over a multifaceted career, Roy has a history of delivering ROI to well-known companies in several industry sectors. Altman is the architect of multiple commercial software products. He has published extensively and has contributed to four other FutureStrategies BPM books. Altman frequently presents at national and global HR and BPM academic and industry conferences and on webinars. He has instructed at several universities. Altman sits on the boards of Professional Exchange of HR Solutions (PEHRS), where he is responsible for their programs and webinars on business technology issues, and Electric Music Foundation, an international not-for-profit music organization.

ALEXANDER BACHMAIER

Research Associate, Database and Information Systems Institute

Ulm University, Germany

Alexander Bachmeier studied at the University of Texas at El Paso and at Ulm University. He completed his Master in Computer Science at Ulm University with a minor in economics in 2013. Since then he has been a research associate at Ulm University. In the scope of his research, Alexander is working on augmenting Business Process Management systems using, among others, localization technologies. His responsibilities include the administration of a Linux computer lab, managing server infrastructure and teaching.

SUMEET BATRA

Senior Product Manager, Fujitsu America, USA

Sumeet leads the development of new Retail Analytics for Retail domain. He has extensive experience building analytics based solutions, prior to Fujitsu he was product management at FICO (Fair Isaac Corporation) building Fraud analytics product, Blue Shield of California, among others. Coming from a technical background, he has strong experience in Product Management, hand on Product development and Program management.

DAVID BRAKONIECKI

Director, European Operations, BP3 Global, Limited, USA

David is a regular conference speaker and thought leader on process and decision management but most enjoys working directly with the BP3 team to solve customer problems in the UK and Europe. David joined BP3 in September of 2014 as part of a their entrance to the European market. Prior to that, he has worked for almost 2 decades in a wide range of industries including consulting, insurance, e-commerce, telecommunications and investment banking in business development, finance and technology functions. This wide range of experience helps him to deliver the best results for his customers. David Brakoniecki holds a B.A. in European History from Northwestern University and an M.Sc. in Economic History from the London School of Economics.

MARK CASEY

CTO / Scientist, Miyian.com, USA

Mark Casey has 42 years of experience in computer science & technology development with national and international corporations, of which 35 years are in healthcare and more than 25 years of post-doctoral level R&D. He is a pioneer in advanced systems for healthcare and other industries, including worldwide systems and computer designs, security and conditional access systems, medical informatics, hospital computer systems, artificial intelligence, virtual reality, EHR, BPM, and advanced complex systems theory and design. He has held CTO/R&D leadership positions with AMI, The Associated Press, Starpoint Systems (Wall St.), and Kudelski-Echostar (Switzerland), as well as a number of technical startups. He is the CTO / scientist at Miyian.com. email:mark@miyian.com

STUART CHANDLER

Vice President-Technology-BPM Practice, Virtusa Corporation, USA

Stuart Chandler is the VP & Global Head of BPM Practice at Virtusa. He has led several business transformational initiatives over the last 20 years, helping many global organizations transform operations to drive greater efficiency and deliver more customer centricity through the business process management discipline. Chandler holds master's degrees in Management Information Systems and Business Administration from Boston University as well as a bachelor's degree in Resource Economics from the University of New Hampshire. Chandler can be contacted at schandler@virtusa.com.

PETER FINGAR

Author, Meghan-Kiffer Research, USA

Peter Fingar is regarded as one of the original promulgators of business process management since the publication of his book coauthored with Howard Smith, *Business Process Management: The Third Wave* (Meghan-Kiffer Press). As a former CIO and college professor, Peter has been working at the intersection of business and technology for almost 40 years. His recent books include *Cognitive Computing, Business Process Management: The Next Wave, Business Innovation in the Cloud* and *Dot.Cloud: The 21st Century Business Platform Built on Cloud Computing*, which have been published in Chinese (Beijing) and Russian (Moscow) editions. He has joined forces with Jon Pyke, founder of the Work-flow Management Coalition (WfMC), and Andy

Mulholland, Global CTO of Capgemini, to pen the influential book, *Enterprise Cloud Computing: A Strategy Guide for Business and Technology Leaders*. Peter delivers keynote talks across the globe and is speaking this year in Asia, Europe, and the Americas. (www.peterfingar.com).

LAYNA FISCHER

Publisher, Future Strategies Inc., USA, ,

Ms Fischer is Editor-in-Chief and Publisher since 1993 at Future Strategies Inc., the official publishers to WfMC.org. In 2001-2006, she was additionally Executive Director of WfMC.org and BPMI.org (now merged with OMG) and continues to work closely with these organizations to promote industry awareness of BPM, BPME, BPMN, Knowledge Work, Case Management and more.

Future Strategies Inc. (FutStrat.com and BPM-Books.com) publishes unique books and papers focusing on BPM-based advanced technologies. As such, the company works closely with individual authors and corporations worldwide and also manages the renowned annual Global Awards for Excellence in BPM and the Awards for Excellence in Case Management.

Future Strategies Inc., is the publisher of the ground-breaking business book series New Tools for New Times, the annual Excellence in Practice series of award-winning case studies and the annual BPM Handbook series, published in collaboration with the WfMC.

Ms. Fischer has been involved in international IT journalism and publishing for over 20 years.

SCOTT FRANCIS

Co-founder and Chief Technology Officer, BP3 Global, Inc., USA

Scott Francis is co-founder and CTO of BP3, a services firm known for innovative software and practices in the BPM market, including Brazos UI, Brazos Charts, and Brazos Portal. Scott is a frequent speaker at conferences, including bpmNEXT, IBM Impact, Lombardi Driven, and BPM Portugal. Scott is also a prolific writer on his blog, at www.bp-3.com/blogs. BP3 has grown more than 10-fold in the last 5 years, with offices in the US, UK, Ukraine, and Portugal. Scott and his team have been responsible for hundreds of successful BPM deployments. Prior to BP3, Scott served as Chief Architect and Director of Technical Services at Lombardi Software, an early innovator in the BPM space later acquired by IBM to anchor the IBM BPM offering. Prior to BP3, Scott was a member of senior technical staff at Trilogy software in a variety of roles. Scott graduated with a degree in Computer Science from Stanford University, and lives in Austin, Texas.

LANCE GIBBS

Co-founder and CEO, BP3 Global, Inc., USA

Lance brings over 20 years of experience in IT and strategic business initiatives to BP3. He is a Certified Master Blackbelt in Six Sigma, an OCEB-Advanced BPM Expert, and an evangelist for customer-centric business process improvement. Lance is the author of many best practice articles concerning Business Process Management. He also has many years of experience rolling out software development lifecycle methods for blue chip companies as a practitioner and educator. Lance was formerly Lombardi Software's Managing Director of Transformation Services, with additional responsibility for creating and innovating Lombardi's BPM implementation methodology, as well as previous positions leading Customer Support, Training, and establishing the service delivery in Europe. Previously, Lance was Managing Partner at USWeb/CKS where he grew the operation from 3 employees to over 100 and was responsible for strategic customers as well as the consulting disciplines for the Austin group.

LARRY HAWES

Principal, Dow Brook Advisory Services, USA

Larry Hawes is the Principal and founder of Dow Brook Advisory Services, (http://www.dowbrook.com) where he advises enterprise software vendors on product roadmap, positioning and messaging, go-to-market, and merger and acquisition strategies. He is also internationally-recognized expert on the application of information management technologies to drive high-value business outcomes and transformation.

Larry's research and presentations are focused on networked business – the nexus of communication, collaboration, social networking, content management and process/activity management within and between organizations. He blogs at Forbes and the Dow Brook blog. Larry's thought leadership has also been featured in The Wall Street Journal, The Financial Times, Wired and many other publications.

SETRAG KHOSHAFIAN

VP of BPM Technology, Pegasystems Inc., USA

Dr. Setrag Khoshafian is one of the industry's pioneers and recognized experts in Digital Enterprises, especially Internet of Things and intelligent BPM. He has been a senior executive in the software industry for the past 25 years, where he has invented, architected, and steered the production of several enterprise software products and solutions. Currently, he is Pega's Chief Evangelist and strategic digital transformation thought leader involved in numerous technology, thought leadership, marketing, alliance, and customer initiatives. Lead author of 10 books and numerous articles.

JOSEPH B. LAIL

IT Business Architect Fellow, Strategy/Business Transformation, Raytheon, USA

J. Bryan Lail is a Business Architect Fellow at Raytheon Company. He works across market pursuits to assess capability gaps for the business from growth strategies and works with a cross-functional team to drive new ways of doing business to fill those gaps. Architecting the business includes rigorous methods for forming new business models, finding new value streams across organizational functions, and innovative use of information to increase probability of win in new markets. Previously he spent three years as the Chief IT Architect driving business discipline into information architecture for Raytheon and teaching business architecture across the enterprise. He was a systems engineer for nineteen years between the Raytheon Company and before that working as a scientist for the Navy at China Lake. He has a Masters in Physics and is a Raytheon Certified Architect, accredited by The Open Group.

VINAYKUMAR MUMMIGATTI

SVP- Head of BPM CoE and Architecture Executive for Shared Operations Services, Bank of America, USA

Vinay Mummigatti is a senior technology executive specializing in business transformation solutions for customer experience, Operational excellence and compliance. In his current role as SVP- BPM CoE leader and Architecture Executive at Bank of America, Vinay is responsible for leading BPM & Case management strategy and delivery for consumer bank. He also heads the technology strategy and architecture for shared services operations (Document and image management, Business activity monitoring and operations across Cash/card/payments/deposits/ CD/lock box).

Before joining BoA, Vinay worked at United Healthcare as BPM CoE leader. Prior to that Vinay headed the global BPM, Content management and CRM practices at Virtusa and Tech-Mahindra, where he worked with most of the leading technologies, delivering technology strategy and solutions across Insurance, Healthcare, Telcom, Manufacturing and Financial services. Vinay's key areas of specialization include Business process excellence, Process automation, Global software delivery, Product development, IT strategy and business transformation. He has also contributed to number of industry white papers, BPM publications and presented at industry forums. Vinay lives in Charlotte, NC with wife and two sons.

YASUMASA OSHIRO

Senior Support Engineer, Fujitsu America, USA

Yasumasa joined in Fujitsu Limited in 1999 and been working as software developer and Product Manager for 16 years. He has been working on lots of Fujitsu middleware product, such as Object Oriented Database, Content Management, Application Server, InMemory Database, and Business Process Management. Currently he is working on Retail Analytics solution in North America as technical lead.

NATHANIEL PALMER

Vice President and CTO, BPM.com, USA

Rated as the #1 Most Influential Thought Leader in Business Process Management (BPM) by independent research, Nathaniel is recognized as one of the early originators of BPM, and has the led the design for some of the industry's largest-scale and most complex projects involving investments of $200 Million or more. Today he is the Editor-in-Chief of BPM.com, as well as the Executive Director of the Workflow Management Coalition, as well as VP and CTO of BPM, Inc.

Previously he had been the BPM Practice Director of SRA International, and prior to that Director, Business Consulting for Perot Systems Corp, as well as spent over a decade with Delphi Group serving as VP and CTO. He frequently tops the lists of the most recognized names in his field, and was the first individual named as Laureate in Workflow. Nathaniel has authored or co-authored a dozen books on process innovation and business transformation, including "Intelligent BPM" (2013), "How Knowledge Workers Get Things Done" (2012), "Social BPM" (2011), "Mastering the Unpredictable" (2008) which reached #2 on the Amazon.com Best Seller's List, "Excellence in Practice" (2007), "Encyclopedia of Database Systems" (2007) and "The X-Economy" (2001).

He has been featured in numerous media ranging from Fortune to The New York Times to National Public Radio. Nathaniel holds a DISCO Secret Clearance as well as a Position of Trust with in the U.S. federal government.

RUEDIGER PRYSS

Research Associate & Consultant, Database and Information Systems Institute, Ulm University, Germany

Rüdiger Pryss studied at the Universities of Passau, Karlsruhe and Ulm. He holds a Diploma in Computer Science. After graduating, he worked as a consultant and developer in a software company. Since 2008 he has been a research associate at Ulm University. In his PhD thesis, Rüdiger focuses on fundamental issues related to mobile process and task support. In particular, he investigates how mobile devices can be integrated with process management technology in a robust and reliable way, e.g., to allow for the autonomous execution of process fragments or single process tasks on mobile devices. Rüdiger was local organization chair of the BPM'09 and EDOC'14 conferences. Moreover, he is experienced with teaching courses on database management, service-oriented computing, business process management, document management, and mobile application engineering.

SURENDRA REDDY

CEO, Quantiply Corporation, USA

Surendra Reddy is the founder and CEO of Quantiply Corporation, an emerging predictive business process intelligence company, being incubated at PARC. Prior to Quantiply, Surendra was the CTO of Cloud and Big Data futures where he was responsible for the applied technology research, business strategy and strategic partnerships for cloud, high performance analytics and big data futures across PARC. Prior to PARC, Surendra served as the General Manager and CTO for SIOS Technology group companies, where he was responsible for defining global cloud strategy and guiding the 200+ strong engineering organization with the technology direction and innovation programs. Before this, he was Vice President of Virtualization and Cloud R&D at Yahoo!, developing a company-wide cloud strategy to increase the operational efficiencies of data centers and reduce operational cost by 20 percent in first two years and up to 50 percent in the third year. Prior to joining Yahoo, he was the CTO and VP of Engineering at Amitive, first cloud based platform for document-driven process automation. Amitive was acquired by GXS and became part of their trading platform. Surendra was also the founder and CTO of Optena Corporation, a pioneer in data center automation and grid computing. He also spent more than seven years as Director of Engineering in Server Technologies at Oracle.

Surendra co-authored RFC 5323, contributed to RFC 3648. He founded the Big Data Foundry, a global initiative to promote the applied research in process intelligence and big data analytics and is an active researcher on business process intelligence, process mining, systems thinking, customer behavioral patterns, case based reasoning, large data sets and data access, security, and integrity issues.

Surendra received his MBA from the Kellogg School of Management at Northwestern University and his Bachelor of Technology in Electronics and Communication Engineering from Jawaharlal Nehru Technological University, India.

MANFRED REICHERT

Full Professor, Database and Information Systems Institute, Ulm University, Germany

Manfred Reichert holds a PhD in Computer Science and is one of the world-leading experts in BPM. Since 2008 he has been appointed as full professor at Ulm University, where he is director of the Institute of Databases and Information Systems. Before, he was associate professor at the University of Twente in the Netherlands and a member of the management board of the Centre for Telematics and Information Technology (CTIT), which is one of the largest academic ICT research institutes in Europe. At CTIT he was coordinator of the strategic research initiative on e-health. Manfreds research interests include business process management (e.g., process flexibility, process lifecycle management, and mobile processes), service-oriented computing (e.g., service interoperability, mobile services, and service evolution) and e-health. Manfred has been PC Co-chair of the BPM08, CoopIS11, EMISA13 and EDOC13 conferences, and General Chair of the BPM09 and EDOC14 conferences. Recently, he co-authored a Springer book on process flexibility and obtained the BPM Test of Time Award at the BPM 2013 conference.

CAROLYN ROSTETTER

Senior Director, Industry Principal - Manufacturing & High Technology, Pegasystems Inc., USA

For nearly 2 decades, Carolyn Rostetter has been a Business Optimization Leader in some of the world's most respected organizations. As a Master Black Belt, she provides vision and experience in areas such as Productivity, Quality, Strategic Planning, Change Management and Communications. She has led large scale Lean Six Sigma development programs in industries including Banking & Finance, Media and Entertainment & Manufacturing. Carolyn has successfully supported enterprise scale programs such as Compliance & Regulatory Services, NPS for Client Services, Organizational Transformation, Revenue Management & Treasury Services, Application Portfolio Optimization, Master Data Management, as well as Vendor Evaluation Services. She is currently Pega's Industry Principal for Manufacturing and High Tech industries.

KEITH SWENSON

VP of Research & Development, Fujitsu America, USA

Keith Swenson is Vice President of Research and Development at Fujitsu America Inc. and Chairman of the Workflow Management Coalition. He was a pioneer in collaboration software and web services, and has helped the development of many workflow and BPM standards. In the past, he led development of collaboration software MS2, Netscape, Ashton Tate and Fujitsu. In 2004 he was awarded the Marvin L. Manheim Award for outstanding contributions in the field of workflow. His new book "When Thinking Matters in the Workplace" is about how managers can support innovation in the workplace. His blog is at http://social-biz.org/.

JAMES TAYLOR

CEO and Principal Consultant, Decision Management Solutions, USA

James is the CEO of Decision Management Solutions. He is a leading expert in how to use business rules and analytic technology to build Decision Management Systems. James is passionate about using Decision Management Systems to help companies improve decision making and develop an agile, analytic and adaptive business. Decision Management Solutions provides strategic consulting to companies of all sizes, working with clients in all sectors to adopt decision making technology. James has led Decision Management efforts for leading companies in insurance, banking, health management and telecommunications.

James is the author of "Decision Management Systems: A practical guide to using business rules and predictive analytics" (IBM Press, 2011). He also wrote "The MicroGuide to Process and Decision Modeling" with Tom Debevoise and "Smart (Enough) Systems: How to Deliver Competitive Advantage by Automating Hidden Decisions" (Prentice Hall) with Neil Raden. He has contributed chapters on decision modeling and Decision Management to multiple books and was one of the original submtters of the Decision Model and Notation (DMN) standard. He regularly speaks, teaches and writes on decision modeling and Decision Management.

Email: james@decisionmanagementsolutions.com.

GREGORY T. TAYLOR

Sr. Strategy Business Analyst, Raytheon, USA

Gregory T Taylor is a Strategy Business Analyst at Raytheon Missile Systems. His responsibilities include strategy research and analysis for IT, support to strategic market priorities, including mobility and collaboration for global growth, and business analytics.

Previously he spent three years as a Business Intelligence Analyst leading the data acquisition team, improving data integration across business unit and corporate systems, refining analytic solution development processes, establishing and maturing the business analyst competency for business intelligence, and driving Mobile and Self-Service BI initiatives.

Greg is a graduate of the Raytheon Leadership Development Program with rotations in Corporate IT Finance, IT Strategy and Business Intelligence over two years. His previous professional experience includes five years as a consulting Network Engineer.

He holds a Bachelor of Science in Management Information Systems from Brigham Young University, and an MBA and Master of Science in Management Information Systems from the University of Arizona.

WIL VAN DER AALST

Full Professor, Eindhoven University of Technology, The Netherlands, Eindhoven University of Technology, Netherlands

Prof.dr.ir. Wil van der Aalst is a full professor of Information Systems at the Technische Universiteit Eindhoven (TU/e). He is also the Academic Supervisor of the International Laboratory of Process-Aware Information Systems of the National Research University, Higher School of Economics in Moscow. Moreover, since 2003 he has a part-time appointment at Queensland University of Technology (QUT). At TU/e he is the scientific director of the Data

Science Center Eindhoven (DSC/e). His personal research interests include workflow management, process mining, Petri nets, business process management, process modeling, and process analysis. Many of his papers are highly cited (he one of the most cited computer scientists in the world and has an H-index of 115 according to Google Scholar) and his ideas have influenced researchers, software developers, and standardization committees working on process support. He has been a co-chair of many conferences including BPM is also editor/member of the editorial board of several journals. In 2012, he received the degree of doctor honoris causa from Hasselt University. In 2013, he was appointed as Distinguished University Professor of TU/e and was awarded an honorary guest professorship at Tsinghua University. In 2015, he was appointed as honorary professor at the National Research University, Higher School of Economics in Moscow. He is also a member of the Royal Netherlands Academy of Arts and Sciences (Koninklijke Nederlandse Akademie van Wetenschappen), Royal Holland Society of Sciences and Humanities (Koninklijke Hollandsche Maatschappij der Wetenschappen) and the Academy of Europe (Academia Europaea).

DAVID WEBBER

Senior BPM Consultant, Horizon Industries, USA

David Webber is an industry recognized practitioner and author on BPM and Information Integration. David manages an open source project for information exchange automation and works on a variety of open standards initiatives. For OASIS he participated in the original BPEL and BPSS standards work. He developed one of the first BPMN visual editors for SmartDraw. David holds two US Software Patents for XML and EDI processing that are cited by over 35 industry patents from IBM, Dell, Oracle et al. David is a Senior Member of the ACM since 2007, and is the DHS appointed industry representative to the NIEM Technical Architect Committee (NTAC). In 2014 PESC gave him a Distinguished Service Award for work on aligning information standards in Education. David holds a degree in Physics with Computing from the University of Kent at Canterbury. David works tirelessly on simplifying solution delivery tools to minimize the gap between business requirements and logical representations that are directly machine processable.

Profile: http://en.wikipedia.org/wiki/David_Webber

CHARLES WEBSTER

President, EHR Workflow Inc,

Dr. Chuck Webster has degrees in accountancy, industrial engineering, intelligent systems and medicine. He earned his medical degree from the University of Chicago. Dr. Webster designed the first undergraduate program in medical informatics, was a software architect in a hospital MIS department, and chief medical informatics officer for an EHR vendor for over a decade. He helped three healthcare organizations win the HIMSS Davies Award, the top industry award for electronic health records excellence in use, and is a judge for the annual Workflow Management Coalition Awards for Excellence in BPM and Workflow and Awards for Case Management. Webster is a ceaseless evangelist for process-aware technologies in healthcare, including workflow management systems, business process management and dynamic and adaptive case management. Webster tweets from @wareFLO and maintains numerous websites including EHR Workflow Management Systems, Healthcare Business Process Management and People and Organizations Improving Healthcare with Health Information Technology.

PETER WHIBLEY

Product Marketing Manager, KANA, United Kingdom

Peter Whibley works for KANA as a Product Marketing Manager. Peter is a senior IT professional with over fifteen years' experience in leading the introduction of products and services within the business applications software and telecommunications industries. Peter's key area of personal interest is customer service and in particular how Case Management and BPM can be used to transform customer service processes. Peter holds a degree in Electrical and Electronic Engineering from the University of Manchester as well as an MBA from the University of Ulster.

Index

Additional Reading and Resources

NEW E-BOOK SERIES

Download PDF immediately and start reading. **Only $9.97 each**

- Introduction to BPM and Workflow
  http://bpm-books.com/products/ebook-series-introduction-to-bpm-and-workflow

- Financial Services
  http://bpm-books.com/products/ebook-series-financial-services

- Healthcare
  http://bpm-books.com/products/ebook-series-bpm-in-healthcare

- Utilities and Telecommunications
  http://bpm-books.com/products/ebook-series-utilities-and-telecommunications

NON-PROFIT ASSOCIATIONS AND RELATED STANDARDS RESEARCH ONLINE

- AIIM (Association for Information and Image Management)
  http://www.aiim.org
- BPM and Workflow online news, research, forums
  http://bpm.com
- BPM Research at Stevens Institute of Technology
  http://www.bpm-research.com
- Business Process Management Initiative
  http://www.bpmi.org *see* Object Management Group
- IEEE (Electrical and Electronics Engineers, Inc.)
  http://www.ieee.org
- Institute for Information Management (IIM)
  http://www.iim.org
- ISO (International Organization for Standardization)
  http://www.iso.ch
- Object Management Group
  http://www.omg.org
- Open Document Management Association
  http://nfocentrale.net/dmware
- Organization for the Advancement of Structured Information Standards
  http://www.oasis-open.org
- Society for Human Resource Management
  http://www.shrm.org
- Society for Information Management
  http://www.simnet.org
- Wesley J. Howe School of Technology Management
  http://howe.stevens.edu/research/research-centers/business-process-innovation
- Workflow And Reengineering International Association (WARIA)
  http://www.waria.com
- Workflow Management Coalition (WfMC)
  http://www.wfmc.org
- Workflow Portal
  http://www.e-workflow.org

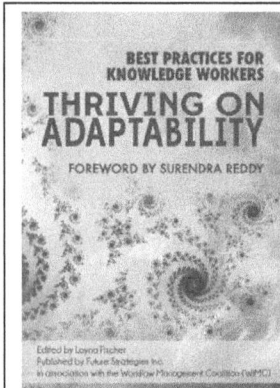	**THRIVING ON ADAPTABILITY: BEST PRACTICES FOR KNOWLEDGE WORKERS** http://futstrat.com/books/ThrivingOnAdaptability.php ACM helps organizations focus on improving or optimizing the line of interaction where our people and systems come into direct contact with customers. It's a whole different thing; a new way of doing business that enables organizations to literally become one living-breathing entity via collaboration and adaptive data-driven biological-like operating systems. ACM is not just another acronym or business fad. ACM is the process, strategy, framework, and set of tools that enables this evolution and maturity: *Surendra Reddy, Foreword*
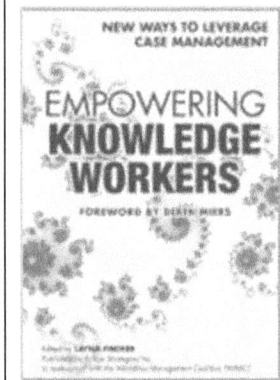	**EMPOWERING KNOWLEDGE WORKERS:** *NEW WAYS TO LEVERAGE CASE MANAGEMENT* http://futstrat.com/books/EmpoweringKnowledgeWorkers.php *Empowering Knowledge Workers* describes the work of managers, decision makers, executives, doctors, lawyers, campaign managers, emergency responders, strategists, and many others who have to think for a living. These are people who figure out what needs to be done, at the same time that they do it, and there is a new approach to support this presents the logical starting point for understanding how to take advantage of ACM **Retail #49.95 (see discount on website)**
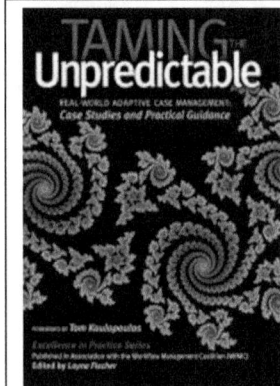	**TAMING THE UNPREDICTABLE** http://futstrat.com/books/eip11.php The core element of Adaptive Case Management (ACM) is the support for real-time decision-making by knowledge workers. Taming the Unpredictable presents the logical starting point for understanding how to take advantage of ACM. This book goes beyond talking about concepts, and delivers actionable advice for embarking on your own journey of ACM-driven transformation. **Retail #49.95 (see discount on website)**
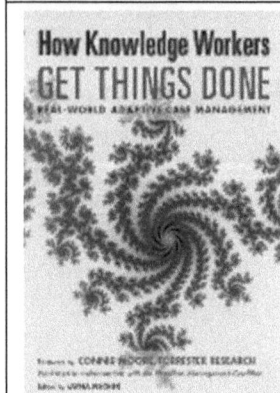	**HOW KNOWLEDGE WORKERS GET THINGS DONE** http://www.futstrat.com/books/HowKnowledgeWorkers.php *How Knowledge Workers Get Things Done* describes the work of managers, decision makers, executives, doctors, lawyers, campaign managers, emergency responders, strategist, and many others who have to think for a living. These are people who figure out what needs to be done, at the same time that they do it, and there is a new approach to support this presents the logical starting point for understanding how to take advantage of ACM. **Retail $49.95 (see discount offer on website)**

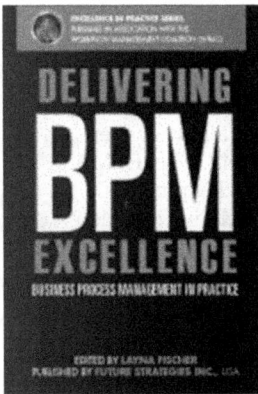

DELIVERING BPM EXCELLENCE

http://futstrat.com/books/Delivering_BPM.php

Business Process Management in Practice

The companies whose case studies are featured in this book have proven excellence in their creative and successful deployment of advanced BPM concepts. These companies focused on excelling in *innovation, implementation* and *impact* when installing BPM and workflow technologies. The positive impact includes increased revenues, more productive and satisfied employees, product enhancements, better customer service and quality improvements.
$39.95 (see discount on website)

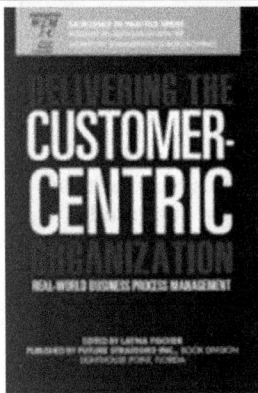

DELIVERING THE CUSTOMER-CENTRIC ORGANIZATION

http://futstrat.com/books/Customer-Centric.php
The ability to successfully manage the customer value chain across the life cycle of a customer is the key to the survival of any company today. Business processes must react to changing and diverse customer needs and interactions to ensure efficient and effective outcomes.

This important book looks at the shifting nature of consumers and the workplace, and how BPM and associated emergent technologies will play a part in shaping the companies of the future. **Retail $39.95**

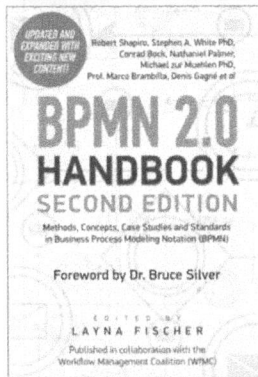

BPMN 2.0 Handbook SECOND EDITION

(see two-BPM book bundle offer on website: get BPMN Reference Guide Free)
http://futstrat.com/books/bpmnhandbook2.php

Updated and expanded with exciting new content!

Authored by members of WfMC, OMG and other key participants in the development of BPMN 2.0, the BPMN 2.0 Handbook brings together worldwide thought-leaders and experts in this space. Exclusive and unique contributions examine a variety of aspects that start with an introduction of what's new in BPMN 2.0, and look closely at interchange, analytics, conformance, optimization, simulation and more. **Retail $75.00**

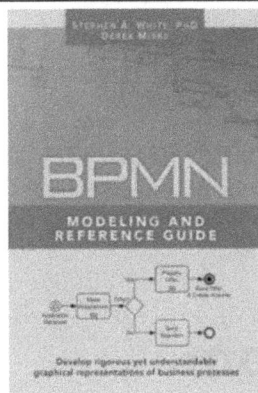

BPMN MODELING AND REFERENCE GUIDE

(see two-BPM book bundle offer on website: get BPMN Reference Guide Free)

http://www.futstrat.com/books/BPMN-Guide.php

Understanding and Using BPMN
How to develop rigorous yet understandable graphical representations of business processes.

Business Process Modeling Notation (BPMN) is a standard, graphical modeling representation for business processes. It provides an easy to use, flow-charting notation that is independent of the implementation environment.
Retail $39.95

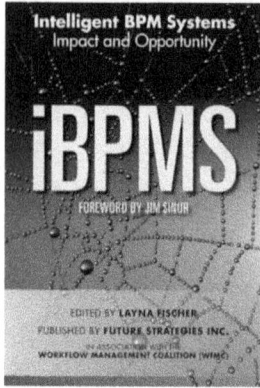

iBPMS - INTELLIGENT BPM SYSTEMS

http://www.futstrat.com/books/iBPMS_Handbook.php

"The need for Intelligent Business Operations (IBO) supported by intelligent processes is driving the need for a new convergence of process technologies lead by the iBPMS. The iBPMS changes the way processes help organizations keep up with business change," notes Gartner Emeritus Jim Sinur in his Foreword.

The co-authors of this important book describe various aspects and approaches of iBPMS with regard to impact and opportunity. **Retail $59.95 (see discount on website)**

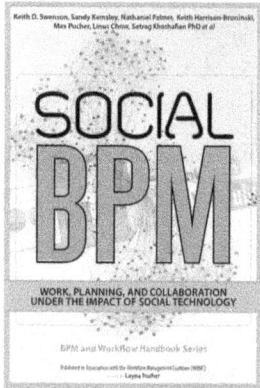

Social BPM

http://futstrat.com/books/handbook11.php
Work, Planning, and Collaboration Under the Impact of Social Technology

Today we see the transformation of both the look and feel of BPM technologies along the lines of social media, as well as the increasing adoption of social tools and techniques democratizing process development and design. It is along these two trend lines; the evolution of system interfaces and the increased engagement of stakeholders in process improvement, that Social BPM has taken shape.
Retail $59.95 (see discount offer on website)

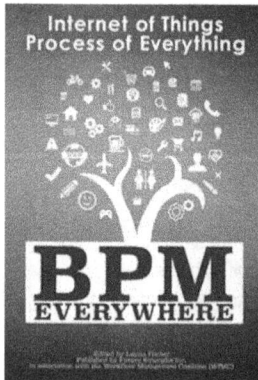

BPM EVERYWHERE

Internet of Things, Process of Everything

http://www.futstrat.com/BPMEverywhere.htm

We are entering an entirely new phase of BPM – the era of "*BPM Everywhere*" or **BPME**.

This book discusses critical issues currently facing BPM adopters and practitioners, such as the key roles played by process mining uncovering engagement patterns and the need for process management platforms to coordinate interaction and control of smart devices.
BPME represents the strategy for leveraging, not simply surviving but fully exploiting the wave of disruption facing every business over the next 5 years and beyond.

Get 25% Discount on ALL Books in our Store.

Please use the discount code **SPEC25** to get **25% discount** on ALL books in our store; both Print and Digital Editions (two discount codes cannot be used together).
www.FutStrat.com

http://bpm-books.com

www.ingramcontent.com/pod-product-compliance
Lightning Source LLC
Chambersburg PA
CBHW080528220326
41599CB00032B/6238